FROM AGNON TO OZ

SOUTH FLORIDA STUDIES IN THE HISTORY OF JUDAISM

Edited by
Jacob Neusner
William Scott Green, James Strange
Darrell J. Fasching, Sara Mandell

Number 126
FROM AGNON TO OZ
Studies in Modern Hebrew Literature

by
Warren Bargad

FROM AGNON TO OZ
Studies in Modern Hebrew Literature

by

Warren Bargad

Scholars Press
Atlanta, Georgia

FROM AGNON TO OZ
Studies in Modern Hebrew Literature

by
Warren Bargad

Publication of this book was made possible by a grant from the Tisch Family Foundation, New York City. The University of South Florida acknowledges with thanks this important support for its scholarly projects.

Library of Congress Cataloging in Publication Data
Bargad, Warren.
   From Agnon to Oz : studies in modern Hebrew literature / by Warren
Bargad.
      p.   cm. — (South Florida studies in the history of Judaism ;
no. 126)
   Includes bibliographical references.
   ISBN 0-7885-0194-1 (cloth : alk. paper)
   1. Hebrew literature, Modern—History and criticism. 2. Israeli
literature—History and criticism. I. Title II. Series: South
Florida studies in the history of Judaism ; 126.
PJ5021.B346   1996
892.4'09006—dc20   95-44129
                                                 CIP

Printed in the United States of America
on acid-free paper

In loving memory of Lois

Table of Contents

Preface

The idea of collecting a number of published articles and essays in an anthology was conceived when I happened to peruse a Scholars Press book of articles written by Mayer Gruber, a biblical scholar at Ben-Gurion University of the Negev, and a former colleague at the Spertus College of Judaica in Chicago. When I met Jacob Neusner after his move to Florida, he graciously offered to interest the Scholars Press in considering this anthology of articles on Hebrew literature for publication. I am deeply grateful for his efforts and generosity on my behalf.

Beyond these coincidental events, however, I had been thinking about looking back at some of the work I have done over the past twenty-odd years since my first published articles, both in 1972, one in *Hadoar* (on Amalia-Kahana Carmon's first novel, *Veyare'ah be'emek ayalon*), and another (on Hayim Hazaz's "Hadrasha") in *Molad*, both in Hebrew. The article on the emergence of *Siman kri'a* in the context of a history of Hebrew journal manifestoes broadened my perspectives on the development of Israeli poetry and prose. The essays on Amalia Kahana-Carmon's works have been quite gratifying, as has been our twenty-year friendship. The more recent pieces on Amir Gilboa and "Poems of Saul" have been challenging and intriguing pieces of work as well. Surprisingly, the piece on Amichai's earlier volumes, the least "scholarly" item in this collection, has had the most citations and other feedback from readers and scholars around the world. The late Ronald Sanders, once the editor of *Midstream*, encouraged me to pen the article; I am still in his debt.

*   *   *

I want to acknowledge the permissions given by the various publishers and the journals in which these articles, essays and reviews have appeared. Especially I want to thank the editors who labored with care to improve these texts. Some of the texts bear slight changes, none of which alters their general sense. The editors and sources are as follows.

****Midstream* [published by The Theodor Herzl Foundation, Inc.]: eds. Roland Sanders and Joel Carmichael.
  *"Children and Lovers: On Yehuda Amichai's Poetic Works," 21, 8 (October, 1975): 50-58.
  *"Amos Oz and Art of Fictional Response," 22, 9 (November, 1976): 61-64.
  *"Innocent Victims" [review of S.Y. Agnon's*A Simple Story*, translated by Hillel Halkin]: 33, 2 (February, 1987): 61-62.

****Judaism* [published by the American Jewish Congress]: eds. Ruth B. Waxman and the late Robert Gordis.
  *"Exclamations, Manifestoes, and Other Literary Peripheries," 23, 2 (Spring, 1974): 202-211.
  *"The Poetics of Allusion and the Hebrew Literary Tradition," 26, 4 (Fall, 1977): 481-488.

****Hadoar* [published by the Histadrut Ivrit of America]: ed. Isaac Ivry.
  *"Aharon Appelfeld: The Lost Past Seeks Remembrance," 51, 14 (February 11, 1972): 214-215 [in Hebrew].
  *"And Moon in the Vale of Aijalon: A Lyrical Novel by Amalia Kahana-Carmon," 51, 36 (September, 1972): 616-618 [in Hebrew].

****Prooftexts* [published by The Johns Hopkins University Press]: eds. Alan Mintz and David Roskies.
  *"S.Y. Agnon and German Neo-Romanticism," 1 (Spring, 1980): 96-98.
  *"Amalia Kahana-Carmon and the Novel of Consciousness," 2 (Summer, 1981): 172-184.
  *"Four Poems of King Saul: A Semiotic Approach," 10 (1990): 313-334.

**Hebrew Annual Review* [published by the Division of
    Hebrew Language and Literature, The Ohio State
    University]: ed. Yehiel Hayon.
  *"The Image of the Arab in Israeli Literature," 1 (1977):
    53-65.
  *"Elements of Style in the Fiction of Amalia Kahana-
    Carmon," 2 (1978): 1-12.

**Migvan*: Essays in Honor of Jacob Kabakoff (Lod, 1988):
  *"Three Monologues on Zionism: Agnon, Hazaz, Oz -- A
    Deconstructionist Approach": ed. Stanley Nash.
    Habermann Institute, pp. 53-62 [in Hebrew].

**Jewish Book Annual* [published by the Jewish Book Council,
    New York]: ed. Jacob Kabakoff.
  *"Realism and Myth in the Works of Hayim Hazaz,"
    41 (1983-84), pp. 40-48.

**International Journal of Middle East Studies* [published by
    Cambridge University Press on behalf of the Middle East
    Studies Association of North America]: a review of *Israeli
    Mythogynies: Women in Contemporary Israeli Fiction* by
    Esther Fuchs, 21, 2 (1989): 281-283. Book Review ed.:
    Aida Bamia.

*   *   *

I owe debts of gratitude to my teachers and mentors in
Hebrew literature, especially to Arnold Band, who provided a
model for the pursuit of Hebrew literary research; to Ruth
Rosenberg, my first professional instructor; to Shmuel Werses
and Gershon Shaked, my teachers at the Hebrew University,
whose courses were always informative and challenging. The
central influence on my career has been the work of Benjamin
Harshav (Hrushovski), who in the mid-1960s introduced me to
Russian Formalism, the offshoots of which attracted me to his
stylistic/linguistic methods in theory and criticism.

I want to express my appreciation to a number of
individuals for their assistance with the preparation of this

anthology. To Norrie Ersoff, who formatted and typed the original manuscript; to Carlene Smith, who helped undo frustrating complications with patience and forbearance; to Michael Cohen, Graduate Assistant to the Center for Jewish Studies and computer operator extraordinaire, without whom this book would never have been born into the world; to Ali Harari who typed the Hebrew articles; to Dr. Dennis Ford and the editorial and production staffs at the Scholars Press; and to Arlene, for her being an extraordinary, loving partner these thirty-some years.

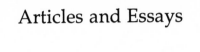

Articles and Essays

Exclamations, Manifestoes, and Other Literary Peripheries[1]

In December, 1971, the Israeli daily, *Davar*, published the first issue of its newly refurbished Friday literary supplement called *Masa*. In a leadoff article, one of *Masa*'s editors, the well-known Israeli writer, Aharon Megged, spoke of the period since the Six-Day War as "a time of letdown after a great exaltation." In a later issue, Megged called on the Israeli literary community to counter the national doldrums by founding a new journal for literature led by "dynamic, devoted editors" like those the Yishuv (pre-state Palestinian Jewry) had known in the years between the First and the Second World Wars.

> [We need] something young, fresh, iconoclastic arrogant, rebellious, exciting, and inspiring. . . . [We need] the time of the Six-Day War, the Six-Day War itself, the four years which followed it, with all the celebrations, the great hopes, the expectations, the disappointments, the frustration, and the fears. . . . All this was a great experience, very great and new, which awakened new powers and created a new style -- we don't perceive it yet, but it's so, it created a new style. . . and [this new style] must be expressed by a younger generation, and they need a new journal, a journal open to the *times*, open, that is, to all the problems of the times and our country, not only to the problems of literature -- and if [such a journal] comes into being, it will bring a new spirit to *all* literature.[2]

Not long after the appearance of these pronouncements by Megged, a group of young writers, critics, and scholars did indeed initiate a new Hebrew literary journal called *Siman kri'a* ("Exclamation Point," or, as a pun, it may also be translated as "an indication of what to read"). One can only speculate as to any direct, causal connection with Megged's exhortations, but *Siman kri'a*'s introductory statement of purpose is undeniably reminiscent of Megged's fervent rhetoric, if not of his somewhat sentimental sense of history.

Siman kri'a did not appear *ex nihilo*, historically speaking. In coming to public notice when it did, it neatly, but only coincidentally, celebrated the fiftieth anniversary of the

1

first important "new frontier" literary journal to appear in Mandatory Palestine, *Hedim* ("Echoes"), which was first published in 1922 under the editorship of Jacob Rabinowitz and Asher Barash. Highly influential, though it was of modest dimensions and only moderate duration, *Hedim* had proclaimed that in "days of spiritual weakness and apathy toward our Hebrew literature" it aimed "not at a transvaluation or renewal of values," but simply at a way [to express] a new feeling, a vibrant idea."

Siman kri'a's manifesto is far less romantic in its tone and far more specific and forthright in its rebellious posture. Reflecting some aspects of the *New AmericanReview*, but much more ambitious in size and intent and more variegated in the spectrum of its materials, *Siman kri'a* aims at nothing less than becoming the main purveyor of "what is central and worthy of notice in contemporary [Israeli] writing." *Hedim*'s editors, in calling for relevance, had employed euphemisms like "feeling," "purity," and "truth"; but *Siman kri'a*'s stance is clearly moralistic and, in an aesthetic sense, humanitarian. Its spokesmen claim that Israel today is vitally in need of a literary journal which will truly cater to "the needs of [current literature] itself and to the needs of its reading audience." Ambitious yet vague, this statement is clarified mainly in terms of literary politics and aesthetics.

The political implications of *Siman kri'a*'s birth become evident in the course of its self-definition as a remedy for the absence of a journal of "real, vital depth," a journal able to provide a "meaningful framework" for literary endeavor. By presenting the "best" of Israel's current literary output, *Siman kri'a* hopes to end the "amorphous mass of cacophonous, dilettantish, and pseudo-scholarly prattle" which, its editors believe, has long plagued the Israeli literary scene. Such highly charged rhetoric blatantly reflects *Siman kri'a*'s quasi-political self image: a vote for *this* journal means a vote for unity and order, professionalism and relevance.

Siman kri'a's explicit statement of intent to change an old-guard state of chaos into a new, effective frontier is not unprecedented. Ironically, it echoes the opening editorial comments of Israel's oldest, mainstream literary journal, *Moznayim* ("Scale," or "Balance"), founded in 1929 as the organ of the newly constituted Hebrew Writers' Association. *Moznayim*, for the past two decades at least, has borne the brunt of persistent ideological attacks, especially by writers involved in new ventures in literary journalism. But its original editors, Y.D. Berkowitz and Fischel Lachower, saw in *Moznayim* an antidote for the state of "decline" and "deterioration," the loss of "clear direction," which, in their view, plagued contemporary Hebrew letters. They, too, intended their journal to be an instrument of renewal, of "clearing the literary atmosphere," and, especially, of "gathering together the scattered forces and restoring the impaired unity" of the Yishuv's literary effort.

Moznayim's call to unity some forty years ago parallels the mandate which *Siman kri'a* has currently imposed on itself; and yet it would be a mistake to equate the factors motivating these two periodicals. *Moznayim*'s editors exhibited a sensitive awareness of their actual historical context. It was, they felt, the thrust of history which had brought *Moznayim* into being; it was a matter of determined necessity, not a willed choice. By the early twenties, they knew that the Soviet regime had effectively shut down the formerly prolific Hebrew presses of Russia and the Ukraine; and Odessa, long the center of the Hebrew renaissance, had had to be abandoned. But even beyond the reach of Soviet officialdom, Hebrew literary life seemed on the wane in Europe. By the mid-twenties, the Berlin community of Hebrew literati, including Bialik and Agnon, for example, was in the process of breaking up and moving gradually to Palestine. By 1929, *Hatekufa*, the giant of Hebrew literary journals, already transferred from Moscow to Warsaw and then to Berlin, was floundering along with the whole Stybel Press enterprise, which, since 1917, had been so significant in financing the development of modern Hebrew literature. Linked to its Zionist-Hebraist ideology and constituency, the Hebrew literary establishment had been transplanted virtually in its entirety, by the end of the twenties, to Tel Aviv. This historical reality prompted *Moznayim*'s editors to see as their mandate the reunification and reinforcement of the entire post-World War I generation of Hebrew writers and readers, a generation whose forces were regrouping in the new Palestinian environment.

> Amid the great turmoil which has befallen Jewish communal life with the disintegration of its main center in Eastern Europe, our literature has not suffered a spiritual revolution which carries within itself the seeds of future renewal; instead, it has suffered total anarchy and ideological chaos. Our literature had an inner unity, which. . . made it a vital, productive force in the life of our people, but that unity has now been shattered. Our best writers. . . have wandered off out of an overwhelming sense of powerlessness and despair. . . . [We need now to] reinstate our literature's inner unity, torn asunder by the ravages of our time.

Moznayim obviously assumed for itself a role dictated by forces well beyond the ambit of purely literary endeavor. The historical perspective evident in *Siman kri'a*'s manifesto is, however, quite different. The editors of *Siman kri'a* appear to be responding, not to an extrinsic dimension of historical reality, but to an intrinsic condition of aesthetic development. They propose to provide new directions in literary offerings and analysis; they demand "newness," "vitality," the fulfillment of contemporary, aesthetic "needs"; they reject what they consider to be passé values in each of the four main categories to be included in the journal's "mixed literary" bag: 1) original fiction and poetry; 2) Hebrew translations of important contemporary works; 3) articles of literary analysis and research; and, finally, 4) reviews of recent Israeli literary works. Much of the manifesto is devoted to explicating *Siman kri'a*'s position in regard to each of these categories. In each case, the tone is quite outspoken, strained, even pugnacious.

Beyond the catch-all terms "centrality" and "worthiness," the editors of *Siman kri'a* clearly pride themselves on what they see as the revolutionary nature of their journal's published prose (though no such claim is made for its poetry, which appears to be more distinguished, if not more avant-garde).

> We are happy that our first issue has been able to present stories which depart from the mainstream of current prose. . . The three works of fiction presented differ from one another, but they have in common liberation from the pillory of Agnonesque and are far from [duplicating] his stylistics. The stories are not a puzzle of meanings, they are devoid of heavy-

handed, ironic twists, and they lack the patterns of allusion [or the allegorical implications] that weigh so heavily [on the reader].

In the editors' view, the fiction published in this first issue offers its readers "an observation of fundamental realities, [*gufei metzi'ut*]"; furthermore, it is purported to "flow properly from the literary possibilities of Israeli reality"; and, finally, its language is "narratively determinative [*sipurit-tahlitit*] and does not stew in its own juices. . . ."

The current needs, as the editors have determined them here, are obviously an unambiguous "realism" and a contemporaneity in both theme and style. Of course, the assumptions implicit in these statements of policy and self-description are that, until now, Israeli literature has been overly obtuse, or allegorical, or allusive; that its language has been too euphuistic or "old-fashioned"; and that it has been remote from an authentic "Israeli reality." Such assumptions cannot go without challenge, however. Why should Agnon, two years after his death at the age of 81, suddenly become the focal point, even symbolically, for a revolution in Hebrew literature? Why Agnon, whose major works (if they are, in fact, to be considered non-"Israeli" or non-"realistic") were published before 1948? Has there, indeed, been no development of an indigenous Israeli literary tradition "realistic" enough to counteract the "excesses" of Agnon's generation? Do the editors of *Siman kri'a* mean to say that works by the "'48-ers," writers like S. Yizhar, Benjamin Tammuz, Moshe Shamir, and Aharon Megged, are generally too allegorical and that their language is too contrived? And are the works of the second generation of Israeli authors -- prose-writers like Amos Oz, A.B. Yehoshua (who both serve on the editorial board of *Siman kri'a*), and Amalia Kahana-Carmon -- mostly "unrealistic"?

Ingenuousness aside, over the years there certainly has been much discussion of the "place" of Israeli literature in the development of modern Hebrew letters. the debate peaked in the sixties, in the wake of the late Baruch Kurzweil's essays which argued that Israeli literature was discontinuous with, and even antithetical to, the entire development of the Hebrew literary tradition in modern times. The historical question itself has since abated, but *Siman kri'a*'s spokesmen seem either to ignore the issue's prior existence or to reshape Kurzweil's outdated indictments into current desiderata. In any case, the inference is that *now* is the time for the *real* revolution in Israeli literary development.

The most troubling aspect of this part of the *Siman kri'a* manifesto is the suggestion that, somehow, Israeli literature has hitherto neither reflected sufficiently (if at all) an "Israeli reality" nor arisen out of its "literary possibilities." To make such a claim about the various social and psychological novels by Yizhar, Shamir, and Megged, among others, is ludicrous, even utterly specious. But there is another historical irony here, at least as far as the rhetoric of literary manifestoes is concerned. In 1945, Moshe Shamir, then 24 years old, composed a manifesto of sorts, called "With My Contemporaries" (*Im bnei dori*), for *Yalkut hare'im* ("The Friends' Magazine"), a "little" magazine founded by a group of young writers during the Second World War. Shamir's demand, employing a rhetoric similar in its hyperbole to that of *Siman kri'a*'s manifesto, was that the new Hebrew literature of *his* generation had to be totally, excruciatingly "realistic."

> We shall never be able to cut ourselves off from life, we shall never be able to escape it, we shall never fear it. . . . The world was not created for the beautiful, the wise, the good -- the world was created for washerwomen, for those who dream of beauty, wisdom, goodness. . . for those who will never be completely victorious. . . . There is no hiding place, no dark corner of human life that does not demand expression, there is not a drop of our blood which is not a part of our whole life experience. . . . All of the "friends" -- they're my contemporaries. Nothing unites us more than a feeling of responsibility to our generation; above and beyond the perplexities of creativity and the songs of modernism. . . what drives us on is the feeling of complete, one-hundred-percent belonging to the *revolution* of *humanity* . . . . Perceiving the world and life as they really are, without illusions, does not conflict in any way with the deepest idealism. On the contrary: it's the very first condition for the existence and development of idealism. The day of cynicism is over. . . . But it will not be replaced by a pleasant, euphuistic, sweet, naive, literature; it will be replaced by a revolutionary, realistic, *merciless* literature.

Shamir's notion of "utter realism" was not only rooted in a naturalistic context, it was also weighted with the utilitarian role of an activist social revolution. Literature, in this view, was conceived as being both *about* the people and *for* the people; and the literature produced by Shamir's "friends" was to be responsible for radically reforming the everyday, common "Hebrew reality" that it depicted. This idea or philosophy of literature had been given numerous ideological formulations -- from Ahad Ha'am's didactic view of Hebrew literature as something necessarily "sober" and "rational," something designed to inculcate the proper Jewish "national feeling"; to Soviet hard-line cultural concepts of "socialist realism" which aim, primarily, at dramatizing the success of Marxist-Leninist principles; to the recently expressed insistence of Black ideologues, that all art is essentially political and that artistic endeavor should be, primarily, a tool to further the cause of Black consciousness and national liberation.

It is immaterial whether one accepts this basically ideological point of view, or any of its variables; or, more specifically, whether Shamir's concept is actually fulfilled in the works of Israel's first generation of writers. The fact is that this mandate, the plea for "realism" in *Siman kri'a*'s manifesto, constitutes, at best, only the most recent eruption of periodically reactivated cries for "relevance" in Israeli literature.

At least two other journals, issued between Shamir's essay in 1945 and Megged's comments in 1971, have pointed to the same pressing need. The founders of *Likrat* ("Toward"), a modest, short-lived but historically important journal, first published in 1953 by another "group of young writers," (mostly students of Hebrew literature at Jerusalem's Hebrew University), noted in their manifesto "the weighty responsibility" they felt in the face of Israel's "new reality" during the early fifties. Their struggle, as they saw it, was with

> individual perplexities. . . the lack of a firmly rooted cultural tradition. . . the partisan atmosphere. . . the crisis of immigrant absorption . . . the loss of real contact between the honest work [of literature] and the reader [and] the lack of understanding on the part of veteran writers.

Especially disturbing for the editors of *Likrat* was their conviction that the old-guard Hebrew writers never really recovered from the shock of the Yishuv's transition to sovereign statehood and, hence, "have not contributed a single new word to our literature" since the War of Independence in 1948. For *Likrat*, therefore, relevance meant confronting an historically imposed "new reality" (here we have an echo of *Moznayim*'s manifesto), an unfamiliar, still vaguely-shaped socio-cultural milieu which, in itself, constituted a mandate for change in aesthetic expression.

In 1955, a few years after *Likrat*'s manifesto, a similarly resounding statement of social consciousness introduced the first -- and only -- issue of *Akhsanya* ("Forum"), edited by the late publicist, Shlomo Grodzensky, and the poet-critics Ezra Sussman (recently deceased), and Natan Zach. One of the goals they mentioned was to provide an avenue of expression for literature of better quality (more "personal, spontaneous, responsible") than what had been appearing "amid the tumult of the daily press." *Akhsanya*'s basic philosophy of literature was, however, the Marxian view that literature, along with all other aspects of human endeavor, was to be measured by its socially utilitarian function. The artist-writer, therefore, was bound to emerge from, and respond and contribute to, his social context:

> A journal for belles-lettres alone is not possible today [especially] in our society which is being constructed out of the remnants of shattered and destroyed worlds and in a world constantly threatened by extinction. . . . The unique and sole right to existence which the humanist has is to observe, to think, to analyze, to question, to feel. . . . This role. . . is surely the unique, the ideal social contribution of literature.

Unlike *Likrat* and *Akhsanya*, *Siman kri'a* is quite ambiguous in demonstrating any similar sort of socially-oriented philosophy. What it does propose is to meet the "needs" of its contemporary audience by providing its readers with examples of good taste. The new journal's basic loyalty to the reading public is, therefore, mainly an aesthetic act; but its promise to present more "realistic" fiction, the essence of its aesthetic viewpoint, remains unfulfilled in this first issue. The three prose works published here are neither more nor less "realistic" or "relevant," either in their content or in their language, than much of the younger mainstream fiction published over the last twenty years. Not only does *Siman kri'a* seem to overlook the historical and aesthetic facts of Israeli literary "realism" since 1948, it also reflects no definitive historical consciousness, other than to state a rather vague intention of moving in an entirely new aesthetic direction. Hence, both claims, the social and the aesthetic, seem to fly in the face of historical and literary realities; and since both claims have been stated before, under various auspices, a certain measure of *déjà vu* is inescapable.

What, then, is unique in *Siman kri'a*? What is distinctive in its self-view? What model do its editors have in mind when they assert that "the contemporary Israeli literary scene. . . has no journal fashioned to meet its needs or the needs of its readers"? And what motivates the effort to issue this type of literary magazine, with such grandiose literary aims and high aesthetic standards, at this point in time?

A partial answer is to be found in *Siman kri'a*'s manifesto, in the section on criticism. Echoing again the argument for a literature directly responsive to contemporary needs, the editors' quarrel with Israel's literary critics is, in the main, that "they have increasingly cut themselves off from the living literature." Unlike the Russian Formalists and the New Critics in their respective times, the editors declare, most Israeli critics have not "asked the questions which are important for and relevant to literature [but only] those which are of interest solely in the small, confined world of the scholar."

Aside from their vaguely democratic aim, these remarks actually reveal a key motivating factor in the founding of the new journal. To a great degree, *Siman kri'a* seems to have been established as a complement to (or antidote for) *Hasifrut* ("Literature"), Israel's leading journal for the study of literature, founded in 1968 and edited by Professor Benjamin Hrushovski (Harshav). Self-proclaimed in its manifesto as "the first [journal] of its kind in Hebrew" (note the similarity in tone to *Siman kri'a*'s opening statement), *Hasifrut* saw itself as beginning "a new stage in Israeli literary study." It would dedicate itself, not to "the criticism of current literature . . .

journalism or ideology," but to a high, "international" standard
of study in the fields of Hebrew literature and poetics. The
Hebrew reader, *Hasifrut* hoped, would "learn that studying the
details of literary works can be more important, more
meaningful, and more interesting than currently accepted
generalizations on literature and writers." But *Hasifrut*'s
stated primary aim, "serving the progress of scientific study,"
appears to have aroused considerable alarm in the literary
community concerning the isolation of literature from the
common interests of the reading public. *Siman kri'a*'s
manifesto reflects this apprehension in its clear warning of the
danger that the present generation of Israeli intellectuals might
suffer alienation from the world of Hebrew literature, its study
and its appreciation.

> A generation of young people who think about literature
> has ceased to ponder literary value, literary taste, and the
> literary mode of expression.   [The result has been an
> accumulation of] verbiage on works of literature, without any
> responsibility toward the specific-essential [aspect] of the work
> being discussed, and without any attention paid to its literary-
> cultural context.

In these remarks *Siman kri'a* does indeed demand a more
humanistic, socio-cultural perspective on literature and
reading; it even evinces a quasi-moralistic emphasis on probing
art's "essence" and evaluating its "meaning." However,
"responsibility," as the editors use the term, seems to connote a
notion of relevance that is quite ambivalent. On the one hand,
at several points in the manifesto the editors underscore the
writer's accountability to his immediate social environment, to
his audience, to his "literary-cultural context" -- a point of view
parallel, in essence, to *Likrat*'s and *Akhsanya*'s agitation for
social awareness. On the other hand, for *Siman kri'a*, in its
totality, relevance apparently means aesthetic transvaluation
for its own sake or for the sake of impelling literary or linguistic
development -- a philosophy parallel, in essence, to *Hasifrut*'s
demand for high standards of literary study in the name of
meaningfulness.
     Evidently, *Siman kri'a* is attempting to don two caps at
once, one of social consciousness, and one of aesthetic

progressiveness. Although these roles are to be shared, the former is mainly the responsibility of the critic in his interpretive work, and the latter mainly the responsibility of the writer in his creative work. However, this journal's basic loyalty is still aesthetic; for the editors go on to state that "*Siman kri'a* has consciously limited its publication of research and criticism in deference to literature which can and must stand at the center of the literary experience of today's writers and readers." It seems obvious, too, that the brunt of these remarks is again directed at *Hasifrut's* assumption of a "purely scientific role."

Two additional motivating factors are evident in the founding of *Siman kri'a*: the revival of a journalistic model to fulfill all the variegated roles of literary presentation to the Israeli reader; and the need simply to create more publishing space for works by younger writers. The choice of models -- I use the phrase in the sense of spiritual continuity within a literary tradition -- is clearly *Akhshav* ("Now"), founded in 1959 and defunct since 1968. It is no accident that *Siman kri'a's* initial issue includes the first installment of reminiscences on *Akhshav's* founding and history; and two poets, David Avidan and Ory Bernstein, formerly involved closely with *Akhshav*, are now major contributors to *Siman kri'a*. Moreover, the new journal's manifesto parallels, in outline at least, the editorial comments that appeared in *Akhshav's* first issue. The second factor is one of literary economics: for various aesthetic and ideological reasons the existing channels are deemed inadequate, and *Siman kri'a* hopes to offer more prestigious space for up-and-coming Israeli writers, the group it purports to represent.

Thus, the appearance of *Siman kri'a* reflects a combination of journalistic, social, and literary ingredients: "economic," in the sense of fulfilling the need for additional breathing room for younger writers; "political," in the sense of offering these writers and their readers, alike, a unified front and an organ for more effective expression; and "aesthetic," in the sense of promising to publish more refreshing (or avant-garde), more realistic (or relevant) original works, to print criticism which is analytic and yet more palatable to the general reader, and to present Hebrew translations of "modern classics."

Siman kri'a's translation policy, discussed at length in the
manifesto, demonstrates that the journal intends not merely "to
acquaint Hebrew readers with the modern classics of world
literature." Its main goal is language oriented, to make Hebrew
itself more flexible, "to free it," as the editorial puts it, "from the
Mendele-Berkowitz-Shlonsky tradition of exaggerated
linguistic purism" (pejoratively referred to as *melitza*).
Although the new translations which appear in this issue --
selections from Woolf, Faulkner, and Richard Brautigan --
really do not go very far in liberating Hebrew from its
euphuistic chains, they firmly convey both the continuation of
this "liberal," culturally broadening tradition in Hebrew literary
journalism and the ever-sharper turning toward Western
European and American works of an innovative character.
Significantly, too, the journal contains an announcement of
Siman Kri'a Publications, which plans to publish an extensive
list of translated works, including novels by Gide, Nabokov,
Fitzgerald, Lowry, Genet, Updike, and Grass.

Its declared intent of focusing on belles-lettres
notwithstanding, *Siman kri'a* allots only forty pages to poetry
(though eleven poets in a wide-ranging selection are presented)
and one hundred thirty pages, more than one-third the
journal's space, to criticism of various sorts. Ironically, some of
these essays are highly specialized and resemble the academic
articles so characteristic of *Hasifrut*. However, since most of
these essays deal quite readably with contemporary writings --
including close readings of works by Gabriel Preil, David Fogel,
Natan Zach, and A.B. Yehoshua -- they are genuinely useful
aids for the sophisticated reading and proper understanding of
the authors and works they discuss. In any case, both the
proportion of critical essays and another announcement of
several projected volumes of criticism under the aegis of Siman
Kri'a Publications demonstrate the editors' central
preoccupation with poetics, in spite of their stated preference
for literature over criticism.

In several aspects of its first issue, especially in its
pronouncements of self-definition, *Siman kri'a* seems to be
caught in the vortex of the games journals play. Its overstated,
outdated nihilism and its self-indulgent mouthings serve only to
create a tone of empty competitiveness which conflicts with the

editors' own dedication to improving the quality of contemporary Hebrew language and literature. One might have hoped that the manifesto of *this* journal would have reflected a more measured self-consciousness as well as a more sensitive awareness of journalistic history and tradition, without necessarily sacrificing its serious -- or even its revolutionary -- sense of purpose.

Fortunately, however, most of the shortcomings discernible in *Siman kri'a*'s introductory issue remain within the realm of the peripheral. In view of its generally outstanding literary and critical offerings and the great promise of future issues and of its accompanying publications enterprise, *Siman kri'a* stands suddenly, but clearly, at the center of literary activity in Israel. It should surely be given regular attention by all who are interested in the current ambience of Modern Hebrew Literature.

Judaism: A Quarterly Journal of Jewish Life and Thought,
Spring, 1974: 202-211.

---

[1] Remarks on the appearance on *Siman kri'a*: A Diversified Quarterly for Literature, edited by Menahem Perry and Meir Wieseltier. (Tel Aviv: University Publications), 1, 1 (Sept., 1972).
[2] I have purposely rendered all my translations from the Hebrew in this article in a rather literal style. -- W.B.

Children and Lovers: On Yehuda Amichai's Poetic Works

> I who stand in the midst of my days
> like water in a pitcher
> love the things that really don't matter.

Were the institution of poet laureate to be initiated in Israel, Yehuda Amichai would most likely be the popular choice. Not that he is the Grand Old Man of Israeli poetry; there are those who predate him, yet speak, as he does, in a contemporary mode; there are those who began their careers, as he did, in the wake of Israel's War of Independence; and there are those who have been as engaged as he with Israel's triumphs and trials. It is Amichai's unique poetic voice that has proved so appealing through the years, a voice consistently in consonance with the spirit of his people and his times.

Not merely contemporary in a topical or linguistic sense, Amichai has displayed a charm and a wit which have endeared him to both an Israeli and an international reading audience. In an historical vein, his affinity mainly to British and American models of poetic expression has made him a founding father of Israel's literary modernism. Though they are generically and stylistically varied, Amichai's works -- so far, there are four volumes of poetry, one of short stories, one of dramatic writings, and two novels -- reverberate with relevance and insight, with aesthetic challenge and pleasure.

One of the most distinctive elements of Amichai's poetry is its disarming simplicity. In reading his poems, one often has the feeling of reading a diary without days, a record of someone's personal impressions or intellectual musings, set down at random. This perception is prompted by several of the poetry's central characteristics: the quasi-autobiographical voice, the aphoristic nature of many of his lines, his patently casual, candid tone, his way of creating sequence through seemingly disjuncted images or metaphors.

Two figures predominate in his poetry: the child and the lover. Both give rise to a tone of intimacy and innocence; both supply a resonance of sentiment and sensitivity; both seem temporarily well protected and secure, insulated by parents' love and by lovers' passion. At the same time, however, they are obviously quite vulnerable to separation and loss. The child grows up, parents are gone, the world and its wars are impassive to warmth and feeling. In "Lovers in Fall" the irony focuses on the idea that, like a clock itself, lovers are oblivious to time, yet they are mirrors, so to speak, of its passing. Childlike fantasies, reminiscent of familiar fairy tales or certain paintings by Chagall, form a protective shell for lovers who attempt to escape painful realities.

> All night the moon worked like mad
> to blur all conflict, to appease blood and
> water.

But the recurring, mocking refrain -- "I told you it would be like this, but you didn't believe it" -- makes it clear that even lovers, with all their beguiling ingenuity, cannot evade the dual fate of life and death. One of humanity's basic struggles, says Amichai, is to realize that the "world" and "love" are not separate entities, that all are bound to recognize the ultimate ends of things, even of love itself.

Of course, the images of children and lovers are merely configurations of all those who would wish naively for continued happiness and goodness, the true believers, in a sense, of faithful mankind. However, Amichai's point of view is not really as tragic as it is sardonic, chiding, bemused. The poet's "I told you so" implies that whatever one's hopes and dreams, people are often turned emotionally into disappointed children or betrayed lovers, victimized not by oppressive social forces or flippant personal behavior but by the normal course of time and change.

Amichai's numerous recurring symbols -- ships, trains, roads, trips, tides, migrating birds, changing seasons -- emphasize the inexorable transitoriness of being, "the sawdust of time." Ironically, the only items of permanence evident are the everpresent reminders of elusiveness and transition: the living memory of a father, the imaginary return to places and times, the "now" and the "other days" that quickly become "then," the ambiguous "you see" which bespeaks the obligatory acceptance of things under the guise of their being explained.

Above all, there are those very "things" themselves, namely, *die Dinge*, borrowed from Rilke's rather philosophical view of the finiteness of objects, and transformed in Amichai's parlance into the ambiguous but intractable order of existence. The only way around these "things" is the questioning voice, an awareness of the need continually to seek meaning. In other words, it is the consciousness of the poet, that reminds us of our being always in mid-passage, in "the spaces between the times," forever muddling our way through "the great rambling expanse" of the hopeless soul.

If there is any philosophical messge to be found in Amichai's poetry, it is that one is sure only of being and having been, never of where, how, or why one is going. But resisting both escapist hedonism and somber existentialism, Amichai's philosophy steers a middle path. A lingering despair combines with a sound sense of humor and a healthy appreciation of irony. The result is a kind of celebration of humanity's futile yet often amusing attempts to survive through intimacy and sensibility. We are all children, lost in the world; the further we move through life, the closer, paradoxically, we stay to childhood. As humans, as mature creatures in control of being, we at best make only dubious progress.

This central irony -- the gradual recognition of essential changelessness along with the certain knowledge of time's unalterable advance -- is evoked most poignantly in Amichai's elegies. In the "Elegy on the Lost Child," images of lovers, faces, landscapes and everyday household items such as doors, cups and chairs are presented in a slowly swirling, metaphorical spiral. The interwoven sequence in itself suggests the mere interchangeability of situations and feelings rather than any real development of being. Figurative places such as "the land of forgetfulness," "our little room," and "the houses of tomorrow" express the ongoing need for insulation, for putting up defenses in the face of life's cold verities. Love provides inadequate protection; it is "like a blanket that's too short." And the quest for value and self-fulfillment usually reveals "all that sought to remain uncovered."

The real object of the search, "the lost child," is Amichai's symbol for all potential naivete in pathetic conflict with the apparently fixed world order. At first the child merely appears to be "lost," but in the poem's development he becomes increasingly distant: he's "disappeared," he "cannot be found," and, finally, "he died in the night." But between these stations leading to his demise, the child reappears and ironically seems to live with increasing vigor and unabated permanence: "He, not we, hears the stones singing"; he stays on after the lovers part, "and he began to resemble the mountains, winds and olive tree trunks." The paradox is highlighted structurally; the only real movement in the poem is the child's advance toward death. That, indeed, seems to be the motivation for the elegy itself. Yet it is not the child's death that is the source of tragedy. Far more than any so-called loss of innocence, it is rather an ambiguous adulthood that is mourned in this work. The very quest is an exercise in futility, for the fate of man-child is his transience. In a characteristically ironic twist, Amichai presents him not as a child born a *tabula rasa* proceeding then through a developmental existence, but rather as a perpetual child who, having lived, dies "clean and white as a sheet of paper." After the child's death, the elegy closes with a masterful understatement which points up humanity's unawareness of its own paramount oblivion.

> But it seemed to us that something had
> Happened: we heard a ringing,
> Like a coin falling. We stood up.
> We turned around. We bent down.
> We didn't find anything; so we kept on going.
> Each to his own.

The elegies evince much of what may be called the universalistic Amichai. More particularistic, in a geographic and an emotive but not an ideological sense, are the poems about Jerusalem, Amichai's home for more than three decades. It appeared in some early poems of the fifties, but played a rather peripheral role, usually as symbolic setting. After the 1967 War, however, Amichai composed a long cycle of poems called "Jerusalem 1967," several of which appear in the translated collection *Songs of Jerusalem and Myself.*

In this cycle Jerusalem has many faces. It wrestles with its several names, thus reflecting in its varied identity the vicissitudes thrust on it by a long history of frequent conflict; its golden hues beam with "all this great light" of recent victory, yet its skies are dotted with stars "like the bubbles of drowning men," flooded with the memory of those who died so recently for its reunification; it seems poised always on the brink of history, like a runner at the start in an international Olympic event.

But there is humor here as well. In a poem near the end of the cycle the ancient Temple Mount is portrayed as a great luxury liner "always arriving, always departing." The stones of the Western Wall are its portholes; joyous Hasidim, all dressed in white for Yom Kippur, its busy crew. With great satiric wit Amichai transforms the new-old Jerusalem, with its incessant post-1967 hubbub, into "the Venice of God"!

Like this later treatment of Jerusalem, Amichai's popularity throughout the fifties and sixties can be attributed to his blending various themes, voices, and images with dominant issues in contemporary Israeli life, mainly war and soldiering, and their effects on the Israeli psyche. Much of Amichai's poetry in those years portrays his sense of the ironic gap between the notion of national heroism and the need for individual equanimity. Amichai handles the dual tension of historical and psychological survival with masterful combinations of compassion and wit, tragic irony and spirited humor. In one poem, for example, he parodies the usual heroic standard of "dying with one's boots on" by offering the refrain, "but I want to die on my bed." The antiheroic stance bespeaks no cowardice or weakness; it aims rather at an individualized portrayal of the dilemma inherent in Israel's political situation.

Mirroring aspects of recent debates on the so-called "Masada complex," Amichai's poetry has long exhibited considerable insight into the Israeli psyche regarding war. The Israeli-as-soldier is confronted as much by his own mythic predecessors -- warrior-victors like Joshua, Samson and Trumpeldor -- as he is by his contemporary enemies. He is a kind of child-soldier pitted against his forefather-hero. In one poem he is depicted as bivouacked in a nursery school, surrounded by toys, a teddy-bear for his pillow; but he is ever cognizant of the "fires" that loom beyond the window. The central conflict, however, is an inner one: how to maintain a basic humanism in the face of the terrible necessity of doing

battle. War confronts the soldier-poet with the possible loss of those aspects of his existence which constitute his daily, human situation. His very normalcy or identity is so threatened by the warrior role that he must take on that everything dear to him is continually hovering in his consciousness: a worried father, a concerned (though dead) mother, a passionate lover. But duty demands his total denial of personal wants. Again, in the war poems, the child and the lover predominate, both superseded by the soldier dedicated to his role of protector, who is himself so much in need of security and protection.

In that these soldier figures are essentially children and lovers, temporarily disestablished for a purpose so reasonable yet so emotionally disabling, Amichai's poetic works may be seen as lyrical versions of the consciousness S. Yizhar created for his adolescent soldiers in the epic novel, *Days of Ziklag* (1958). There, too, the young men are locked in a battle for survival, but their hearts and minds spill over with the reminiscent warmth of girlfriends, families, fields and villages.

Amichai, however, does not stop short at war's melancholy abrogation of love and innocence. The understated, incredulous voice of the child-soldier in "A Body on the Battlefield," conveys through ironic juxtaposition the horror of the maiming and dying.

> His blood was tossed hastily, sloppily,
> like clothes
> of someone too tired.
> How big the night grew!
> Windows were right,
> like my parents when I was a boy.

At the sight of the bloodied corpse, the observer turns into a wide-eyed boy, wondering at the darkness of it all, acknowledging -- only to highlight the sense of naivete, of course -- that there really must have been some truth to those parental warnings after all. The appalling if unwitting pettiness of the suddenly infantilized comrade-in-arms thrusts into relief the grim recognition of man's fragility and the ugly finality of death. This awful truth, perceived in the "windows" -- a recurring metaphor for the reality principle -- conveys a

flash of awareness which projects the world's natural, uncontrollable harshness and disorder.

As seen in other of Amichai's war poems, the disarray is cosmic; the entire universe, even God, the veritable creator of order, seems to have gone awry.

> God has mercy on kindergarten children,
> less so on schoolchildren.
> And for adults he has no mercy at all;
> He leaves them alone,
> and at times they must crawl on all fours
> in the burning sand
> to get to the aid station
> and they're gushing blood.

Divine mercy appears misplaced; the ones who seem to need it the most go begging.

Like those who seek to regain the irrecoverable elements of life -- "to revise the map of my life," in Amichai's phrase -- the poet defines himself as someone facing a great puzzle, a perfectly powerless being "who uses only a small number of words in the dictionary," yet is continually "forced against his will to solve riddles" about how the world really works. Expressing some reluctance even to play this passive role as a poet ("he thought he would write for a while/till he'd find what he really wanted to do"), Amichai nods his head in resignation, acquiescing to, if not quite agreeing with, some inscrutable higher wisdom that says, knowingly, this is the way it must be.

> As for the world,
> I'm always like Socrates's students: I walk by
> his side,
> listening to his seasons and history,
> and what I can say is:
> Yes, that is indeed true.
> You're right again.
> Certainly, you are correct.

These themes are by no means unique. "Pack up your troubles," "The girl I left behind," "I won't forget you," "War is hell," "The world's gone mad" -- the slogans are the stuff of romantic ballads, wartime ditties, and protest songs. Several factors,

however, distinguish Amichai's artistic versions of these motifs. The first is mainly extrinsic. By combining his casual tone and rhythms with oblique but obvious commentaries on the national character and events of the day, Amichai became the heir apparent of the famous poet Natan Alterman, who, throughout the forties in his "Seventh Column," had published droll political poems with catchy puns and tongue-in-cheek references that helped the Yishuv through some of its darkest days.

Related to Amichai's position as a major transmitter of the modern Hebrew poetic tradition is his deft blending of traditional and colloquial Hebrew diction. Avraham Shlonsky, Leah Goldberg, and Alterman had energized their poems with heavy doses of traditional phraseology, taken from biblical, rabbinic, and liturgical sources familiar to their readers; and poets contemporary with Amichai, such as Amir Gilboa and Haim Gouri, mixed modern idioms, even Israeli slang, with weighty, mainly biblical turns of phrase. Amichai's particular talent is his juxtaposing an obviously archaic phrase to one blatantly contemporary, much as he often blends the seriousness of dramatic situation with the playfulness of his tone. Sometimes the method is parody, as it is here in his use of the last verse of the *Kaddish* prayer.

> The jet plane
> makes peace in its high places
> upon us and upon all
> those who love in the fall.

At other times, instead of twisting meanings, he obstinately presses for the literalness of a familiar phrase, in order to convey an ironic message. Such is his use of the opening line of the *Yizkor* memorial prayer in a poem which expresses the clash of the reality of human experience with the stock, traditional -- and for Amichai, bitterly paradoxical -- response.

> God full of Mercy [*El male rahamim*]
> If it weren't for God's being full of mercy
> there might be some mercy in the world
> and not just in him.

> I who have picked flowers on the mountain
> and looked into all the valleys,
> I, who have brought back bodies from the
> hills, can tell you that the world is empty of
> mercy.

A more humorous approach is evident in Amichai's play with colloquial idioms, already noted in the "I told you so" poem quoted earlier.   Following Auden's lead, though Alterman's inveterate punning is again a main influence here, Amichai adroitly transforms the come-on line "If you've got the time, I've got the place" into

> We were together on my time and at your place.
> You offered the place and I the time.

The familiar phrase "the calm before the storm" becomes the ironic reverse:

> Now, in the storm before the calm,
> I can tell you things I couldn't in the calm
> before the storm . . . .

And the Israeli children's chant, "We won't go to sleep, we want to fool around" (*lo rotsim lishon, rotsim lehishtage'a*), also changes radically, if not so humorously.   As the lovers mature over the years, their passion diminishes, their relationship dwindles; so they say, "Now we just want to go to sleep."

Amichai's forte, however, is his extraordinary skill in the use of figurative language.   Since many of his similes have a homey, "down-to-earth" ring to them, this aspect of Amichai's figurative language is probably responsible for the superficial labels of "gentleness" or "simplicity" which often describe his poetry in general. But Amichai is no poetic Grandma Moses. With impressive original force he has turned aside Alterman's symbolist tendency -- Alterman's lyrical poetry is infused with highly abstract figurative patterns -- and has consciously opted for more concrete linguistic structures. At times the results are comic. The triumphant lover, for example, approaches his girl with the line, "So you're finally alone, like a bank at night,/with all the gold that's in it, that's in you." At others the effect is to heighten seriousness: the person sensitive to the ways of the world perceives "how people who leave [in the morning] intact/are returned home at night like pieces of small change."

Another major technique employed by Amichai is a chain-like series of seemingly disparate metaphors which actually links the poem's parts into a unity of meaning. In "God Has Mercy on Kindergarten Children," for example, the varied images presented are children of different ages, adults, soldiers, "true lovers," a shady tree, a man sleeping on a park bench, "we," and "the last coins of kindness" bequeathed by mother. The reader is forced continually to consider the connective elements of each abstruse image as it is added to the growing metaphorical design. Because of this technique, it may be said that many of Amichai's poems develop in burgeoning blocks of figurative patterns, instead of direct, vertical lines. The reader must set these blocks in order, as it were; one must employ a creative intelligence in order to discover the common denominators of objects which at first glance, at least, seem highly dissimilar.

Often there are sustained lighter sides to Amichai's works, particularly in many of his short stories. Though poetic in style and serious in implication, they are motivatd by a dramatic, theatrical imagination which blends Kafka's grotesquerie, Agnon's dreamy surrealism, and Ionesco's absurdity. In "The Battle for the Hill," for example, a hurried army mobilization is presented in purposely disjointed scenes and dialogues. As the impending battle draws near, the dramatic and the verbal actions become chaotic.

> Cars drove through the streets at a whisper, children ceased to shout. My wife took in the wash from the roof; women soldiers dressed in pajamas stood by the antennas and spoke into space. . . . Jews maddened by the Psalms stood in courtyards, trumpeters and drummers practiced in the youth centers. Proclamations were pasted to human backs. . . Girls in hoop skirts parachuted in public squares. Metallic sounds filled the air. Commands were whispered. Loudspeakers were set up. Silent speakers frightened the sleepers.[1]

As in many of the poems, the humor and the aesthetic appeal flow from Amichai's talent for ironic juxtapositions in both phrasing and context. Since the entire narrative is really a fanciful expedition into plangent reminiscenses of war's disruptiveness, the battle never happens at all. The narrator-soldier emerges from the impressionistic scene of memory and ends up waiting for a haircut -- a favorite image in Amichai's works for the passage of time and ironic change. When his former captain flashes past in the mirror, the narrator thinks to himself: "Sometimes my whole life passes before my eyes in the barber's mirror."

This same type of intertwined time and scene sequence is employed as the structural design of Amichai's 1963 novel, *Not of This Time, Not of This Place*. In this book the main character, Joel -- another quasi-autobiographical figure -- meanders emotionally and even physically, or so it seems, between two conflicting worlds: the agonizing return to the now all but *Judenrein* Germany of his youth, and the pleasurable but otherwise similarly overwhelming love affair with a non-Jewish American nurse in Jerusalem. The sensuousness of the love trysts (with a woman so uninvolved spiritually in inner Jewish perplexities) is clearly a ploy to keep Joel in Jerusalem, away from the painful recognition of the Holocaust and the consequent loss of contact with his own past. Because of the staggered sequence, the reader too waivers continually between Jerusalem and Germany; one is certain only of the imposed simultaneity of symbolic action, of the spiritual schizophrenia which gives the tragic hero no rest.

Eroticism as escape is the main objective and theme of Amichai's *Lolita*-like 1971 novel, *Who Will Give Me Shelter* (a direct reference to Jeremiah's wish to flee to the desert because of the rampant moral decay in Judea; but the title may also elicit the more contemporary "Gimme Shelter" by the Rolling Stones). The work presents a rather repulsive, burlesque treatment of a formerly prolific Hebrew poet who leaves Israel for New York City, only to become a Humbert Humbert type, rooming in a fleabag hotel, bogged down in abject promiscuity with the adolescent Ziva (splendor) and in his ridiculous job advertising women's lingerie. The grotesque sensuality heightens the plight of the alienated loner, beset by the loss of family, hope, or any grasp on the central, controlling forces of life, a situation reminiscent, too, of John Updike's *Rabbit Redux*. Amichai's novel, however, ends with no sense of return or even accommodation. Faced with the imminent outbreak of the 1967 War, with his son called up for service (instead of on his way to visit him in New York), the ex-father-poet is indeed abandoned in the wilderness, pathetically impaired by his own paralysis.

In the late sixties and early seventies Amichai seems to have become more sensuous in his writing, not casually or playfully, but rather in a way that suggests a personal hungering for self-insulation, an uncontainable need for immediacy and privacy. This trend is particularly evident in the "Achziv Poems" of his third collection, *Not Just to Remember* (1971), and is continued -- with an emphasis on a tone of personal remorse -- in his latest collection, *Behind All This There's Great Happiness Hiding* (1974). These later poems are characterized generally by a pronounced colloquial, far less figurative style. The rhythms are much more akin to casual speech than ever before; "live" voices, speaking in brief, poignant phrases, emerge from within nostalgic scenes or sentimental reflections. In the *Great Happiness* collection the mood is, for the most part, dejected, the voice partial to trauma, engrossed in sadness. This tone is especially pronounced in the post-Yom Kippur War cycle, "Songs of the Land of Zion Jerusalem," a phrase borrowed from the last line of Israel's national anthem, "Hatikvah" (hope), thus heightening the tragically ironic disparity between the long-standing dream and the current, crushing reality. In these elegiacal poems, which embody Amichai's responses to the Yom Kippur War, both the child and the lover are acutely vulnerable victims of the blind vagaries of conflict. Love affairs, one poem states, always happen "after World War II" or "a day before the Six-Day War," but never, it seems, before or "during the peace." Referring in another work to his infant son David, born only a few months before the 1974 War, Amichai writes:

> Our baby was weaned in the first days of the
> war. And I ran to look

over the awful desert.

At night I came back to see him
asleep. He's beginning to forget his
mother's nipples
and he'll keep forgetting until the next war.

And so, still so little, his hopes are sealed off
and his pleas open up, never to be quieted again.

The message is clearly grim: innocence is surrendered practically before it is attained.

In a personal reminiscence of Auden published in a recent issue of *The New Yorker* ("Reflections," January 20, 1975), Hannah Arendt speaks of an innate "animal *tristesse*" she perceives underlying the poet's range of emotion. His poetry, she suggests, really belongs to the post-World War I generation, "with its curious mixture of despair and *joie de vivre*." Much the same, allowing for the appropriate time change, could be said of Amichai and his poetic works. His impish disdain for rules and formalities, his casual but potent projections of inconsistent realities, his penchant for paradoxical portraits of children and lovers -- all these qualities characterize Amichai, too, as one of *les malheureux* in the world of contemporary poetry.

The broad affinity notwithstanding, there is something in Amichai's works that makes him very Jewish, very Israeli, something beyond his kings and prophets, beyond his landscape and language: it is his resurgent response to his people's plight, his capacity for conveying the national grief as a personal elegy. Though fairly flippant in his early commitment to "things that really don't matter," Amichai has internalized the shock waves of the Yom Kippur War and admits to a searing speechlessness, to a forced renunciation of all insight -- quite an anguished state of mind for a poet of such genius.

The poem called "I Have Nothing To Say" ends with a biting but weary mock-affirmation of a world order which defies reason yet demands acquiescence. This ironic confirmation-from-despair of a twisted existence is, in the words of Randall Jarrell, the "monumental certainty" that gnaws at Amichai's ambivalent soul and, at the same time, makes him a great poet.

> And because of the war I say once again,
> for the final, simple sweetness of it all:
> The sun revolves around the earth, yes it does.
> The world is flat, like a lost piece of lumber that
> flowers, yes it is.
> There is a God in heaven, yes there is.

Midstream, October, 1975: 50-57.

---

1 *Israeli Stories*, ed. Joel Blocker (Schocken Books: New York, 1965), p. 214f.

The Image of the Arab in Israeli Literature

One of the first and, by now, classic confrontations between Arab and Jew in modern Hebrew literature is depicted in a short vignette by Yosef Hayim Brenner (1880-1921). Walking homeward through a Jaffa grove one evening in 1921, Brenner happened to meet a young Arab boy whom he recognized as a citrus worker. Casually questioning the boy, Brenner learned to his dismay that the boy was working an inordinate number of hours in the groves for terribly meager pay -- a few pennies per day. The writer, long sensitive to the plight of the impoverished working class, sympathized with the boy and pondered his plight from the point of view of the Jewish settlers' moral liability.

> My young brother! It does not matter whether the scholars are right or not, whether we are blood relations or not; I feel you are my responsibility. I must enlighten you and teach you the ways of human relationships. [Not socialism or revolution or politics at all] though we might be involved in these out of despair, because we have no choice. No, not these. But the contact between one human being and another. . . now and for generations to come. . . with no other purpose or goal. . . than the wish to be a brother, a companion, a friend. . . .[1]

Brenner's perception of the young Arab is that of a soul brother, a fellow sufferer, a victim of powerlessness and economic persecution. The boy's naiveté has been exploited, his innocence and youth defiled both by local landowners and by generations of socio-cultural forces. Though Brenner's pose in this vignette is apolitical, all his social and political thinking comes to bear in this brief encounter. His rhetoric of "despair" and "no choice" sums up his basic-human-rights philosophy for the Jewish settlement in Eretz Yisrael, a philosophy which presumes to move beyond conventional systems of social thought and action (much the same as the notion of non-violence has done in recent times), in order to project a deeply moralistic, even spiritual tenor of unequivocal justice. In this sense, the young Arab boy is a symbol of all downtrodden peoples whose inalienable rights have been abrogated; and

28

Brenner's declaration of responsibility to and mutuality with this symbolic figure of the Arab bespeaks his view of the plight of the Jew at that time. Identification, not tolerance, is the issue; Arab and Jew are brothers, not enemies; they are united, in Brenner's egalitarian vision, by common human needs and goals.

Brenner's death at the hand of Arab marauders in Jaffa, only a few weeks after this sketch was written, is certainly a terribly tragic irony of history.[2] His symbolic perspective stands, however, as a keynote journalistic piece in the annals of modern Hebrew literature's treatment of the Arab. Most later writers who offered fictional portraits of Arab figures followed Brenner's example by projecting through these images central aspects of their own self-views, aspects of their own feelings and experiences in pre- and post-1948 Israel.

In the early decades of the century, much of the literature depicting Arabs consisted of a folkloristic or local-color type of fiction. In *B'nai arav* (People of Arabia), stories of Moshe Smilansky (1874-1953), and the collected works of Yitzhak Shami (1889-1949), for example, the reader is presented with varied, quasi-ethnological portrayals of Arab life: their customs, tribal ceremonies, rivalries, foods, love relationships.[3] Generally this genre of literature depicts Arab society as a self-contained world, with little or no intrusion by alien outsiders; it is akin to the glimpses of inner, native life rendered by Cooper and Kipling in nineteenth-century fiction.

The image which dominates this local-color literature is the nomad, the Bedouin. Representing a reality so far removed from the circumscribed experience of the *shtetl*-born Jew, the Bedouin was a most romantic figure. He was a primitive being, at home in the untamed, natural setting of the fearsome desert; an exotic figure, full of mystery, intrigue, impulsive violence and instinctive survival; at once a bold victor and a vulnerable victim of political power struggles and inimical surroundings.

It was probably more for his naturalness, his ways of accommodation to a hostile environment, that the Bedouin represented for these writers their own encounter with the pristine land, their own wish for a settled adjustment to the unfamiliar, recalcitrant, new country. These vicarious notions of "naturalness" and "rootedness" seem to have attracted the

Hebrew writers to the nomad as a central character.⁴ Beyond
these factors, the Bedouin also may have represented a figure
parallel to the Jewish watchmen (*shomrim*): gallant,
swashbuckling horsemen, the epitome of dashing, romantic
heroes. The Bedouin was the Eastern version, it may be said,
of a combined cowboy-Indian chief persona. (Hollywood's
depiction of Valentino as "The Sheik" combines several of these
highly romanticized ingredients.) Both the Bedouin tribesmen
and the *shomer* were thus figments of a frontier society
imagination.

Shami's rendition of the Bedouin's unmitigated love for
his horse (with the accompanying jealousy) exemplifies these
elements of the fiction:

> Mansur went inside the tent and entered the women's
> compartment to give his instructions. While he was thus
> engaged, the slave slowly approached the mare until he was
> within two or three paces of her. Looking about. . . he stared
> intently into her eyes and whispered a magic spell.
>
> The mare stared back at the slave, as if studying him. He
> went up to her, passed his finger tips caressingly over her
> head and along her back, rubbed her head, patted her flank
> and legs, and wound her long glossy tail about his arm. . . .
>
> As Mansur came out of the tent, he was astonished to see
> the slave embracing his mare's head, kissing her forehead
> and giving her a handful of parched corn mixed with grains
> of salt. . . .
>
> A shadow of apprehension, jealousy and anxiety crossed
> Mansur's face. The sight of the Negro courting his mare
> disturbed him. . . . Coldly he said: "The food is ready. Go and
> eat in God's name."⁵

This genre of literature is blatantly naive. (Perhaps
changing tastes on the part of a readership removed from the
particular milieu described in the fiction have accentuated an
already apparent quaintness.) The "noble savage" figure of the
Arab, however, overcame this naiveté by projecting a vital,
romantic model for the "new Jew" in Eretz Yisrael. The Jewish
pioneer was then forging a totally new, vigorous existence for
himself in an unfamiliar land. He saw himself as a *halutz*
(pioneer), actively fulfilling A. D. Gordon's notions of the
return to and unity with nature, the soulful, "religious"

immersion in toil, the cosmic repair and regeneration of Jewish roots in new, healthy soil. The Bedouin thus represented for the Jew in the Palestinian Mandate period wishful possibilities of his own self-renewal as a deghettoized, liberated, "natural" human being.

Another prominent theme in this Arab-oriented literature is the love affair. Here, too, certain motifs parallel those already current in contemporary Hebrew fiction about Jewish love experiences. For example, Smilansky's story about a Sheik's daughter,[6] promised against her will to someone she does not love, parallels similar depictions of misguided matches in stories by M. Y. Berditchevsky and Ya'acov Steinberg. Steinberg's "Bat harav" (The rabbi's daughter),[7] bears an especially close resemblance to the Smilansky story.

The lamentable situation of both heroines is heightened by their respective social prominence and imposed public responsibility. More effective (and melodramatic) is the love affair between Arab and Jew. Perhaps the most extended portrayal of such a taboo-ridden relationship is to be found in the novel *Ba'al be'amav* (Master of his people) by Yehuda Burla.[8] Doomed from the start, the secret love affair between Gideon and Hamada is reminiscent of similar "strange loves" in earlier fiction by Berditchevsky and Hazaz. Predominant in these works is the notion of taboo. Love for the outsider eventually meets with downfall and despair in a romantic, psychological sense, if not in socio-cultural terms.[9]

The first generation of Israeli writers -- among them S. Yizhar, B. Tammuz, M. Shamir, and A. Megged -- produced a number of short stories about Arabs.[10] For the most part, these stories reflect issues of concern with regard to the "Arab problem" in the newly-founded Jewish state. The central issues are Arab displacement from their land and property, the victimization of innocent villagers by forces beyond their control, and the agonized feelings of loss in terms of personal relations or possibilities of peace. The point of view is sympathetic; the tone, whether strident or understated, is clearly moralistic.

One of the best known stories of this generation is "Hashavuy" (The prisoner) by S. Yizhar.[11] Once again the central Arab figure is a Bedouin, a shepherd who, though merely an innocent bystander, is taken captive by an Israeli patrol during the 1948-49 War of Independence. The narrator's view of the platoon commander is bluntly sardonic; he seems impelled to take "some action," to accomplish "something concrete" no matter how trivial or inane. The story's dramatic effect derives mainly from the underlying conflict between the empty purposefulness of the military command (the shepherd is interrogated and beaten harshly) and the strong ambivalence of the soldier-narrator, who struggles with his sense of duty and his concomitant feelings of basic, human empathy.

From the very start the dualism of character and theme is fixed. The soldiers are the strong, booted interlopers, who trample the peaceful field of grain and capture the harmless shepherd. They intrude into the quiet, idyllic scene to complete their questionable task. Yet the inner view the soldiers have of themselves is close to that of the innocent Bedouin. They, too, in their consciousnesses are immersed in "golden valleys of grain -- the kind of world that fills you with peace." They yearn for the "good, fertile earth" and the kibbutz harvest, "not to be one of the squad which the sergeant was planning to thrust bravely into the calm of the afternoon."[12]

The caustic irony turns moralistic in the story's sequence. The dilemma of responsibility vs. conscience, however, goes unresolved; for the jeep, which carries the prisoner off to the next (presumably more intensive) bout of interrogation, travels over a flat, undefined plain "of no river beds, no hills, no ascent or descent, no trees, no villages. . . a vast expanse stretching to infinity."[13] Through parallel structuring of the story's opening and closing passages, Yizhar alters the scene from lush vegetation, the scene of the crime, to boundless flatlands, the locus of unattainable answers.

At the dramatic center of this work is the individual conscience. But it is the view rendered of the group, the unit of soldiers themselves, which supplies much of the story's tone of bitter recrimination.

> One man was taking pictures of the whole scene, and on his next leave he would develop them. And there was one who sneaked up behind the prisoner, waved his fist passionately in the air and then, shaking with laughter, reeled back into the crowd. . . . And there was one wearing an

undershirt who, astonished and curious, exposed his rotten teeth; many dentists, a skinny shrew of a wife, sleepless nights, narrow, stuffy rooms, unemployment, and working for "the party" had aggravated his eternal query of "Nu, what will be?"

And there were some who had steady jobs, some who were on their way up in the world, some who were hopeless cases to begin with, and some who rushed to the movies and all the theaters and read the week-end supplements of two newspapers. And there were some who knew long passages by heart from Horace and Prophet Isaiah and from Chaim Nachman Bialik and even from Shakespeare; some who loved their children and their wives and their slippers and the little gardens at the sides of their houses. . . some who were not at all what they seemed and some who were exactly what they seemed. There they all stood, in a happy circle around the blindfolded prisoner, who at that very moment extended a calloused hand. . . and said to them: "Fi, cigara?" Got a cigarette?[14]

Several elements of Israeli society are included in this group portrait. Yizhar points his finger at them all, from the most common to the most educated, from the most predictable to the most pretentious. They all encircle the Bedouin in mirthful camaraderie. However, the passage bears a more subtle meaning as well. All these soldiers seem torn from their normal milieus, from their familiar houses and newspapers. Like the shepherd, torn suddenly from his idyllic ambience, the soldiers themselves are victims of aberration and uprootedness. The Bedouin's innocent request merely highlights the totality of innocence which the war has harshly abrogated.

Among the other prominent writers of Yizhar's generation Benjamin Tammuz is particularly to be noted for his literary treatment of the Arab problem. In his well-known story, "Taharut sehiya" (The swimming race),[15] Tammuz poignantly portrays the loss of all possibility of friendship between Israelis and Arabs through a three-tracked passage to an ironic maturity: from boy to soldier, from swimming race to battlefield, from ingenuous playfulness (with a little Arab girl) to gratuitous killing (of the girl's uncle). The paradox of losing (in the race) and winning (in battle) projects the author's feelings of a fruitless, tragic progression. In a similar though more strongly allegorical vein, the 1972 novel *Hapardes* (The Orchard), evinces Tammuz's sympathy for the defeated Arab, displaced by war, cheated by power and history. With fratricide its central disaster, the family chronicle and the lovely orchard embody Tammuz's rather transparent political commentary on the sins of State and society.[16]

Far more subtle and oblique is the treatment given the Arab by a number of second generation Israeli authors. In a story called "Navadim vatzefa" (Nomad and viper),[17] written relatively early in his career, Amos Oz attempts to render through symbolic action a condition of double jeopardy regarding Arab-lsraeli relations. The scene is the kibbutz, which, in Oz's imagination, becomes the quintessential setting for modern Israel's inner conflicts. The kibbutz members are seriously considering some sort of paramilitary action to discourage Bedouin shepherds from grazing their flocks too close to kibbutz farmland. The themes of encroachment and projected retaliation intensify within the framework of a dual perspective. The Bedouins are starving, pitiful, primitive innocents, and simultaneously they are seen as foreboding, sensual, unfathomable aliens.

The Bedouin shepherd in this story is obviously the literary descendant of Yizhar's captive; but in his depiction Oz emphasizes the dichotomous feelings of attraction and obsessive hatred engendered by the Arab in the Israeli consciousness.

In his dense style, combining both lyric and gothic qualities, Oz weaves a story within a story which projects a fictional social psychology of attitudes toward the Arab. The kibbutz members are united in their recrimination; but Geula, the twenty-nine-year-old spinster coffeemaker, pays no heed. A loner, frustrated in love and hemmed in by group living, Geula walks about in the orchard (described as "heavily laden and fragrant") during the romantic evening hours. Here she confronts Bedouin in a sensual scene of mutual but hesitant, unfulfilled seduction. Sickened, presumably, by the Arab's "loathsome touch" -- but more probably, by the revulsion at her own illicitness, her flagrant breach of taboo -- Geula roams about fitfully. Just as the kibbutz discussion of the external threat reaches its climax, she returns to the orchard to meet her bizarre fate. Sexual fantasies and a strangely quiescent death bring the story to an ambiguous close.

> The earth had not succumbed to the cold, but continued to exude a subdued warmth. Red, green, red, green, red winked the planes in the sky. The flashing lights did not distract the viper crawling alongside the girl's body. Rage swept over the serpent, who raised his head and shot out a forked tongue. The viper's anger was not capricious. The girl had chosen to stretch out in the thick of the bushes and in doing so had blocked the entrance to his hole with her body. He wanted to return home, but he could not. His eyes bulged with a dull glassiness. . . . His body was grey-green and outstretched. The zigzag line stressed his outstretched pose and exaggerated it by contrast. Lost in her poetic reverie, the girl was unlikely to notice the snake. Her eyes were shut, and they did not open when the viper thrust a pair of sharp, venomous upper fangs into her ankle, the lower ones lending stiff support. Geula lifted her foot at the sudden pain and rubbed it with a warm hand. She tried to pull out the thorn which had been thrust into her flesh.
>
> Freed of his venom, the serpent experienced release. In lazy loops he made off from the scene. Exhaustion prevented him from going far. . . . His eyes were ever-open. Geula's eyes, too, were open. A heaviness pressed against her ankle. A dull pain, a tender pain penetrated her bloodstream and soothed her whole body, while a sound as of distant bells warned her to get up and look for people. The heaviness overpowered her, and her eyes closed once more. Her knees betrayed her and refused to bend. Weakly she rolled over on her side, curled up and rested her weary head on her arms. A shudder of pleasure rippled over her skin. Now she could listen to the sweet wave sweeping through her body and intoxicating her bloodstream. To this sweet wave Geula responded with complete surrender.[18]

Heavy-handed allusiveness and obtrusive symbolism notwithstanding, the orgasmic killing of Geula-Eve by the serpent-lover conveys a dual sense of fulfillment and guilt. Geula's attraction to the Bedouin meets with deadly overdoses of pleasure and pain, reward and punishment. Oz, the social moralist, perseveres through forcefulness of style and bizarre situation to generate a drama of complex psycho-social attitudes toward the Arab. Here, too, it is a vision of self, a heightened, dual vision of hostile repulsion and wished-for intimacy, which dominates the story and transmits its central meaning of torn emotions.

Adam ben kelev (1969) by Yoram Kaniuk is a masterful, grueling novel of Holocaust survivors who have become inmates at a fictional "Institution for Rehabilitation and Therapy" in Arad, a settlement in Israel's northern Negev desert.[19] In "One Flew Over the Cuckoo's Nest" fashion, Kaniuk offers a jaggedly grotesque, theatrical narrative of madness, interspersed with poignant, ironic flashes of sober awareness. These are the indelible scars, says Kaniuk, which the Holocaust has bequeathed: people reduced to a dog-madness which often envelops more than just the survivors themselves. Humanity in its totality is sick; these "survivors" are merely its most bloodied victims.

Near the end of the novel, its movement marked by a growing sense of debasement, the inmates escape into the surrounding desert. Stripped naked by her fellow escapees, bound by chains and wrapped only in newspapers, the elder, sixty-year-old Schwester sister wanders about seeking God. Instead, she confronts a group of Bedouin smugglers. "Shepherds," she says to them, "you're obviously shepherds,"[20] and asks them for help. They laugh at her naiveté, her nakedness, her helplessness. Then, one by one, they proceed mercilessly to rape her.

> The Schwester sister doesn't emit a sound. As though she were dead, as though the heat and the shame had erased her existence. An old woman like me! Actually, she herself couldn't ever believe that the insects loved her with an honest passion. Now she catches sight of the Bedouin laden with watches. His face is riveted upon hers, his eyes do not stir from her white old body. She sees his leg muscles, his huge hands, his eyes that sow fire. If he were to tell her that he was God, she would believe him. His blemished smile, his gold tooth, his leching body, his tortured features impose on her mind the memory of thoughts of ascent, the memory of distant dreams. She will now get her revenge for the humiliation of her empty life, revenge against her idiotic sister, against her failure, her husband, her mustache, against shaving razors, forests, the camp, Cyprus, barbed-wire fences,

against the wretched boat, against hostile Israel, against the children who eat bananas and sour cream and chant patriotic songs.[21]

Instead of revulsion and degradation, the Schwester sister feels a certain personal redemption. She even discovers a miracle. In the rainbow colors of a Bedouin's cascading urine she sees an angel, a sign that "God is not dead," and she thanks the Bedouins all for what they have done. The ironic blend of debasement and salvation bears Kaniuk's message of an ambiguous, senseless survival.

As in most of the works mentioned in this discussion, especially Yizhar's "The Prisoner" and Oz's "Nomad and Viper," the Bedouin shepherds are not really people at all, not even fully developed fictional characters. They are merely figments of emotions or ideas, only embodiments of motifs: innocence, love-hatred, cruel indifference.

The inhumanity shown the Schwester sister by the Bedouin rapists is a further sign of humanity's sordidness, its instinctive lack of compassion. Even if there were such compassion, Kaniuk intimates, it would probably be useless for those who have become, through the trauma of torture, nothing more than incarcerated, unwanted outcasts. Kaniuk's portrayal of the desert nomads merely enforces that brutal image of humankind as a self-gratifying, unconscionable victimizer of the defenseless.

Amalia Kahana-Carmon's work *Veyare'ah be'emek ayalon* (And moon in the vale of Aijalon, 1972) also has little to do with the Arab problem. It is a novel of resentment, focused on the figure of a Tel Aviv housewife, Noa Talmor, and narrated in a variety of stream-of-consciousness modes. Mrs. Talmor feels desolately alone, abandoned by her husband and his world of "doing," left on the periphery of activity, conversation, romance, and social life. The outlook is grim; the tone, quietly despondent.[22]

Near the center of the novel, Mrs. Talmor tours Beersheba with her husband and Philip, a British business associate, toward whom she feels some definite, but undefined and unrealized affection. Outside a small restaurant (inside the talk consists of typical male-chauvinist bar chatter) she catches sight of a Bedouin woman, patiently waiting for her husband. Noa ponders the Bedouin woman's apparently peripheral place in the social order. Her interior monologue projects a chilling still-life portrait of isolation.

> Suddenly the sky turned dark: I am night. Of dirt, debris, and dust. With a tin bracelet, her mouth veiled, a swollen face, eyeless: a woman beast. A black Sudanese woman. Black Bedouin clothes and a black child, a black hen set before her, she squats and waits outside on the sidewalk. Man is born to toil. And woman, like me, to be forgotten. Who can know your life in darkness, in dust, O black woman. The Bedouin men in the restaurant, poker-faced. You cannot guess which one she belongs to, which one she is waiting for.[23]

The passage is brief but central, for it captures and conveys key aspects of Noa Talmor's own situation. The inner, lyrical voice (similar to that found in parts of Virginia Woolf's *The Waves*), the tone of restrained despair, the themes of abandonment and emotional ambivalence -- these understated elements characterize Noa's inner, desperate alienation. Here, too, the depiction of the Bedouin woman projects a problematic dimension of self.

It seems ironic, but is indeed typical, that most of the Arab (or Bedouin) figures which appear in contemporary Hebrew literature are portrayed not as the enemy but as reflections of the varied human conditions and concerns on the Israeli scene: social, moral, philosophical, or psychological. The intrinsic study of the image of the Arab in this fiction also demonstrates main trends in Israeli literary history, from the quasi-documentary realism of the twenties and thirties to the current variety of symbolic narrative modes.[24] In any case, the several authors discussed here, representative as they are of the wide spectrum of Hebrew literary creativity over the past several decades, clearly have utilized the figure of the Arab to express a variegated, changing montage of Israeli self views.

Hebrew Annual Review, 1977: 53-65.

Chapter 3:

1 In Brenner (1960, p. 212). My translation. -- W.B.
2 The piece, entitled "Mipinkas," appeared in *Kuntres*, April, 1921. Brenner was killed on May 1.
3 See Smilansky (1927) and Shami (1972).
4 Cf. Shamir (1969, p. 184). See also Citrin (1973, pp. 10ff).
5 "Bein holot hayeshimon," in Shami (1972, p. 132). Quotation taken from "Hamamah: A Tale of the Arabian Desert," in *Tehilla and Other Israeli Tales* (London and New York, 1956), p. 122. Translated by I. Schen. See also "Hasheikh vesusato," in Smilansky (1927), vol. II, pp. 196-216.
6 "Bat hasheikh," in Smilansky (1927). vol. 1, pp. 47-52.
7 In Steinberg (1957), pp. 122-129.
8 Published as a volume in Burla's collected works, *Kitvei Yehuda Burla*. (Burla's Collected Works [in eight volumes), Masada Publishing, n.d.). On this subject see also "Latifa," in Smilansky (1927), vol. I, pp. 1-6.
9 Other authors of this generation who wrote on the Arab include Y. Aricha, P. Bar-Adon, M. Stavi, and Y. Bar-Yosef. See Bachur (1964).
10 Bachur (1964) briefly surveys some of this literature. His point of view, however, is apologetic and his classifications somewhat superficial. Citrin (1973) notes an anthology of short stories on these themes which includes works by several first generation Israeli writers, e.g., Aricha (1963).
11 *Hirbet hiz'eh--hashavuy* (Merhavia, 1949). Also collected in Yizhar (1959), pp. 113-138.
12 Taken from "The Prisoner," in J. Blocker, ed. (1965), p. 153. Translated by V.C. Rycus.
13 Blocker (1965), p. 173f. On these aspects of landscape background, cf. Miron (1962), pp. 283-297.
14 Blocker, pp. 158-159.
15 First published in *Luah Ha'aretz* (1951), pp. 239-249. A translation appears in *Israel Argosy* (Spring, 1953), pp. 69-84.
16 Citrin (1973) discusses *Hapardes* at length (see pp. 119-174). I have omitted from my discussion another rather transparent (though interesting) work which both Citrin (pp. 91-118) and Bachur (1964, pp. 46, 58) treat: Yehoshua's (1968, pp. 9-55) "Mul haye'arot" (translated as "Facing the Forests," in Yehoshua, *Three Days and a Child*, New York, 1970).

[17] First published in *Ha'aretz*, February 7, 1964. Collected in Oz, *Artsot hatan* (1965), pp. 25-41).
[18] Michener (1973, pp. 305-306). Translated by N. de Lange. The text is taken from the first edition of *Artzot hatan* (Lands of the Jackal), 1965.
[19] The novel appeared in English entitled *Adam Resurrected* (New York, 1971), translated by S. Simckes.
[20] *Adam Resurrected*, p. 321.
[21] Ibid., p. 323.
[22] See my review of this novel in *Hadoar* 51, 36:616-618.
[23] Kahana-Carmon (1971, p. 133). My translation. -- W.B.
[24] Cf. Alter (1977).

BIBLIOGRAPHY

Alter, R. 1977. "Afterword: a problem of horizons." *TriQuarterly,* "Contemporary Israeli Literature," 39:326-338.
Aricha, Y. (ed.) 1963. *Sippurim ivriyim mehayei ha'aravim.* Tel Aviv.
Bachur, Y. 1964. "The Arabs in modern Hebrew literature." *New Outlook* 7, 3:40-46, 58.
Blocker, J. (ed.) 1965. *Israeli Stories.* New York.
Brenner, Y. H. 1960. *Kol kitveiY. H. Brenner* II. Tel Aviv.
Burla, Y. [n.d.] *Ba'al be'amav.* In *KitveiYehuda Burla.* Tel Aviv.
Citrin, P. 1973. *The Arab in Hebrew Literature Since 1948.* Unpublished M.A. Thesis, Hebrew Union College. Cincinnati.
Kahana-Carmon, A. 1971. *Veyare'ah be'emek ayalon.* Tel Aviv.
Kaniuk, Y. 1969. *Adam ben kelev.* Tel Aviv.
Michener, J. A. (ed.) 1973. *First Fruits.* Philadelphia.
Miron, D. 1962. *Arba panim basifrut ha'ivrit bat-yameinu.* Tel Aviv and Jerusalem.
Oz, A. 1965. *Artsot hatan.* Tel Aviv.
Shami, Y. 1972. *Sippurei Yitzhak Shami.* Revised edition. Ed. A. Barash. Tel Aviv and Jerusalem.
Shamir, M. 1969. *Hayay im yishma'el.* Tel Aviv.
Smilansky, M. *1927. B'nai arav.* 2 volumes. Jerusalem and Tel Aviv.
Steinberg, Y. 1957. *Kol kitveiYa'acov Steinberg.* Tel Aviv.
Yehoshua, A. B. 1968. *Mul haye'arot.* Tel Aviv.
Yizhar, S. [Smilansky, Yizhar] 1959. *Arba sippurim.* Tel Aviv.

The Poetics of Allusion and the Hebrew Literary Tradition

There has been much discussion in recent years regarding the problem of composing a literary history of a particular literature. The discussion has focused on various elements, such as the rubric "literary tradition," the notions of change, development or decline in an historical evaluation of literary works, and the central issue of delineating the historical parameters of literary art.[1] Definitions and solutions vary, but the view which seems most convincing is that any literary history must pay some primary attention to the intrinsic configurations of individual works. The literary historiographer, at least one who sets about writing an account of a particular national literature, should take into account the "*formative* principles of particular works. . . the special artistic intentions and processes of individual authors in particular cases."[2] Such "formative principles" are determined, no doubt, by the author's use of literary conventions, and a proper literary history is, by and large, a history of individual styles and uses of literary conventions.[3]

Two points of reference from within the modern Hebrew literary tradition shed light on aspects of this dual theory of literary history and convention: a remark made in a new Israeli literary journal about a particularly eminent Hebrew author, the Nobel Prize winner S.Y. Agnon, and the employment of a particular literary convention in works by Agnon, i.e., allusion.

In their 1972 manifesto, the editors of the new journal, *Siman kri'a*, were emphatic in delineating what they saw as the revolutionary nature of the Hebrew prose that they were publishing. They were, in fact, proclaiming a new age for Hebrew literature, one that would be free from what they saw as undesirable, cumbersome elements of the previous literary age. Singling out Agnon in particular, they announced the following.

> The three works of fiction presented [in this first issue] have in common a liberation from the pillory of Agnonesque. . . . The stories are not a

41

> puzzle of meanings; they lack his heavy-handed
> ironic twists. . . and they are devoid of the *patterns
> of allusion* which weigh so heavily [on the reader].[4]

Now it is true that Agnon (who died in 1970 at age 81)
created many works of fiction which are highly allusive, but his
uses of allusion are quite varied. There are allusions to Biblical
contexts, to classical and medieval rabbinic texts, to folkloristic
myth and legend, and even to other stories by Agnon himself.
Some allusions are oblique, others direct; some are
semantically weightless, serving only to create an archaic tone,
while others join contexts to highlight inner meanings. Agnon
also wrote many stories and even novels with very few
allusions and often none at all. It is somewhat superficial,
therefore, for the editors of *Siman kri'a* to have identified
Agnon mainly as a master of inaccessible allusion. Their
central mistake, however, is to have declared a new age for
Hebrew fiction on the basis of "a liberation from. . . patterns of
allusion", for this proposition demonstrates a basic
misunderstanding of the varied writers, and by Agnon in
particular. The literary historian, too, should note the
particular uses of this and other conventions and not label a
writer or an age with such generalizations.

The problem may be illustrated by the varied types of
allusion that Agnon used in three separate works. The first
two, which I shall note only briefly, are found in stylized
folktales. One is a direct allusion to a biblical text, the other a
more oblique allusion to a rabbinic context.

In the introductory sketch to the collection called "Polin:
Sipurei Agadot" (Poland: stories and folktales), Agnon
narrates in quasi-historiographic style how the Jews first came
to Poland. It was really quite simple, says the folk-narrator of
"Kedumot" (Antiquities). The Jews were suffering terribly in
Western Europe (under the yolk of the Holy Roman Empire)
and were, indeed, seeking another place to live. A piece of
notepaper floated down from heaven bearing the message:
"Go to Poland."[5] And so, states the narrator, quoting from
Genesis (12: 5), "And they went forth and came unto the land of
Poland," (*vayelkhu vayavo'u artza Polin*). Of course, "Poland"
is substituted for the name "Canaan" in the Abraham story, but

the parody has a definite purpose: Agnon is creating the myth-
-only to break it down later in the "Polin" cycle--that the Land
of Poland stood, indeed, next to the Land of Canaan in the
spiritual geography of the Jewish people. The medieval exodus
to Poland, presented as a temporary substitute for Canaan, is
thus portrayed as a preconfiguration of the future messianic
return to the Promised Land. This optimism is shattered in
most of the tragic tales to follow, but the direct allusion to the
Abraham story serves well to evoke Agnon's mythical and
subsequently ironic import.

A more oblique use of allusion occurs in the short story
"Agadat Hasofer" (The legend of the scribe; *Elu ve'elu*, pp. 131-
145]. It tells of Raphael and his wife, Miriam, he a scribe of
Torah scrolls and she a housewife. Despite Miriam's manifold
devotions and folk cures, she remains childless. Heartbroken,
she soon dies, and Raphael sets out to write a Torah scroll in
her memory. But, in a Gothic, fantasy ending, as Raphael
completes the scroll, Miriam comes before him in death,
dressed in her wedding gown. He and his scroll seem suddenly
overwhelmed by fire and fall to the floor, covered over by the
white gown.

The story, generally to be treated as a tragic romance, is
given much greater depth of meaning through the use of an
oblique allusion. While Raphael sits at his holy work on one
side of the room, Miriam is depicted on the other side doing all
the cooking, darning, sewing, and cleaning. The room is
divided by a tall partition, and Miriam never ventures from her
place of daily chores into Raphael's realm of the holy.

> How good the proper sequence of things. Since we have
> described the course of his holy work we shall now mention
> the place of his holy work. He worked in his small
> apartment near the Great Synagogue and the public bath
> house (pardon its inclusion here) which contains the ritual
> bath. His apartment was small and modest, consisting of one
> room divided by a wooden partition. On the other side of the
> partition stood an oven and a stove and between the oven
> and stove sits the modest mistress of the house who cooks
> and bakes and brews and darns and weaves and knits and
> tends to the household chores. They had no children.
> Because the Holy One, blessed be He, craves the prayers of the
> righteous He kept her childless (*Elu ve'elu*, p. 133).[6]

Miriam's household work is described by way of allusion to the laws of Sabbath infractions as delineated in Tractate *Shabbat* (Chapter 7, mishnah 2). That is to say, in contrast to Raphael's continual immersion in holy acts, Miriam's chores are redolent with a certain anti-sanctity, a profaneness identified with acts of breaking the halakhic laws of Sabbath holiness. Agnon alludes to this motif again later in the story, when the narrator, in apparent praise of Miriam and the calm grace and charm of her home, notes that "were it not for her busy hands one could mistake every day for the Lord's Sabbath." These allusions transform the work from a simple romantic tale into a complex, ironic drama of the holy and the profane. The story, by means of its underlying, metaphorical design, depicts an underlying struggle between the abject "pureness" and the "impure" human acts of desire and loving. The subtle allusions tell the reader that it is an overwhelming sense of the holy which, by denying anything deemed "unholy," ironically causes the characters' childlessness and tragic sorrow.

The third example is a particularly conspicuous allusion used by Agnon, not in one of his stylized folktales, but in a realistic social novel called *Sippur pashut* (A simple story), published in 1935. The novel is set at the turn of the century in a small town in Galicia (southern Poland), a town which appears to be thriving on all fronts: political, economic, and social. The town, Shibush (gone awry), displays a developing socialism, a new industrialization, and a rising middle class. At the center of the novel is the sad story of Herschel Hurwitz, son of the well-to-do shopkeepers, Baruch Meir and Tsirel Hurwitz. Herschel has fallen in love with his poor orphaned cousin, Bluma (flower), but his parents find Mina Ziemlich much more acceptable, since Mina is the daughter of the well-to-do rural grain merchants, Gedalia and Bertha Ziemlich ("suitable"). The match between Herschel and Mina is cleverly engineered, but, several months into the marriage, Herschel, who all the while is mourning the loss of Bluma, has a severe nervous collapse: he is found lying in a field croaking like a frog and crowing like a rooster. Subsequently, he is sent to a clinic in Lemberg where Dr. Langsam (slowly or gradually) effects a cure with a kind of self-disclosure, empathic therapy: he tells Herschel about his own childhood growing up in a small Jewish town. Herschel eventually returns to Mina and to his parents' store and becomes--or at least so it appears--a devoted husband and father and an upstanding member of the community.

This particular passage has eluded the attention of literary analysts, probably for the very reason that it is so obviously allusive. It is highly digressive as well. The narrator interrupts the scene, so to speak, a festive meal at the Ziemlich estate in honor of Herschel and Mina's engagement, and deliberates on the various laws of kosher poultry as they relate to the particular bird which Bertha Ziemlich has prepared for this significant dinner.

> The main course, which Bertha feared her guests would not sufficiently savor [because they were stuffing themselves with the marinated mushroom hors d'oeuvres] was the meat-in-gravy of a bird called "Grecian chicken." There was some doubt at first as to whether this chicken was kosher, since it was so weirdly shaped, even though its eggs were normal, with one sharp and one rounded end. But then came along our renowned Galician sages and permitted its consumption without any doubt or hesitation, because it had the necessary three signs of purity: a craw, an easily skinned stomach membrane, and a hind toe. In addition, it had long been the custom to eat this bird. . . and there also have been reliable witnesses who have testified that this chicken is common in the Holy Land and it is eaten there without hesitation. However, in spite of their being acceptable, these birds were not readily available. . . and only wealthy landowners bred them in their private yards. That's why Bertha was so anxious for her in-laws to come into dinner with a hearty appetite, so that they'd know full well what it was they were being served.[7]

The specific allusions in this passage are to the laws of kosher poultry found in Tractate *Hulin* and in later codes of Jewish law.[8] Though the use of such specific detail may require further analysis and interpretation, the reader can readily account for at least three thematic components here: the unfamiliar chickens served by Bertha recur in Herschel's reluctant metamorphosis into a strange bird; like the "Grecian chicken," Mina was considered "acceptable" for Herschel, while poor Bluma was considered "unkosher"; and lastly, Bertha clearly has gone out of her way to make an impression on Tsirel, a reminder that this work is, in great measure, a novel of middle class manners.[9]

To go a step further, the various elements in this allusive passage, which functions as a dramatic focal point, radiating with meanings throughout the novel, may be classified in three thematic categories: 1) the world of "tradition" or social convention; 2) the motif structure of "birds and eggs;" 3) the themes of doubt, difference of opinion, duality and, by extension, ambiguity.

By quoting from the halakhic texts, the narrator establishes both himself and the novelistic milieu as rooted in a traditional ambience. But, while the laws of kashrut are still observed, Shibush is depicted as a town rapidly entering into the modern age. The ancient, traditional laws are validated, as are the new methods of psychotherapy. Indeed, it is this very dichotomy of traditionalism and modernism which quashes Herschel's romance and brings about his fall. Though he is part of a society in transition, he becomes an ironic victim of entrenched custom. Furthermore, Bertha is not at all concerned with tradition; she cares only about impression. Thus, the passage highlights a second ironic clash, that between the notions of a "traditional society" and a "social tradition" or bourgeois convention. Such a specific reference to the laws of kashrut in the *social* context becomes a means of satire by way of parody. Tsirel Hurwitz makes the subtle mockery quite obvious. With masterful one-upsmanship, and with masterful anticlimax on the part of Agnon, Tsirel ignores the prospect of "Grecian chicken" and tells Bertha how terribly full she seems to be getting on those wonderful mushrooms!

With regard to the pervasive motif of "birds and eggs," a brief commentary will suffice to show the intricacy and persuasiveness of Agnon's artistic design in this novel. Just after the quoted allusive paragraph, the dinner is launched with soup dished out of a large bowl shaped like a goose, "its beak twisted in anger."[10] The matchmaker who brings Herschel and Mina together is named Yona Toiber; both his names mean "dove." At the very beginning of the novel

Herschel imagines Bluma as a nightingale, with lovely birds hovering overhead in an idyllic scene. By contrast, his mother Tsirel is described as constantly gorging herself with food, "leaning over her chicken and filling her plate like a poultry saleswoman about to feed her birds" to fatten them up (for slaughter, that is). And finally, just before Herschel's breakdown, the old men in the synagogue fill in the time between prayer services by discussing, of all things, the various Talmudic laws concerning the kosher slaughtering of poultry.

The final category of thematic development which derives from the excerpt quoted above is that of doubt, difference of opinion, duality, and ambiguity. There is, of course, great difference of opinion over Bluma within the Hurwitz family, but Tsirel's plans hold sway. Herschel obviously lives a life of duality, at least in emotional terms: he is married to Mina but yearns for Bluma. And in his breakdown, he becomes both a rooster and a frog, in a way both the highest and lowest of creatures, a middle-class prince in a lowly form, waiting for his lover to rescue him. There is also disagreement among the witnesses who had seen Herschel just before his breakdown: some said he seemed fine, others claimed he looked very ill indeed. (The theme of testimony, reminiscent of those who had witnessed the consumption of "Grecian chickens" in the Holy Land, also comes to mind here.) And there is the debate which arises over Dr. Langsam's therapy. Is it "scientific" or not? Is it a bona fide method of therapy or not? Agnon exacerbates this issue by describing, through his narrator persona, how Langsam generally shunned routine therapeutic methods, especially medication. In fact, the only reason that he used medication at all was "in order to differentiate himself from the Hassidic Rebbe of Alesk" and his folk-cures! (Ginaton edition, p. 190).

But Agnon takes us beyond these aspects of plot and background. He suggests that an entire *cosmic* duality is at work in the world of the novel. Humankind, notes the narrator (quoting a famous midrash from *Bereshit Rabba* 8, 1), was created a Janus-faced being, a dual image looking in opposite directions. However--the narrator continues with his own cosmogony--in the later generations of humanity, "each individual is created unto oneself alone, and is not bound to

look back behind" (p. 220). This confirmation of the individual
personality, stated near the end of the novel, seems to apply to
Herschel's recent recovery. He is to look forward now, not
backward. What's past is past; Herschel is now reconciled with
his parents, his wife and family, and his work in his parents'
store.

Agnon, however, maintains the ambiguity--the dual
possibility of reconciliation or victimization--to the very last.
Sippur pashut ends with a definite, purposeful sense of
irresolution and irony.[11] Close to the novel's end (Chapter 37),
there appears another festive dinner scene at the Ziemlichs',
and the meal is begun again with soup from the same bowl of
the irate goose. (The narrator playfully comments that he
cannot understand the obvious discrepancy between Bertha's
happy face and the angry look of that porcelain bird!) And who
should turn up at the party but Arnold Ziemlich, Bertha's
brother-in-law from Germany who hasn't visited since
Herschel and Mina's wedding. At that time he had come to
Shibush to set up a local branch of his business, and now he has
returned to check on its progress. His business: the poultry and
egg trade, of course! Arnold Ziemlich, the modern
businessman, according to Herschel's father, symbolizes all
that is well with the world. And who knows, muses Baruch
Meir Hurwitz, perhaps there will be more marvelous matches
between the Ziemlichs -- the German Ziemlichs, that is -- and
the Hurwitzes. Chickens and eggs, Ziemlichs and Hurwitzes,
in continuous progression. He dreams of a future dynasty!
Business, progress, and continued fruitfulness, that is what is
important in the world. Herschel becomes a living symbol, or
victim, of this implied bourgeois ethic. Bluma will forever
remain beyond his grasp, but not beyond the realm of fictional
rendering. In an amusing ploy, which actually stresses this
"simple" story's implied meaning, Agnon ends the novel with a
mock statement of purpose:

> The story of Herschel and Mina is ended, but not so
> the story of Bluma. Bluma's story is a book in itself
> . . . . How many pens and how much ink will it take
> to tell the story of [all those] involved in our simple
> story. God knows when we'll have the time.

Bluma, in other words, may be out of reach for Herschel, but not for you, dear reader. Bluma and all that she represents still live, at least as a prospective figment of one's wistful imagination.

In this discussion of *Sippur pashut* I have clearly gone far beyond the quoted passage of allusion -- but that is precisely my point. The literary analyst, when interpreting a work's meaning, should not, and cannot, isolate a particular passage or a particular allusion from the literary work as a whole. And likewise, though in a much wider context, the literary historian should not isolate the use of allusion as a static convention or a detached stylistic technique.[12] The comments in *Siman kri'a*'s manifesto notwithstanding -- and surely one can readily see that their remarks on Agnon are merely part of a well-meaning but somewhat overstated declaration of renewal--each use of allusion should be treated individually within its artistic context by the literary critic. All "patterns of allusion" should be recorded and evaluated by the literary historian according to their particular usage and aesthetic effectiveness. From the point of view of both aesthetics and history, it may be said that there is *no* full-fledged "*poetics* of allusion" in modern Hebrew fiction (in contradistinction to most medieval and much of modern Hebrew poetry). There are *allusions*, used artistically with more or less success by a variety of writers, both older and more recent. It would be a mistake, therefore, to see allusiveness as somehow old hat and unworthy of continuation in an alleged new age of Hebrew prose fiction.

Art, as history, is continuous; and artists, too, may live through several so-called literary periods in their lifetime. Such is the case with Agnon. He is a true example of the writer who represents a "conjuncture" of literary and cultural experience, as well as a staggering virtuosity of technique in the modern Hebrew literary tradition.[13] And like any other literature, modern Hebrew literature represents a "tradition" only in the sense that eminent works of the past, such as those by Agnon, stand before the contemporary writer, reader or critic as already canonized opera; they may be confronted either with adulation or critique, but always with proper understanding. The literary historian, like the young writer, must recognize the "essential continuity of the written word."[14]

In this sense of continuity, *both* Agnon *and Siman kri'a*, with their respective modes of expression and intent, become the stuff of literary history. In recording the ever-evolving interplay between the old and the new, the literary historian must analyze and interpret the theories, genres, styles and conventions which, in themselves, constitute the aesthetic conjunctures of literary art.

Judaism: A Quarterly Journal of Jewish Life and Thought, Fall, 1977: 481-488.

Chapter 4:

[1] See, for example, R. Wellek and A. Warren, *Theory of Literature* (Peregrine ed., London, 1963), pp. 38-45; Geoffrey H. Hartman, *Beyond Formalism* (New Haven, 1970), pp. 356-386; and Claudio Guillén, *Literature as System* (Princeton, 1971), pp. 420-510.

[2] Robert Marsh, in P. Damon, ed., *Literary Criticism and Historical Understanding* (New York, 1967), p. 12.

[3] On convention as "collective style," see Harry Levin, *Perspectives on Criticism* (Cambridge, Mass., 1950), p. 77.

[4] *Siman kri'a* [Exclamation Point]: *A Mixed Literary Quarterly,* 1 (Sept., 1972), p. 8. (My emphasis. -- W.B.) For a historical discussion of the appearance of this journal, see my article, "Exclamations, Manifestoes, and Other Literary Peripheries," *Judaism,* 33, 2 (Spring, 1974): 202-211.

[5] *Elu v'elu* [Vol. II of Agnon's collected works], 6th edition (Jerusalem and Tel Aviv, 1960), p. 353. In this short piece Agnon was elaborating on a well known Jewish folktale. See Diane K. and David G. Roskies, *The Shtetl Book* (New York, 1975), p. xiii.

[6] See my complete translation in *The Jewish Quarterly,* 23, 1-2 [83-84] (Spring-Summer, 1975): 25-30, 59. Another translation, by Isaac Franck, appears in S.Y. Agnon, *Twenty-One Stories,* ed. Nahum N. Glatzer, (New York, 1971), pp. 7-25.

[7] Schocken paperback edition, with explanatory notes by Naftali Ginaton (Jerusalem and Tel Aviv, 1968), p. 83. The novel has traditionally appeared in Volume III of Agnon's collected works, *'Al kapot haman'ul* (last revised, in its 13th edition, in 1971). (My translation. -- W.B.)

[8] The specific halakhic references here are to the shape of the eggs, the "three signs of purity" (kashrut), and the matters of custom and of testimony by eye witnesses. See Tractate *Hulin,* Chapter 3, especially mishnah 6. For additional references, see the *Jewish Encyclopedia* on "Clean and Unclean Animals" (subsection: "Birds"), and "Dietary Laws" (subsection: "Milk and Eggs").

9 Cf. Gershon Shaked, *Omanut hasippur shel S.Y. Agnon* (The Narrative Art of S.Y. Agnon," Merhavia and Tel Aviv, 1973), pp. 197-227.

10 Cf. Lev Hakak, "Motiv hatarnegol *beSippur pashut leS.Y.* Agnon" (The Rooster Motif in S.Y. Agnon's *Sippur pashut*), *Hasifrut* 4, 4 (Oct., 1973): 713-725. Hakak mentions the theme of "religious problematics, i.e., the matters of slaughtering and kashering [poultry]," but he does not make this particular context a specific aim of his deliberations. In my discussion I have chosen only a few out of tens of possible examples.

11 On the issues of ambiguity and resolution, cf. Arnold J. Band, *Nostalgia and Nightmare: A Study in the Fiction of S.Y. Agnon* (Berkeley and Los Angeles, 1968), pp. 242f, 252-254; William Cutter, "Setting as a Feature of Ambiguity in S.Y. Agnon's *Sippur pashut*," *Critique*, 15, 3: 66-79; and Baruch Hochman, *The Fiction of S.Y. Agnon* (Ithaca, N.Y., 1970), pp. 94ff, 108-111. My own view is closest to Hochman's idea of Herschel's "ironic reconciliation" with Shibush and its mores.

12 On the process of "actualizing" a literary allusion, see Ziva Ben-Porat, "The Poetics of Literary Allusion," *PTL: A Journal for Descriptive Poetics and Theory of Literature* [ed. Benjamin Hrushovski [Harshav], Tel Aviv University], 1, 1(Jan., 1976): 105-128.

13 On "conjuncture" and "continuity" in literary historiography, see Guillén, *Literature as System*, pp. 435ff, 449ff, 461-469.

14 Ibid., p. 498.

Elements of Style in the Fiction of
Amalia Kahana-Carmon

The writings of Amalia Kahana-Carmon may be categorized as "lyrical" prose, as fiction which reflects the artistic attempt to put into words the world of personal, inner experience.[1] In general, her works demonstrate an interweaving of outer, objective events with an inner, subjective view of those events. In creating this blend, Kahana-Carmon has utilized the various technical tools -- narrative, dramatic, and linguistic -- of lyrical prose: interior monologue, both direct and indirect; "poetic" descriptions of landscape and background, filtered through the consciousness of the narrator or character; a stream-of-consciousness exposition, based on a psychological mode of free association; and a structure involving the disjunction or montage effect of time, place, and dramatic voices.[2] Above all, her stories are infused with varied designs or recurring patterns of metaphorical images, motifs, and other symbolic structures. This sort of design replaces plot, the "story-line" of more conventional realistic prose. It focuses attention on dimensions of inner experience, and, to a great degree, it is probably responsible for the term "lyrical," which has been used to describe this complex genre of writing.[3]

Various critics (including myself) have already discussed some of the general characteristics of Amalia Kahana-Carmon's mode of writing, especially the main themes, the narrative structures, and the image of the narrator.[4] It seems, however, that much of the criticism written about her works has been weakest where it might have been strongest, namely, in the analysis of her style. For the most part, the articles which have dealt with this aspect of her works have been vague and ambiguous. For example, Kahana-Carmon is praised, on the one hand, for her "poetic language," for the "forcefulness of [her] imagistic language," her "delicate perception" of things, and her "inward writing, with all its sensitivity and grace."[5] On the other hand, her works are sharply criticized for their undue "verbosity," for the "exotic esotericism" in her linguistic usages, and, in the opinion of one writer, for her "phantom-like, monsterish language," which fosters a repulsive sense of "falseness and artificiality."[6] Taken individually, these sorts of comments do not relate at all to factors of meaning in Kahana-Carmon's writings; they ignore altogether the essential relationship between the language of literature and other meaning structures within the literary text.[7] Moreover, such vague, imprecise remarks only muddle further the terms "lyrical" and "poetic" when utilized in the analysis and interpretation of prose fiction.[8]

Style, of course, is a central conveyor of meaning in all literary texts, whether prose or poetry. In the genre called "lyrical" prose, however, style often becomes the most important semantic ingredient. Particular uses of language and syntax in this genre play a central role in creating an illusion of the dramatized, inner consciousness. Though they surely are not used exclusively in lyrical prose, individual words or phrases are often utilized in this genre to reflect symbolic dimensions and to embody dynamic motifs. These usages thereby contribute subtly yet significantly to the development of the particular work's sense and to its effective artistic design.[9]

Such linguistic phenomena appear often in Amalia Kahana-Carmon's fiction as semantic vehicles. My aim here is to discuss three stylistic devices -- the archaism, the cliché, and the euphuistic expression *(melitza)* -- and to analyze their utilization as conveyors of meaning in one of Kahana-Carmon's short stories, "Livnot lah bayit be'eretz Shinar" (To Build Her a House in the Land of Shinar."[10] I have chosen these three elements of style, because they are particularly salient features of Kahana-Carmon's writings in general; they function often as prime vehicles in the projection of narrative tone, in characterization, in the structuring of both dramatic and metonymic action, and in the creation of motif designs. In view of their recurrent use, the archaism, the cliché, and the euphuism should be perceived as central stylistic elements in the structure and semantic content of Kahana-Carmon's fiction.

These linguistic devices have three basic, common features. First, they are difficult to define with absolute clarity. (This is especially true of the term *melitza.)* For the purpose of this discussion, succinct definitions, as unambiguous as possible, are best: (1) An archaism is an old-fashioned or outdated phrase no longer generally used in common parlance. Its Hebrew sources are usually the Bible, rabbinic literature, or the liturgy. (2) A cliché is a common phrase which has lost most of its cogency because of overuse.[11] (3) And *melitza*-- according to Even-Shoshan's *New Hebrew Dictionary* -- is an "inflated phrase," or "verses or parts of verses [from the Bible] interwoven" in everyday speech or writing, or "very high diction."[12] A second common feature of these linguistic formations is the difficulty often confronted in attempting to differentiate the three. For example, a Hebrew euphuism is usually constituted by archaic language; and often, depending upon the particular utterance, a *melitza* may also be considered to be a cliché.[13] By the same token, the Hebrew cliché is often marked by a flowery diction which can readily be called *melitza*-like. Thirdly, these three usages reflect and form part of the generally high level of stylistic expression in Kahana-Carmon's works. Most of her writings are infused with an obscure, difficult vocabulary, complex syntactic structures, and a high, formal diction. The reader is immersed in what appears to be a stylistic blend of Hebrew linguistic purism and an intricate artistic expressiveness.[14] Within this general framework, however, one can clearly delineate the use of the three linguistic elements, which are the focal points of this discussion.

"To Build Her a House in the Land of Shinar" is a short story whose "plot" may be summed up briefly. The setting is a new frontier town close to the Mediterranean coast, bordering on the northern Negev desert. A man and wife, apparently in their late thirties or early forties, have recently settled in the town. The housewife appears to be going through a depression of sorts; she is suffering from boredom and a lack of any hope or goal for the future. Her relationship with her husband has deteriorated of late (a typical Kahana-Carmon situation). She recalls from her childhood in Europe the time she had come with her mother to a residential part of the city, near a hospital, and she remembers the impression a glimpse of the medical staff had made upon her. Through the window she glances at a ship on the horizon, changing its direction, an experience she no longer has any hope for. And, finally, she serves tea to the "expert-on-nutrition-and-home-economics," a kind of visiting government social worker who has come to town to assist the new residents in organizing their new homes and lives. The nutritionist's advice to the housewife: take on a part-time job as a dental assistant; the job will make life easier and more interesting. The story ends with the housewife serving refreshments -- followed by an unambiguous feeling of personal irresolution. In essence, the short work portrays the gap between a superficial, pragmatic view of life and the inner, emotional needs of the individual. The expert argues, "It's a question of organization"; the housewife responds, "No. It's life, one's fate."

The story begins with a street conversation (overheard by the housewife) between the nutritionist and the town council chairman. The nutritionist remarks, "On the way here I saw a woman and her child going down into the heart of the wilderness." The phrase "going down into the heart of the wilderness" (a literal translation of *yardu belev hashemama*) technically is a metaphoric expression, but it has no real figurative connotation. The phrase is reminiscent of similar Hebrew expressions, like *yardu bimtsulot* (the Egyptians "went down into the depths" of the Red Sea, Exodus 15:5) or "in the heart of the sea" (*belev yam*), or "seas" (*bilvav yamim*, Jonah 2:4) meaning, in each case, "in the midst of the ocean."[15] One could say that by bringing to mind dimensions of sea, desert and depths, the phrase neatly projects the frontier town backdrop of the story.   But the expression bears a more significant meaning. By virtue of its high diction -- the phrase evinces both archaic and euphuistic dimensions -- *yardu belev hashemama* raises a simple mother-and-child stroll to a higher level of activity.

The diction here suggests a kind of courageous, quasi-heroic act, the act of venturing undauntedly, one could say, into the midst of a vast wilderness. Through its semantic connotation the phrase reflects a sense of heroism inherent in confronting the dangers and challenges of life in a new frontier town.   This connotation, however, clearly bespeaks the "establishment" attitude of the government nutritionist. Hence, the euphuism "went down into the heart of the wilderness" becomes an ironic motif in the story, a motif which develops with increasing intensity. Heroic notions, even pragmatic ones, only exacerbate the housewife's inner, psychological debilities. In confronting other ironic themes in the story's duration and similar euphuistic expressions as well, the reader is thrust back to this initial *melitza* and recognizes its significance as an empty cliché (on the part of the nutritionist) with definite sarcastic overtones (on the part of the author).

The object of sarcasm is the notion of a neat, organized life style, accompanied by a tenor of optimistic progressivism, which is being promulgated by the government expert. This vigorous approach to life, touted as a panacea for life's problems, clashes with the housewife-heroine's emotional sensitivities. (It appears to clash as well with the author's sympathetic point of view.) People do not live by clichés, the connotation seems to be. Life is far more complex, too difficult for superficial answers. Beyond its own semantic weight, however, this particular ironic cliché becomes linked with similar phrases later in the story. Taken together, not only do these phrases form a significant motif design in the work, they also engender a sense of structural rhythm. A central function of these stylistic devices, therefore, is to emphasize continually the story's ironic motifs (such as the virtue of "newness" and the urban version of the pioneering ideal in Israel) and to remind the reader of the abiding sarcastic tone.

As the story progresses, the housewife waits for her temporary lodger (the nutritionist) to return to her apartment. While the housewife waits, the narrator reveals her inner feelings. She tried her best, the reader is told, "to gain the attention and the affection" of the expert. But for that very reason "she harbored a slight hatred toward her" (*natra lah eiva kala*). The euphuistic nature of the Hebrew phrase (which I have tried to render in the English wording, "harbored a slight hatred") accentuates the housewife's mixed feelings toward the nutritionist. In this way the device contributes centrally to the characterization of this ambivalent personality. The character is caught in a difficult, dualistic situation, torn between wanting to please and wanting to divulge her actual feelings. The phrase also stresses the story's main dramatic theme: the clash between an outer, surface mien and an inner dimension of emotive expression. Moreover, the oxymoron *eiva kala* ("a slight hatred") subtly conveys its own inner contradiction. One might say "a slight disaffection" or "some resentment," but not "a slight hatred." (The Hebrew might provide *tina*, or perhaps *tina kala*, though the combination is not generally used.) Thus the oxymoron in itself projects both the inner inconsistency of the situation and the character's understated but seething unhappiness.

Soon the three characters -- the nutritionist, the housewife, and her husband -- sit at the table for light refreshments, and the conversation turns to the various ethnic foods the nutritionist has encountered over the years in her advisorial work. Suddenly, the husband is reminded of a favorite dish from his childhood. "You remember," he remarks to his wife, "where we lived they used to eat doves, dove pudding." Since this is the first time, after a long hiatus, that he has spoken to her directly at all, the wife is quite taken aback: "His words flew at her like a loosed arrow." The language of this response is blatantly archaic. (I have attempted, at least, to render archaicly the archaic sound of the original Hebrew *kehetz shalu'ah avaru'ah.*) The use of the archaic grammatical form *avaru'ah* emphasizes the wife's surprise at her husband's revived communication. The archaic (or euphuistic) sounding simile, *kehetz shalu'ah*, also accentuates the pathetic, demeaning aspects of this minor trauma.

The entire context is essentially ironic: the husband does indeed end his long silence and speaks to his wife; but at the same time it is clear that by his reference to ethnic foods he is siding, so to speak, with the enemy, namely, the nutritionist. Moreover, the very subject of his nostalgic statement is ironic; the eating of doves at weddings refers to romantic notions of love and happy marriage, notions which have long since disappeared from their lives. In a structural sense, too, the brevity and flatness of her husband's nostalgic comment evince an ironic contrast to his wife's memories, filled as they are with emotive sentimentality and expectation.

In her subsequent, weary argument with the nutritionist's whole point of view, the frustrated housewife explains, "After sixteen years of marriage I simply need some strength." At this point the narrative voice, a voice sympathetic to the housewife throughout the story, describes the character's inner feelings as she speaks out: "Her voice sounded different than usual, an echo of days gone by, when she still considered herself something of value, someone "whom all delighteth to honor." The language of this emotive response evinces a variety of usages. *Shelo ketadir* ("different than usual") and *mishekvar hayamim*, ("days gone by," a recurring motif in Kahana-Carmon's works), both somewhat archaic and euphuistic, are phrases which combine to express the housewife's sad sense of distance between the possibilities of "then" and the realities of "now." And on the heels of this emphatic combination comes the familiar euphuism, borrowed, with a small variance, from Esther 6:6, *asher hakol hafetzim bikaro* ("whom the King [here, "all"] delighteth to honor" -- the words so ironically misunderstood and later forced upon the villainous Haman, after his sudden reversal, to declare publicly in praise of his rival, Mordecai). The euphuistic phrase has a dual function in this psychological context. On the one hand, it alludes to a classic tale of expectation-turned-disappointment, and, on the other, to a story of near-tragedy-turned-celebration, thus providing an ironic background reflection of the housewife's plight. In addition, the mock-heroic tone of the allusion both projects the motif of the harsh decline in the housewife's fortunes and characterizes her once again as a rather helpless figure. She is constrained by the painful contrast of a stagnant present vis-à-vis an evocative past. The high-flown phrase becomes a stylistic device, an "emotive style,"[16] used to highlight her pathetic situation.

The climax of dramatic irony in "To Build Her a House in the Land of Shinar" is located in the government nutritionist's ensuing advice to the unhappy woman, that she take on a part-time job. "Just think," says the expert to the housewife, "an easier sort of life; I believe in being comfortable." The housewife's response is rendered partly by another euphuism (though, in English, it sounds like a cliché): "The housewife listened, but her heart was not in it." The euphuistic diction of *veliba bal imah* (taken from Proverbs 23:7) heightens the woman's emotiveness in contrast to the nutritionist's utterly superficial, impersonal solution. The housewife mocks this superficiality with a sarcastic response: "A new land, a new life, eh?" The phraseological doublet *eretz hadasha, hayim hadashim,* may be perceived as a kind of ideological cliché, a patriotic, frontier motto which, in the context of this story, at least, has lost both its magnetism and its viability. By converting the motto into an empty cliché, not only has the housewife struck back, though limply, at the nutritionist, she has also voiced her disdain toward the lofty -- and fallacious -- notion of heroic, frontier settlement. In this sense, her response expresses something far beyond the individual psyche: it is an intense, emotive protest levelled at fervid but shallow socio-political slogans, slogans which had promised (in the late fifties and early sixties) "redemption" and renewal in the new colonization of the Negev region. At its dramatic center, therefore, the story evinces a social sense which transcends the psychological focus of the narrative. The blend of a personal condition and its social ramifications is, at once, the most deliberate theme and the most engaging tendency in Kahana-Carmon's writings.

In the wake of the motto-turned-cliché comes the story's denouement. Night falls and the lights in the surrounding buildings begin to be extinguished. "Worlds go out in violet, worlds in grey. In line with the whitewash tint. But the earth abideth forever." Interposed as it is in the narrative description without special markings, the direct quotation from Ecclesiastes 1:4, *veha'aretz le'olam omedet,* may be considered to be a *melitza,* a euphuistic expression denoting a timeless continuity, the unending sameness of things (according to its sense in the biblical context). Hence, both by way of allusion and by way of rhetoric, the phrase again accentuates the housewife's particular dilemma. She is doomed, the phrase connotes, to a continued sense of stagnation and hopelessness. Progress exists only in high-flown slogans, only in surface views of quasi-heroic potentialities. For her, nightfall, with its ominous tone of recurrent frustration, symbolizes only a fruitless, unchanging future.

The story's closing scene is replete with a final, devastating irony. The housewife, acting the part of conventional hostess and homemaker, serves tea and cake to her husband and her guest. Pointing one last time to the clash between inner and outer dimensions, the narrator again utilizes archaic expressions to highlight the housewife's feelings of helplessness -- a linguistic coup de grâce, one could say, in the story's recurrent emphasis of an emotive inwardness: "The housewife wanted with all her might to say what was in her heart but could not find the words." Evincing both archaic and euphuistic characteristics, the phrases *hafetza bekhol me'odah* ("wanted with all her might") and *lomar et asher im bilvavah* ("to say what was in her heart") express the final, pathetic irony. Not only does the poor woman not have the strength to protest, she even thinks to herself -- as the narrator would have the reader perceive -- in terms of empty, impotent clichés. Her victimization, one could infer, is thus complete.

Throughout the course of this brief narrative, clichés, archaisms, and euphuisms -- the story's most salient stylistic devices -- play a variety of roles. In very specific yet subtle ways, they contribute to the work's motif structure, to the characterization, to the overriding irony and sarcastic tone, and to the very organization of narrative materials. Taken together, therefore, these stylistic tools clearly constitute "expressive linguistic facts" which, by their "affective content,"[17a] focus the reader's attention on the psychological and underlying social senses of the text.[18]

By virtue of their being distributed over the whole body of narrative, these stylistic, phraseological units also reflect the story's rising and falling dramatic line. From the early expression "going down into the heart of the wilderness," to the pathetically climactic "A new land, a new life," and to the denouement helplessness of "wanted with all her might" -- each phrase has become an integral part of a whole, dramatic structure. Thus the "stylistic value"[19] of these expressions is multilithic, subtly pervading, and aesthetically effective.

Before closing, some brief mention of the story's title would be fitting. "To Build Her a House in the Land of Shinar" (*Livnot lah bayit be'eretz Shinar*) seems to bear within it at least three of the story's main motifs: "house" (*bayit*), as in *kalkalat-bayit*, "home economics" or "domestic science," the government nutritionist's field of expertise; "land" (*eretz*), as in *eretz hadasha, hayim hadashim,* the sardonic response of frustration on the part of the housewife; and "to build her a house" (*livnot lah bayit*), a phrase which evokes the story's general, ironic theme of frontier progressivism. The title also seems to project a certain exoticness, with Shinar (the biblical name for Babylonia) sounding somewhat like "Shangri-la." The clash between exotic, appealing possibilities and desperate, personal realities further heightens the story's central irony and plaintiveness.

Actually, the name of the story reflects far more irony and sarcasm than those inherent in the motif structure. Borrowed directly from a particularly metaphorical prophetic text (Zechariah 5:11), the title refers to the prophet's vision of a symbolic exorcism: a female figure of "wickedness," set into a measure, is carried off to the distant land of Shinar, presumably connoting the prophet's message of the need to remove evil and to mend one's ways. Thus what on the surface appears to be a reference to a positive view of building and development (inherent in the settling of the Negev) becomes -- once the title's origin is noted -- the not so subtle suggestion of a moralistic admonition. Furthermore, beyond the thematic irony, the very form of the title takes on a special significance: as a direct, biblical quotation, the words *livnot lah bayit be'eretz Shin'ar* constitute an archaic sort of utterance, a phrase which reverberates with the lofty diction and metaphorical imagism of prophetic passages.

In its embodiment as an allusive archaism, the title is joined both morphologically and semantically with the succession of similar phases in the ensuing text. The reader is thereby confronted continually -- from the very beginning of the story and throughout its duration -- with the work's dualistic design. In this particular story and in other works by Amalia Kahana-Carmon,[20] the semantic weight of these types of stylistic usages should not be underestimated.

Hebrew Annual Review, Vol. 2 (1978): 1-10

Chapter 5:

[1]   See Freedman (1963), pp. 1-17).

[2]   See Humphrey (1965), pp. 62-104).

[3]   On the notions of "design" and "pattern," see Humphrey (1965), pp. 85-112); Brower (1962), pp. 3-16, 123-137); Freedman (1963), pp. 1-19 and *passim*.

[4]   See Bargad (1972), Kalderon (1972), and Shaked (1974), pp. 168-174, 205-219).

[5]   Excerpted, in the order given, from Shaked (1974), pp. 176, 220), Tsemah (1973), p. 195), and Telpaz (1971). Cf. also Wieseltier (1966).

[6]   Tsemah (1973), p. 200), Sandbank (1972), p. 327, and Ben-Herzl (1971).

[7]   In contrast to these vague evaluative comments, Shaked (1974), pp. 175, 220-221) has cogently analyzed certain syntactic usages in Kahana-Carmon's works.

[8]   Freedman has based his definitions mainly on epistemological theories and their artistic configurations. My attempt here is to delineate aspects of Kahana-Carmon's "poetic" style strictly in terms of descriptive stylistics.

[9]   See Humphrey (1965), pp. 90-99, on "word-phrase motifs."

[10]   First published in *Al hamishmar*, September 14, 1966. Collected in Kahana-Carmon (1966), pp. 111-117.

[11]   On the cliché as a variable, stylistic phenomenon, see Riffaterre (1955).

[12]   Shahevitch (1970) does not entirely succeed in his attempt to define the term *melitza*. Its literary utilization remains an open issue.

[13]   Voegelin (1960) uses the linguistic term "noncasual [or "formal"] utterance," which might be appropriate for *melitza*, but the term seems somewhat too general for this particular analytic context. "Noncasual utterance" also does not differentiate the varying register or tone of the three usages discussed here.

[14]   See Stankiewicz (1960) on the different norms ("innovating" and "archaic") at work in every speech community. In discussing the general influences of tradition and culture in the formulation of a literary language, Stankiewicz notes specifically that the use of heterogeneous elements from different language systems or layers "often becomes in poetry a purposeful, artistically exploited device" (p. 76).

[15]   All translations of biblical quotations are taken from *The Holy Scriptures* (1960).

[16]   This particular use of "emotive language" is reminiscent of S.Y. Agnon's style in the neo-romantic story "Bidmi yameha" (In the prime of her life). In this story, Agnon used the euphuistic and archaic formations to evoke a lyrical -- and ultimately ironic -- tone of innocence and infatuation in characterization. On the stylistic characteristic called "emotive style," see Todorov (1971), p. 36f.

[17] Giraud (1974), p. 946f. Cf. Stankiewicz (1964), especially his remarks on expressiveness achieved "through the substitution of grammatical forms and constructions" (p. 243).
[18] See Mukarovsky (1964), p.18f, on utterance "foregrounding." He also notes how these foregrounded components contribute to the unity of the literary work (p. 21).
[19] Giraud (1974), p. 950.
[20] This is especially true of the style and archaic motif design in *Veyare'ah be'emek Ayalon.*

BIBLIOGRAPHY

Bargad, W. 1972. *Veyareah be'emek ayalon:* haroman haliri leAmalia Kahana-Carmon." *Hadoar* LI, 36:616-617.

Ben-Herzl, Y. O. 1971. "Nitzhon haneo-melitza."*Yedi'ot aharonot,* 20 August.

Brower, R. A. 1962. *The Fields of Light.* New York.

Freedman, R. 1963. *The Lyrical Novel.* Princeton.

Giraud, P. 1974. "Rhetoric and Stylistics." *Current Trends in Linguistics* 12, 2: 943.

The Holy Scriptures. 1960. Philadelphia.

Humphrey, R. 1965. *Stream of Consciousness in the Modern Novel.* Berkeley and Los Angeles.

Kahana-Carmon, A. 1966. *Bikhfifa ahat.* Merhavia.

Kalderon, N. 1972. "Ma'ase hoshev." *Siman kri'a* 1:321-326.

Mukarovsky, J. 1964. "Standard Language and Poetic Language." *A Prague School Reader on Esthetics, Literary Structure, and Style.* Ed. P. L. Garvin. Washington, D.C.

Riffaterre, M. 1955. "Sur un singulier d'André Gide: Contribution á l'étude des clichés." *Le Français Moderne* 23: 39-43.

Sandbank, S. 1972. "Lehitbazbez al hatzedadi: al *Veyare'ah be'emek ayalon* leAmalia Kahana-Carmon." *Siman kri'a* 1 :326-328.

Shahevitch, B. 1970. "Bein amur la'amira: lemahutah shel hamelitza." *Hasifrut* 2, 3: 664-668.

Shaked, G. 1974. *Gal hadash basiporet ha'ivrit.* Second, expanded edition. Merhavia and Tel Aviv.

Stankiewicz, E. 1960. "Linguistics and the Study of Poetic Language." *Style in Language,* pp. 69-81. Ed. T. A. Sebeok. Cambridge, Mass.

Stankiewicz, E. 1964. "Problems of Emotive Language." *Approaches to Semiotics,* pp. 239-264. Eds. T. A. Sebeok *et al.* The Hague.

Telpaz, G. 1971. "Ha'isha bamoshav ha'ahori." Ma'ariv, 25 June.

Todorov, T. 1971. "The Place of Style in the Structure of the Text." *Literary Style: A Symposium,* pp. 29-39. Ed. S. Chatman. New York and London.

Tsemah, A. 1973. "Ma'amad vetzeruf shel ma'amadot: 'al sippurah ve'al sipureha shel Amalia Kahana-Carmon." *Siman kri'a* 2:195-202.

Voegelin, C. F. 1960. "Casual and Noncasual Utterances within Unified Structure." *Style in Language,* pp. 57-68.

Wieseltier, M. 1966. "Anashim—hadavar hanifla beyoter." *Akhshav* 17-18:158-160.

Agnon and German Neo-Romanticism

> [Dr. Rechnitz] stayed in his room devoting himself entirely to his work. He would take up some piece of seaweed, cut it and examine it under the microscope, then attach it to a sheet of paper, fold the sheet, place it in his great album and note down its name, its habitat, and the date when he had drawn it out of the sea. . . . The sea gave forth its daily harvest, and at night, under the moon, the daughters of Jaffa took their walks by the shore. . . . But you will not find Rechnitz there . . . . That album is the bliss of his eye and soul.
>
> (S.Y. Agnon, "Betrothed," Two Tales, translated by Walter Lever (New York, 1966, pp. 117-119)

S.Y. Agnon's *Shevu'at emunim* ("Betrothed," 1943) is the story of Jacob Rechnitz, a respected botanist, and his various entanglements: seaweed, six young Jaffa women, and Susan Ehrlich, his childhood sweetheart. In outline, the story tells of Jacob's divided life. Though devoted to biology -- he is a rising star in his profession -- Jacob often is seen taking evening strolls with the six young ladies. (Together, notes the narrator, they form a fixed constellation of sorts, the "Seven Planets.") Rechnitz is not at all torn between the two realms; apparently he enjoys them both. His botanical research is central and solid, his romantic involvements casual and complementary. The balance, however, is soon disturbed by Susan Ehrlich's sudden reentry into his life. Visiting Jaffa while on a world tour with her father, the Consul (Rechnitz's former patron), Susan reminds Rechnitz of their childhood vow, an "oath of betrothal" (of the story's title) to one another. She makes him repeat the oath and elicits his promise to keep his word. Jacob does so, but the incident sets him into an emotional quandary. His equanimity lost, Jacob attempts to ward off the predicament by total immersion in his work (described in the introductory excerpt). The matter is held in abeyance by a strange sleeping sickness which has affected Susan. Meanwhile, the Jaffa maidens converge and press Jacob for some entertainment: one evening they snatch him from his room for a walk on the beach. In a playful mood, the girls suggest a race, the winner to be crowned with a garland of seaweed from Rechnitz's laboratory. In the midst of the race, Susan appears mysteriously among the runners. She wins, and takes the seaweed wreath and places it on Jacob's head.

"Betrothed" has received a thorough treatment by Agnon critics. Analyses and interpretations of the story run the gamut from careful tracings of motif structure, to suggestions of psychological import, to determinations of all-out allegory. My own view is to identify the story centrally as an ironic love story, and thus to remove it from allegorical projections which seem superimposed. The pervasive patterns of ambiguity in the narrative -- a complex irony which has been the main cause of the great variety of interpretations -- are located primarily in the central character's areas of conflict. Rechnitz is caught between the innocent-turned-serious oath to marry Susan and his rather casual, and preferred, relationship with the other six women. His real passion has been his scientific work with species of seaweed; the uncommitted nature of his social relations has allowed him to lead a controlled existence. With Susan's willful resurrection of a long forgotten commitment, Jacob's equipose is shattered. Susan's victorious crowning of Jacob brings the dilemma to its climax, and the reader is left with Agnon's oft-used ploy of purposeful irresolution.

It is not so much a proper interpretation of "Betrothed" which has engaged my attention; rather, it is a query into the story's roots, into its literary genealogy. Most of Agnon's love stories contain heavy doses of irony and ambiguity; many are only peripherally "Jewish" in character and theme (e.g., *Giv'at hahol* [The hill of sand, 1920], *Bidmi yameha* [In the prime of her life, 1923], *Tehilah* [1950], *Edo ve'Enam* [Edo and Enam, 1950]). The presence of a traditional milieu tends to be either a neutral backdrop or, more often, a reinforcing element of irony (e.g., *Agadat hasofer* [The Legend of the Scribe, 1919]). Whatever the particular blend of ingredients or thematic focus, these stories reflect an abiding interest on Agnon's part in the ironic love tale. In turn, this interest seems to infer a distinct source of his literary imagination.

The source I have been exploring is German Neo-Romanticism, an area generally overlooked in Agnon research. The term "Neuromantik" seems to include within it several distinct but overlapping trends and periods in German literature and art from about 1890 to 1920. (Agnon lived in Germany from 1912 to 1924.) The particular mode of expression, which appears most relevant for Agnon studies, is called "Jugendstil," meaning, in literal terms, the style generally attributed to authors and poets who contributed to or wrote in the manner of the turn-of-the-century literary magazine *Jugend*. Broadly speaking, Jugendstil constituted an artistic reaction to naturalism Though by no means a unified group, its writers were concerned not with worldly issues but with aesthetic expressibility and appeal. Their aim, in one critic's definition, was to write "harmless, stylized vignettes." Topics reflected in Jugendstil writings include the life of leisure, recreation, beauty, nature, and casual flirtations. Closely related to Agnon's works, the love stories in particular, are the Jugendstil motifs of a restrained eroticism and a purposeful vagueness.

Once placed within this particular genealogical parameter, *Shevu'at emunim* reads like a Hebrew version of a Jugendstil creation. The study of botany, for example, becomes a consuming pastime during the Jugendstil period; one writer characterizes the entire trend as "the green love of algae." Main fictional characters are pampered young women of the upper middle classes, and many are dreamy maidens who seem suspended in sleep or in a trance-like state (Schlafbefangenheit). Figures of water nymphs and mermaids, often bedecked with flowers and crowns, appear frequently in Jugendstil art and literature. Main activities, in German life as well as the arts, include recreation in parks and at beaches, athletic events, and races. The sea and its underwater world of plants possess natural and secret properties which inspire both mystical and artistic possibilities. Young girls, some boy-like in manner and physique, some wearing flower garlands or bearing roses, populate the scene and participate in the leisurely, sportive events. Paintings of the period depict nymphs wearing crowns of flowers or seaweed; they rise from the sea bearing crowns aloft, their hair resembling seaweed, trailing into the water.

These selected motifs play a role, dramatic or descriptive, in "Betrothed." Although the aspects of theme, character, or action do not in themselves embody the gist of the story, which

Agnon has woven so effectively, they do evince undeniable evidence that the Jugendstil mode must be considered a central source of Agnon's romantic tales. Beyond this genre and beyond Jugendstil itself, the wide range of German Neo-Romanticism, from Impressionism, to Gothic Revival, to Expressionism, should prove to be a fertile field indeed for Agnon research.

Prooftexts 1, Spring, 1980: 96-98

Amalia Kahana-Carmon
and the Novel of Consciousness

In the late 1950s and early 1960s, the first decade of her literary career, Amalia Kahana-Carmon languished on the periphery of Israeli writing. Her stream-of-consciousness style and her intense concentration on inner realms of being set her apart from the mainstream of Israeli prose fiction (Tammuz, Shamir, A. Megged, et al.), which focused for the most part on national issues and social realities. The publication of her first collection, *Bikhfifa ahat* (In one bunch, 1966), confirmed the basic image of unconventionality. But this array of eighteen stories made it impossible to deny that although she was not assimilable to the current norms in writing, Kahana-Carmon did possess considerable talents. She combined an ardent sensitivity to emotional states of mind with a forceful agility of language. Linguistic verve, inwardness, and psychological universality eventually came to be acknowledged and appreciated as qualities that distinguished Kahana-Carmon from her literary contemporaries.

From the beginning of her career Amalia Kahana-Carmon has been a writer of lyrical or nonrealist prose. Her hallmark has been the mastery of techniques derived from stream of consciousness fiction, including the varied kinds of interior monologue and represented speech, the dramatization of inner awareness and emotion, and the blending of inner and outer experience.[1] Her fiction is supported by sub-structures of metaphorical motifs that crystallize random associations of mind into unified meaning.[2] There is a strong vein of social criticism as well. Kahana-Carmon contraposes bourgeois manners and entrenched social mores with the ambivalence and uncertainty of individual sensibility. Most often it is the woman, her feelings and fate in contemporary society which engage her imagination.

Most of Amalia Kahana-Carmon's stories focus on the emotional impact of one incident, one occurrence, a brief encounter, a transient but incandescent moment, the individual flicker of emotive, often pathetic self-recognition.[3] The lives of her characters, in their projected inwardness, resemble, in

Virginia Woolf's words, "a luminous halo, a semi-transparent envelope."[4] They and their experiences are enclosed by a bell-jar which keeps them separated from reality, yet unprotected from the permeating lights and shadows. The characters live in a constant state of diaphonous ambiguity.

In style and focus, Amalia Kahana-Carmon's works do, in fact, bear a general resemblance to the fiction of Virginia Woolf. Like Woolf, Kahana-Carmon has ever more finely and intensely endeavored not only to probe the individual mind but "to convey this unknown and uncircumscribed spirit,"[5] to portray the vulnerabilities of heightened consciousness. The characters who populate Amalia Kahana-Carmon's writings are vulnerable precisely because they are capable of intense inward lives. They are ironic victims of their own acute awareness. Ne'ima Sasson, a teenaged character in one of the stories who is hopelessly in love with her teacher, can express the inexpressible only through her ecstatic, stylized poems; the emotive flow and the forced control intermingle and clash inextricably. In another story, the middle-aged housewife in a newly-established Negev frontier town cannot get herself to take the advice of a stolid government nutritionist, who has suggested she merely put some order in her life. Memories of past possibilities, now irretrievable, have created inner needs that conflict with superficial views of either quasi-heroic or pragmatic adjustment.[6] For similar reasons, Noa Talmor, the main character in Kahana-Carmon's first novel *Veyare'ah be'emek Ayalon* (And moon in the vale of Aijalon (1971), finds great difficulty in becoming part of the world of progress and doing; she lives only with a growing, resentful sense of identity loss and quiet despair.[7]

The essential theme of nearly all her short stories and her first novel, is lovelessness, or, better, a fleeting encounter with the amorphous possibility of some close relationship, whether intimate or not. This sort of casual but lingering encounter leaves its victims groping for attachments, seeking to unravel the mystery of inconsequence. An almost-but-not-quite relationship, an understated but uncontrollable involvement, and a desperate, haunting memory -- this melancholy combination forms the thematic base of much of the fiction.[8] Though her themes sound melodramatic in outline, the artistic realization of these emotive and reminiscent states of mind is a real achievement.

Sadot magnetiyim (Magnetic fields, 1977), her recent novel, represents the culmination of a long, continuous effort to portray these essences of inward experience. In this novel Kahana-Carmon presents an artistic chronology of a potential relationship, its germination, its budding, its aborted growth, and untimely death. The work depicts a passing, month-long encounter in London between Zevulun Leipzig, an Israeli playwright approaching middle age, and Wendy Eleanor Otis, an American Ph.D. candidate and instructor in contemporary history. He is doing research for a new play, and she is working on her dissertation on British labor unions. Zevulun falls in love with Wendy, head-over-heels in love, though the romance never comes to fruition. At its center, *Sadot magnetiyim* is less concerned with depicting a brief, unrequited affair than with presenting those moments of consciousness that transmit the entirety of inner response to outer stimuli. The mysterious attraction-repulsion syndrome of emotive magnets is the premise for a deeper investigation, an inquiry into the psychic management of physical and emotional phenomena. As Miss Dennis, a secondary character, puts it, "the plot is only an excuse to say something else" (p. 68).

Sadot magnetiyim is a novel of recollection. By force of his vivid but chaotic memory, Zevulun Leipzig ponders the encounter with Wendy and inquires into its inner meanings. Kahana-Carmon concretizes this psychic process mainly through structure, narrated time, and motif patterns. The first structural device encountered is a kind of double prologue, two episodic narratives placed before the story of Zevulun and Wendy. (Beneath the title *Sadot magnetiyim*, Kahana-Carmon notes the rubric, "A triptych.") The first episode concerns Shoshana, a thirteen-year-old Israeli girl, seduced and abandoned by a young Canadian U.N. soldier during a bus ride home. Shoshana is a combination of naiveté and romantic yearning. She allows the encounter to develop, for she sees herself as the heroine in a sailors' ballad her father often sang: the girl left behind, longing for the sailor gone to sea. She perceives the soldier's advances as a signal both of her demise

and of her future fulfillment. She has met her end, she feels,
yet she has just begun to know life.

> And why aren't they walking any further. . . . And why
> did he throw her so rudely to the ground. . . . She struggles to
> get free, half of her held between his legs and he presses her
> legs together, the top half of her held by one of his arms, he
> just lay on her, hard, with his clothes and shoes, and that's
> all, with his other hand forcing her face toward his face,
> searching out her mouth, as if seeking closeness and desire
> ...what sort of scheme is this, and he sighs and seems so
> excited. And suddenly he's gone. Everything's not clear, not
> good. Surely we were friends. And I, because of him, no
> longer belong to Israel. I belong to the U.N. (p. 19f).

> A U.N. soldier, Shoshana exulted, extended her hands,
> held onto his waist, not wanting to leave. Then she walked
> on with him. (P. 22).

The rape is not against her will; it is beyond her comprehension
as a rape. She senses the harshness, the uncontrollableness,
the badness of it; but she also senses her initiation into some
"secret covenant," into "the world's day-to-day mysteries" (p.
21). As a result, she has matured, become a woman worthy of
love; at the same time she has been diminished and become
more child-like. She's both "the girl of the brigade" and Alice in
Wonderland in her school play. This duality heightens the
dilemmas developed later in the work. In his relationship with
Wendy, his foreign encounter, Zevulun is cast into a trauma of
hope and despair, of fulfillment and loss. Surrendering to
ambiguous dreams, Zevulun eventually must confront a dual
vision of himself, a vision both of renewed vigor and of
encroaching death.

The second panel of the triptych portrays the evocative
return of an unnamed woman to London and its environs, to
places of residence during her early married life with Alex. The
landscape is highly charged with dualistic overtones: "day is
like night," the sunset is lovely but "of drained blood" (p. 29).
The people she once knew are gone, yet all seems the same.
"Where are you. Where am I. . . . Where have we been since
then," she muses (pp. 30, 32). Past and present blend together:
happy laughter of then mixes with quarreling voices overheard

now. But the dualism persists. Fired then from her secretarial job at the Israeli Consulate, the woman-narrator reacts to it as both a demeaning and an uplifting experience. She takes comfort in the sunset: "I watched it. . . in its entirety. Till the end. . . . So what. A stupid sunset. Who needs sunsets" (p. 39). Dualism also persists in the complex structure of narrated times. All is a reminiscence, but several "thens" are called to mind, and several "nows" are depicted. Unordered moments fill the narrative present, which is itself in flux.

Here the reader begins to comprehend the meaning of "triptych." The three main sections of the work are separate pieces which are placed before the reader as a unity. The linear properties of sequence become secondary to the significance of the three sections as contiguous parts. The viewer of the triptych moves his eyes from the first panel to the second, to the third; but after the initial glances the particular order of continued perception is unclear and unimportant. Sequence gives way to contiguity and to simultaneous comprehension. Like the work's central characters, the reader, too, "lives" in more than one time frame, experiencing an endless series of multiple, overlapping times, scenes, voices, and responses.[9]

In like manner, Zevulun Leipzig's interlude with Wendy is constructed as a disjunctive, nearly timeless blur. The last narrated scene of meeting between them is the same as the first. "The T.V. room's over there," Wendy's playful remark outside the British Museum recalls Zevulun's previous directions to her when she first arrived at the Hotel Arundel, their London domicile. I say "first narrated scene" of meeting, because they actually had met before, at the Arundel. This is the first time the *reader* meets Zevulun-meeting-Wendy, as they meet outside the British Museum, sometime after they have met in the Arundel's T.V. room, which is sometime after he had met her -- for the actual first time -- at breakfast. What the reader is continually apprehending, therefore, is moments of reminiscence in Zevulun's mind, moments of consciousness themselves, gestures, conversations, encounters, and feelings. Wholly immersed in this multileveled, memoiristic frame of mind, the reader has constant and "immediate access" to the whole range of Zevulun's past and present.[10] Time-as-expansion becomes time-as-contraction; time as a linear,

sequential force becomes a vertical, simultaneous state. In
other words, time itself -- it's formulation in this work, that is
-- has become synchronic. Furthermore, all experience has
been "made strange" by at once separating and juxtaposing
multiple aspects of inner, psychological being. Thus all
experience has been transformed into an emotive montage of
memory.

In a traditional view of characterization one could note
that Zevulun and Wendy clash with or complement each other
on the basis of their different personalities. He is more artistic,
humanistic, or romantic; she more pragmatic, and above all,
goal-oriented. But this is not simply a story of clash of
characters; it is rather an interwoven series of muddled,
agonized bursts of consciousness on the part of Zevulun.

> And as I remember all these [views of Wendy] today?
> Everything, why, takes on character. Of wrestling, slowly, in
> a dream. Bound by a different law of gravity. Or a foothold, a
> trampoline. Circling and twisting, bending, detaching, knees
> swinging, tumbling. And lift a hand, put down a hand. Take
> hold. As in sleep. Light as mist. And fly to another place.
> All the while, as if floating. . . . And how could I know. As if
> a different possibility of beginning was cast here then, for a
> brief moment, with the speed of wizardry: the flash of a
> glimpse into another dimension. Opening and closing.
> (P. 61).

Wendy possesses no such introspection, no baring of an
interwoven consciousness. Wendy is a linear character; she has
a sequential scale of priorities, a linear plan for her present and
future. Evidence of her linearity is given by her own
uninterrupted, linear narration of an episode out of *her* past, a
recurring but standoffish and ultimately undone liaison with a
fellow instructor at her college. The inherent analogy to
Zevulun is obvious, but far more significant is Wendy's telling
her story in a simple, sequential fashion. We have no such
telling on the part of Zevulun. He is anything but linear; he is
topsy-turvy and inside out. The two activities in which he
participates, writing note after note to Wendy and conversing
with her on the phone and in person, have their linear
properties totally abrogated. Most of the notes are never sent,

and the dialogue is usually aimless, superficial or interrupted by Zevulun's thoughts and non sequiturs. "You fascinate me when you talk," he says, while Wendy prattles on. Zevulun, by extending over time and experience through consciousness, is a static figure, suspended in a timeless web of reverberating memories. Through his stop-action replay of events, "a repeated development of the same photograph" (p. 204), Zevulun floats in the novelistic space, continually attempting to "weave together" the broken threads of the encounter. His constant effort, as he says in the very beginning, is trying "endlessly to understand" (p. 51), wondering what has transpired in both the outer and the inner dimensions of this experience.

Beyond these aspects of characterization and time structuring, Amalia Kahana-Carmon effects the synchronic montage by manipulating several sets of narrative materials. Interjected into the dramatized scenes and varied discourses are four blocks of narrative: (1) Items described in a catalogue to an antique furniture exhibit which Wendy and Zevulun had visited; (2) excerpts from a scientific book on magnetism which Zevulun happened to pick up at the British Museum; (3) part of a radio broadcast on the ordering of one's goals in life; (4) a pamphlet listing gift items offered as premiums to excursion travelers on the Henry Hudson Line ships. (Thinking of following Wendy to the U. S., Zevulun picked up the pamphlet at a local travel agent's office.) Each of these apparently digressive sets of narrative materials is, of course, connected thematically to the story of Zevulun and Wendy. The visit to the exhibit is their first date; the mystery of magnetic fields parallels the hold Wendy has on Zevulun; the radio speaks to the issues of practicality and waste which involve them both; and the lists of food premiums bring us back continually to the lunches and dinners they have eaten in a myriad of foreign restaurants, scenes of their all too brief and unintimate rendezvous. But in terms of the work's structure these narrative blocks project a far deeper significance. By interspersing these static sets Kahana-Carmon is projecting "paradigmatic possibilities" onto the syntagmatic, linear narrative.[11] By existing in their own pattern these sets become metaphorical projections of the character's experience.

Through their contiguity with other parts of the narrative the static parts of the narrative create metonymic associations which convey central components of the work's meaning.[12] Once again, as in the structuring of the "triptych" itself, the reader has before him a contiguous, metonymic whole, a "hermeneutic code"[13] which leads the reader into an understanding of the work as a highly structured, stream-of-consciousness novel of recollection.

Aspects of the work's meaning are also transmitted by the physical properties mentioned in these paradigmatic lists: furniture, magnets, and foods. These physical entities constantly thrust upon the characters (and upon the reader) looming perceptions of concrete objects in the outer world. This is the very realm of Zevulun's dismal failure, the source of his incidental but soulful encounter, the realm of his own aging and contemplated death. These physicalities bring on inescapable associations and memories which expand into scenes and other narrative structures.[14] They combine with the divulged psychic processes to convey Zevulun's need to understand, to disengage emotionally -- and to go on living.

Three central motifs dominate the narrative: child images, the theme of power, and the leitmotif "to know." The three often overlap, and in their intermeshed design they express the central dichotomies of *Sadot magnetiyim*: the irony of growing older but not wiser; the complete lack of control over one's fate, despite maximal exertions of will and desire; the wrenching frustration of discovery without understanding. In Zevulun Leipzig's story the three themes are linked inextricably to his confused narrative of disjuncted time and, ultimately, to his unsettling awareness of aging and his foreboding of death.

Child images abound in the text. The opening motto poem by the Israeli poet Meir Wieseltier, "The Fire of God Upon Children," conveys the abuses children suffer at the hands of well-meaning parents and a hostile world order. Shoshana watches children play in the park as she waits for her father. The U.N. soldier points to his watch and, since it is late, offers to walk the "little girl" home. Everywhere children confront the woman returning to England in the second section of the work. She catches simultaneous glimpses of her first gray hairs and of a lonely, young boy, standing on a soccer field without playmates. Schoolchildren, playing freely, in a park (another recurring motif), sing a resounding song of accomplishment: "Ask and you shall receive, search and you will find." The words haunt her, filling her with feelings of failure, inertia, and loneliness. "Where am I, where are all my children," she laments (p. 41). Zevulun sees Wendy, talking so seriously about her research, as "a child in big slippers, pajamas, with Daddy's hat and briefcase" (p. 53). She seems "just out of jeans [like] a child still in diapers. A twenty-six-year-old child" (p.108). He perceives himself emotionally as "still in kindergarten" (p. 82); he dreams about a child, his son, "a little, laughing boy. . . freckled, with the tiny face of a man of reason, a brilliant scholar" (p. 93), a self-sufficient, secure child in contrast to his uncertain, unneeded father.

The child motif plays several roles. It reflects the dichotomy in the work of youth and old age; it expresses the ironic blending of innocence and growth, maturity and loss; it juxtaposes freedom and playfulness with loneliness and despair; it promises youth and rebirth but brings old age, retreat, and disappointment. These are the problems of life which all the work's characters confront.

The theme of power (or strength or force) is linked to the child motif mainly by its suggestion of self-reliance and control, or their absence. When the soldier takes her ticket and hands it to the conductor on the bus, Shoshana feels suddenly devastated, at a loss, no longer "the eldest daughter [who should be] taking care of herself through her own power" (p. 16). She tries to struggle free during the rape; "But men, how strong they are, she learned" (p. 19). After being fired, the returning woman recalls her "childish words" in response; but as she repeats them, "abracadabra, they flood her with force, with confounding memory" (p. 35). The backdrop to Zevulun and Wendy's walks to restaurants shows "trees approaching middle age, and trees at the peak of their strength and power" (p.63). Wendy tells of a recurring dream: led to execution (by meatgrinder!), she feels "totally powerless [like] a man driving . . . on a snowy night. The car begins to skid. . . and you're powerless, holding onto the steering wheel with all your might but uselessly" (p. 107). In like fashion, Zevulun feels "tossed

with force into the sky [to] a chilling height" by the gears of a
time machine. He muses on what he has read about magnetic
forces and atomic theory; he feels the surge of "this force"
when he and Wendy are jolted together in the subway. But
what transpires in their relationship is the gradual loss of
emotive power. "I'm a middle-aged man. I have no strength
any more," Zevulun admits to himself, surrendering sadly to
the improbability of love.

Power and powerlessness, attraction and repulsion,
youth and old age, the innocent, open force of love and the
crushing, cruel fate of rejection and aging: these themes recur
in multiple scenes, images, and juxtaposed sequences. The
motifs express a painful lament of loss, an unnatural stifling of
emotions which have been cut off from all possibility of
fulfillment.

The fateful, ironic seal of these aroused but smothered
emotions is the motif of knowing. "I'll never know," Zevulun
says, after Wendy closes her door after him for the last time,
implying that he will never understand her feelings or why
things did not work out (p. 254). Recalling her first visit to his
room, he says, "And now that I'm reconstructing [the past]. I
have a question. Am I sorry or glad that I met her? Answer:
I've gained knowledge" (p. 147). What he has learned, what he
knows is that "human relationships. . . . are drifting sands.
One cannot build on them. For a long time I did not know that.
And I did not know. . . that at the end of each relationship my
fate is to be the loser" (pp. 82-83).

All the knowledge and understanding Zevulun gains are
self-defeating, hence paradoxical. He is constantly haunted by
not knowing: "There's a desperate sadness in the lack of
complete knowledge," he muses (p. 50). His ignorance (or
innocence) is bliss. For discovery leads him only to despair.
The more he learns, the more he seeks to know, to comprehend
himself, to understand the brief interlude, the more pathetic he
becomes. To know, to discover, to feel, to attain, to understand
-- Zevulun ironically both succeeds and fails in these
endeavors. Typical of Kahana-Carmon's characters (though
probably the most agonized figure in her works to date), he is
the ironic victim of his own sensibilities.

Two aspects of style and another recurring theme must be noted, since they permeate all three sections of the "triptych": the high level of diction, the use of *diglossia* (English words transcribed into Hebrew), and the recurrent name-dropping of famous personalities.

Elevated, often archaic diction is a conspicuous feature of all of Kahana-Carmon's writings. The function and effect of high diction vary from work to work. Its use generally infuses the text with a tone of heightened sensitivity or perception; it makes the reader aware of an intelligence which, though assuredly emanating from the author, envelops and highlights the particular character, idea, or scene lying at the dramatic center of the narrative. Often the high diction projects a poetic or lyrical image, so as to evoke with intensity a pathetic situation, a sympathetic tone, or even a satirical, mock-heroic point of view.[15]

In *Sadot magnetiyim* the predominant role of elevated language -- in vocabulary, phrasing, and grammatical and syntactical structures -- is to augment the emotive tone of the narrative, and thereby to accentuate the plaintiveness of the central characters. The diction unites Shoshana, the returnee, and Zevulun Leipzig by a common tone of majestic melancholy. A lofty resonance of lament raises the characters from mundane states of lovelornness to a peak of emotional intensity and pathos. In combination with the portrayal of confused states of mind and the disjunctive sequences of time, memory and backdrop, the use of heightened diction impresses the reader with the characters' devastating plight, their insurmountable, tragic loss. Indeed, it is a classic tone of tragedy that is struck throughout all sections of *Sadot magnetiyim*.

Regarding the use of *diglossia*, it seems quite natural for Kahana-Carmon to have used a great number of Hebrew transcriptions of English words and place names, since the background of the story is London. Thus the reader does not balk at the Hebrew transcription of familiar place names like "Hyde Park," "Picadilly," or even the "Vest End"; nor does one think twice about names like "Miss Dennis," "Lord Asqvit," or "Dame Edit Evans" -- and the necessary consonantal changes are taken for granted. However, these usages begin to become more noticeable in certain instances of *combined* English and Hebrew designation. For example, items in the furniture catalogue read (phonetically):*kabinet indo-portugezi* (an Indo-Portuguese cabinet) and *shulhan pembrok elipsi besignon hapluit* (an elliptic Pembroke table in the Pluitt [?] style); food items read: *ugat puding-kristmas* (a Christmas pudding-pie), and *kruvit-kevusha 'pikalili' [2 pint]* (marinated cauliflower 'piccalilli' [2 pints]). In these examples some Hebrew words are used, some English words in Hebrew transcription, and overall the word order is Hebrew. At times, however, the choice seems arbitrary: the title of the tune "Lady Be Good" is transliterated; but *Nuhi, geveret, nuhi*, Bob Dylan's "Lay, Lady, Lay," is translated. And then there is the strange, seemingly erroneous or redundant mix of the two languages. (The redundancy is evident in the menu listings noted immediately above.) For example, "And here is Oxford Street" becomes *vezehu rehov oxford-street*, with the Hebrew word for street, *rehov*, unnecessarily repeated. And the British "Public Records Office" could certainly have been translated; instead, it appears in Hebrew transliteration as *publik rekords offis*. Finally, there is the matter of the main characters' names, one terribly Hebrew and terribly foreign, even archaic sounding: "Zevulun Leipzig"; and the other, very American (and very foreign-sounding, of course, to Zevulun), necessarily transliterated as *Elinor vendy otis*. We hear these names over and over again: Zevulun and Vendy, especially Vendy, Vendy, Vendy. And the title of the novel itself, *Sadot magnetiyim*, also reflects a kind of combined language usage.[16]

It seems that by using this strange, obtrusive blend of Hebrew and English, Kahana-Carmon graphically has combined elements of normalcy and strangeness, elements of a common linguistic usage and an obtrusive foreign effect. The duality parallels the recurring novelistic themes of familiarity and foreignness, of intimacy and alientation; Israeli and American, Hebrew and English, Zevulun and Wendy. These oppositions are the poles about which the work revolves. Consequently, the dual language usage appears to be analogous to the entire situation of ambiguity in the novel: Zevulun wavers between romance and estrangement, between his hopefulness and his dread of the end. His reminiscences are both sweet and bitter, his experience with Wendy double-edged. The reader, too, lives a kind of dual existence. Simultaneously we stand between a foreknowledge of the story's outcome and a retrospective view of how it has come about. The use of *diglossia*, then, is a stylistic tool which creates a semantic irony; and this irony reflects in turn the thematic irony of emotional arousal versus breakdown.

Beyond the link between the linguistic and the thematic, the *diglossia* seem paradoxical in the general context of the work's "high Hebrew" diction. If the author were aiming at a more sophisticated, more "authentic" or "pure" level of Hebrew, the ironic effect notwithstanding, why then would she regularly interpose transliterated English words, instead of seeking a "proper" Hebrew translation? The paradox may be resolved by perceiving the use of *diglossia* as a purposeful, counteractive force to the inflated diction. By recording the names of streets, hotels, offices and restaurants in the English "original," so to speak, Kahana-Carmon creates the illusion of a more immediate, more "real" setting. In this framework of concrete places and things the characters' emotional traumas also become all the more real and harsh. As an antithesis to the lofty language of inwardness and sensibility, the *diglossia*, like the recurring lists of furniture and foods and the digressions concerning magnetism, function as concrete physicalities which make more palpable the individual character's sense of personal pain.

Parallel to the ironic use of high diction is the recurring mention of famous personalities. Movie stars, writers, and royalty abound: Anthony Perkins, Doris Day, Dame Edith Evans, the Duke of Edinburgh, George Bernard Shaw, Ella Fitzgerald, Bob Dylan, Agnon, Bialik, Pinter, and King Kong, among others. The "star" or "Jet-Set" theme injects into the narrative a passing but pervasive sense of the exotic, the faraway world of stage and screen, fame and fortune. "And the movie dashed on. Dashing forward, extending and going beyond itself," Zevulun thinks (p. 158), linking the whirlwind affair with Wendy to the unreal but unstoppable world of the cinema. The Hollywoodesque is ironic; it is also fatal. Zevulun's passion is inflated, charged; the glitter of stars accentuates the unreal possibilities, the stretch of emotive

imagination to which Zevulun falls victim. "We flew too close
to the chariots of the sun. It was an experience that attracted
[*sha'ava*, as with magnets] me," he notes in the same context.
His end, however, is utterly real: an aging, older man,
devastated after a brief, passing affair which leaves him, as in
the beginning, in a ceaseless, mournful state of contemplation.

> And I'll never know. I'll never hear her version of the
> story. Or if she had a version. A few times, how many, five?
> we went out together. As colleagues. Here and there we ran
> into each other and exchanged words. Once I stormed up to
> her room. And there were four or five telephone
> conversations. That's all. What does that tell her? . . .
>   It all happened about a year ago. Nearly a year. As I've
> said. When our paths crossed then; Wendy called out to me,
> in a kind of harsh voice, smileless, pointing in the opposite
> direction: "The T. V. room's over there," -- she moves, they
> move, on. I liked it. As if I'd put down roots on the spot.
>   I had no warning. (Pp. 254-255).

In Amalia Kahana-Carmon's own evaluation, *Sadot
magnetiyim* is a unique achievement. She has written:

> I don't know how much I've succeeded in transmitting
> how I was affected while writing it, the elevation of spirit
> which was even somewhat frightening. As if the angels were
> speaking to me through loud speakers.[17]

For her this work has been one of inspired imagination, of
emotional intensity and precise composition. She recognizes
her writing as being "different." By focusing on the inner
thought complexes of a reflective, "preoccupied character," she
realizes that her work may not be acceptable to all readers. But
Kahana-Carmon has been willing to take the risk, an act of
nonconformism which makes for greatness and permanence.
    Sadot magnetiyim is a central artifact of contemporary
Israeli modernism. It is the product of a writer who is unafraid
to experiment with genre, style, structure and language, and
follows steadfastly the direction of her own artistic
commitment and concerns. She continues the movement in
modern Hebrew literature of great, nonconformist writing,
from Berditchevsky to Agnon, from Gnessin to Yizhar.

Kahana-Carmon's refining and recasting of the lyrical novel shows how vibrant and forceful fiction can be when a masterful writer blends a modern novelistic tradition with the depth of virtuosity and a broad range of language.

Prooftexts 1, 1981: 172-184

Chapter 7:

1   See Ralph Freedman, *The Lyrical Novel* (Princeton, 1963), pp. 1-17.
2   See Reuben Brower, The Fields of Light (New York, 1962), pp. 3-11, 123-37.
3   Cf. Freedman, p. 192ff.
4   Virginia Woolf, *Collected Essays*, vol. 2 (London, 1966), p. 106.
5   *Ibid.*
6   The stories referred to are *Ne'ima Sasson kotevet shirim* (Ne'ima Sasson writes poems) and *Livnot bayit be'erets shin'ar* (To build her a house in the land of Shinar), both collected in *Bikhfifa ahat* (Tel Aviv, 1966).
7   *Veyare'ah be'emek ayalon* (Tel Aviv, 1971).
8   These themes and dramatic situations are reminiscent of the novels of the English novelist Jean Rhys, a writer for whom Amalia Kahana-Carmon has had great regard.
9   Kahana-Carmon's own description of time and space in this work refers to "a constant, wavering movement...as in Op Art." See her discussion of *Sadot magnetiyim* in "They're All Only Partial Truths" [in Hebrew], *Davar*, February 18, 1977. See also Freedman on Virginia Woolf's use of time "as an image, determining the lyrical design" in *The Lyrical Novel*, p. 222.
10   J. Hillis Miller, "Virginia Woolf's All Souls' Day: The Omniscient Narrator in *Mrs. Dalloway*," in M.J. Friedman and J.B. Vickery, eds., *The Shaken Realist* (New Orleans, 1979), p. 108.
11   See Robert Scholes, *Structuralism in Literature* (New Haven and London, 1974), p. 188.
12   See Roman Jakobson, "Aphasia: The Metaphoric and Metonymic Poles", in J.V. Cunningham, ed., *The Problem of Style* (Greenwich, Conn. 1966), pp. 260-65.
13   See Roland Barthes, *S/Z* (New York, 1974), pp. 75-76.
14   Freedman, p. 198.
15   A similar example of the use of a purposely elevated, romanticized style may be found in S.Y. Agnon's love story, *Bidmi yameha* (In the prime of her life). The Kahana-Carmon story, *Ne'ima Sasson kotevet shirim* mentioned above, also utilizes a stylized, high diction which emphasizes the protagonist's inner, emotional expressiveness.

[16] On historical aspects of the use of *diglossia* in Hebrew literature, see I. Even-Zohar, "Toward a clarification of the function of the language of literature in *diglossia*" [Hebrew], *Hasifrut*, 2:2 (1970): 286-302.

[17] See note 9 above.

Realism and Myth in the Works of Hayim Hazaz: 1933-1943
On the Tenth Anniversary of His Death

Hayim Hazaz (1898-1973) should be read and understood as a novelist of ideas. In his fiction he was continually preoccupied with the dramatization of theories on the dynamics of Jewish history. At the same time, his works demonstrate the artistic conventions of the literary tradition of realism. A central characteristic of his writings, therefore, is the blend of philosophical and realistic elements, with the realism often utilized to bolster the "truth" of the philosophy.[1]

This basic Hazazian blend is seen primarily in his character depictions. On the one hand, many of his main characters either embody or speak out on various ideas of Jewish history. On the other, they are presented in heightened realistic fashion, often in caricature: burlesque external description, mimetic, melodramatic speech, and idiosyncratic, emblematic gestures. Most of the characters, therefore, have both ideational and representative dimensions. Hazaz developed this distinctive mix of characterization features mainly in the years 1933-1943. This period, therefore, represents a significant, even decisive transition in Hazaz's career.

The period opens with the publication of "Rahamim hasabal" (Rahamim the porter)[2] and closes with "Hadrasha" (The sermon),[3] the last significant short story of ideas Hazaz was to publish. "Rahamim hasabal" may be seen as the standard Hazazian story of the thirties, especially in terms of its structure. "Hadrasha" evinces the peak of Hazaz's creative ability in his formulation of the story of ideas. The 1933-43 period also shows important thematic and generic shifts in Hazaz's works. He began writing about the Yemenite Jews, and he displayed a renewed interest in the novel.

My purpose here is to point to a number of realistic conventions in each of these stories, especially to characterization, in order to demonstrate Hazaz's transition from the realistic story, which contained certain philosophical overtones, to the genre of the story of ideas, which uses realistic depiction as a purposeful framework for dramatized ideas.[4]

There are several common denominators in "Rahamim hasabal" and "Hadrasha": (1) In their general framework, both are stories of confrontation; at their dramatic center is a meeting of minds concerning a problem purported to affect both sides of the argument. (2) Both focus on a common theme; namely, the response to the traumatic experience of transition from the Diaspora to Erets Yisrael (in theory, if not in fact). (3) In structure and narrative rhythm the stories also resemble each other. External and internal characterization of the main character; comments by the narrator on the character's personality and attitude toward his surroundings; regular references to background details; the meeting or confrontation between protagonist and antagonist; an increasing crescendo toward climax of debate, response and interruption; a climax which includes a moment of silence or quiet introspection; followed by a brief denouement with an open or ambiguous ending, creating a strong sense of irony. (4) The characterization techniques in both stories are also parallel. Mainly these are a realistic presentation by means of idiosyncratic speech and recurring, emblematic gestures; the introduction of a basic contrast or conflict between the characters of confrontation, in both external depiction and in inner characterization; and, most significantly, the presentation of main characters in emotional polarization.

Menashke Bezprozvani, the central character in "Rahamim hasabal," is the descendant of Hazaz's earlier street-wandering figures, such as Meir Heres in "Kevo hashemesh" (As the sun riseth), Yerahmiel Leavitt in "Marie," Budnick, a forest wanderer, in *Beyishuv shel ya'ar* (In a forest settlement), and Reb Pinhas, the old emigré, in Istanbul.[5] Like them, Menashke is also a loner, depressed, angry, and embittered, searching but essentially aimless and perplexed.

> One sunny day Menashke Bezprozvani, lean as a pole, wandered through the streets of Jerusalem, his face seamed and sickly-looking, his mouth unusually fleshy and red, his eyes discontented and disparaging.
> Bitterness gnawed at his heart, piercing through him like some venom. . . the bitter, gloomy quintessence of fever and

hunger, of unsettled wandering from *kevutza* [commune] to *kevutza*, of vexations and suffering and troubles enough to send a man out of his mind and make him lose his strength, and all the other effects of his past experiences, his lack of employment, and his present sickness.[6]

Immediately following this opening description the narrator, in the mode of dramatic irony, reveals to the reader Menashke's inner feelings, the source of his despair, ambivalence, and lack of self-awareness.

All these were the complaints of a dejected, despairing person who, more than he wished to comfort himself, wished to torture himself, to cry out aloud and rebel and remonstrate against the whole state of affairs. But his complaining was only half-hearted. Like it or not, he possessed a great love for the Land and a great love of the Hebrew language. And since his complaints were no more than half-hearted, he complained all the more, denying everything and destroying everything in thought without getting anywhere, and just making himself uncomfortable. (P. 215f)

In contrast to Menashke, when Rahamim the porter arrives upon the scene, he appears to be at peace with the world, sporting "a smile of satisfaction and wonder" which recurs throughout the story.

He was a short individual with thick black eyebrows, a beard like a thicket, his face bright as a copper pot and his chest uncommonly virile and broad. He was dressed in rags and tatters, rent upon rent and patch upon patch, a rope girded around his loins and a basket of reeds in front of him on the donkey's back. (P. 216)

In the story's exposition the narrator points out that Rahamim also has undergone certain travails in his life, including a great disappointment immediately upon his arrival in Palestine: the Jewish Legion, which Rahamim hoped to join, had just disbanded. Therefore, Rahamim, like Menashke, had also lived through a trauma based on the paradoxes of history and individual experiences. The difference, however, between the two characters is first and foremost in their physical dimensions: "lean as a pole" vis-à-vis "short and stocky"; a face "seamed and sickly-looking" vis-à-vis a face "bright as a copper pot"; a mouth "unusually fleshy and red" vis-à-vis a chest "uncommonly virile and broad"; eyes "discontented and disparaging" vis-à-vis the smile "of satisfaction and wonder." These physical differences, of course, are the external signs of the contrasting personalities: one is depressed, the other optimistic; one an aimless wanderer, the other settled, employed and apparently happy; one quiet, the other talkative; one embittered, the other smiling; one introverted and contained, the other open and gregarious; one preoccupied, immersed in introspection, the other outgoing and unburdened. Menashke is controlled and restrained, and Rahamim is free in his speech, gestures, and laughter. And one further set of contrasts should be added: Menashke is middle class, Ashkenazi, ambivalent, and desperate after leaving Kfar Giladi, while Rahamim is a "primitive" (especially in speech), Sephardi, trusting in God, a Jerusalemite bearing palm fronds, and riding on a donkey. Menashke is all too human; Rahamim reverberates with quasi-messianic qualities.[7]

The contrast is drawn all through the story. It is reflected, for example, in the story's structure and time of narration: Rahamim relates lengthy anecdotes, but Menashke only emits an intermittent brief question or response. The contrast is seen also in the mode of discourse used in the narration: Rahamim's adventures are presented in indirect monologue, which is close to imitated speech, while Menashke's thoughts are rendered directly by the narrator. Furthermore, Menashke's depiction remains totally static throughout, with no additions of descriptive detail given while he speaks or listens to the porter; but Rahamim is constantly accompanied by gestures and elaborate similes which accentuate the physicality of his external description.

In summary, "Rahamim hasabal" is based upon the polarized depiction of two immigrant types; the story is structured on a continual contrasting of the characters' physical and emotional dimensions. Without an understanding of this polarized presentation, constituted mainly by conventions of realistic depiction, a proper understanding of the meaning expressed by the story is impossible. It is precisely the blatant, physical attributes of Rahamim, especially his smile and face, which calm Menashke and distract him from his feelings of frustration and melancholy. The concrete, physical aliya to Erets Yisrael is traumatic, but in spite of it all, and, in great measure, due to Rahamim's solicitude, Menashke will overcome the trauma. This message of eventual adjustment and accommodation is the main idea expressed in "Rahamim hasabal."[8]

Many aspects of the analysis and interpretation of "Rahamim hasabal" may be somewhat transparent. But the main point of this analysis is to demonstrate its application as a key to a proper understanding of "Hadrasha," a story whose meaning is far more ambiguous and the subject of a great variety of attempted interpretations. At the center of "Hadrasha" there is also a dramatic confrontation of characters -- Yudke, the speaker, and the council members, his auditors -- who appear in physical and, especially, in emotional contrast. A proper interpretation of "Hadrasha," as is the case with "Rahamim hasabal," depends upon an analysis of the emotional contrast of clashing personalities. The reader, viewing the transition from the one story to the other, must perceive the parallel structuring of both stories and apply the analytic lessons learned to possible interpretations of the more ambiguous "Hadrasha."

*　　　　　*　　　　　*

Like "Rahamim hasabal," "Hadrasha" tries to capture a significant moment of trauma in the life of its protagonist. Here, too, one finds underlying tensions between the main character and his antagonists; but more prominent in "Hadrasha" is the evergrowing, emotive contrast between speaker and auditors. More than a story, "Hadrasha" may be defined as a dramatic "scene of ideas" into which is injected -- through the technique of "making strange" -- a whole panoply of historical notions and theories.[9] These ideas are expressed to the council by Yudke, a hesitant, fumbling, incoherent speaker, a "primitive" in speech like Rahamim, who seems entirely unsuited (according to some critics, at least) to the task. The contents of Yudke's monologues present the auditors and the reader with a virtual mythology of Jewish history.

"The Exile, that is our pyramid, and it has martyrdom for
a base and Messiah for its peak. And. . . and. . . the Talmud,
that is our Book of the Dead. . . . In the very beginning, as far
back as the Second Temple, we began to build it. Even that
far back we planned it, we laid the foundations. . . Exile,
Martyrdom, Messiah. . . . Do you grasp the deep cunning
hidden in this wild fantasy, the cold moonlight with which it
flames. . . ? Do you grasp it? Just think, just think! Millions
of men, a whole people plunging itself into this madness and
sunk in it for two thousand years! Giving up to it its life, its
very existence, its character, submitting to affliction,
suffering, tortures. Agreed that it is a foolish, a lunatic
dream. But a dream, that is, a vision, and ideal. . . . What an
uncanny folk! What a wonderful, awful people! Awful,
awful to the point of madness! For look, it scorns the whole
world, the whole world and all its fighters and heroes and
wise men and poets all together! Fearsome and blind! A
bottomless abyss . . . No, one could go mad!"[10]

The scene is intense, suspenseful in both dramatic and
intellectual aspects. The dual intensity makes "Hadrasha" a
highly effective story of ideas. The contrast it depicts is mainly
between Yudke, who grows ever more vocal, even
obstreperous, and his auditors, the council members, who grow
ever more quiet, even docile. At the same time, a visible,
emotive contrast is continually evinced: the speaker seems
overly sensitized to aspects of Jewish history -- a sensitivity
which appears to have prompted Yudke to address the council
in the first place -- while the audience exhibits scorn,
amusement, hostility, and, for most of the story, indifference
toward what Yudke has to say.[11]

Direct monologue serves to create the realistic illusion in
"Hadrasha." The "live speech," so to speak, also becomes the
framework for Yudke's ideas, which burst forth with great
vigor. Rahamim's outward vividness turns into Yudke's
extraordinary vitality of speech and virtuosity of thought.
Rahamim's optimistic energy overcomes Menashke's silence
and sadness; Yudke's verbal and intellectual energy
overwhelms, or at least penetrates, the mask of indifference
enveloping the council members. Yudke's success, however,

seems short-lived. Just as in "Rahamim hasabal," it occurs only as a brief moment of quiet.

> "I'm finishing. In a word, this is the aim: one people, and above all, a people creating its history for itself, with its own strength and by its own will, not others making for it, and history, not the chronicles of a congregation, anything but *chronicles*, that's how it stands. For a people that doesn't live in its own land and doesn't rule itself has no history. That's my whole idea. I've already told you and I repeat again, and I'll say it again and again, day and night. . . is it clear? Is it clear?" And all at once his words ran together and his voice broke and sputtered with feeling, his eyes flickered to and fro like one who doesn't know which way to go. "With this I've said a great deal, the whole thing. . . everything I had on my mind. . . and now I don't want to say anything more. I have nothing more to add. . . . Enough. . . ." (P. 243)

Just after this silent moment, a moment of confusion, relief, discomfort, or ambivalence, both speaker and auditors apparently revert to their prior poses. Yudke remarks that he has not yet finished, that he has not yet reached "the main thing." Continuing his role as chief auditor, the council chairman asks Yudke to go on, but adds the outrageously ironic comment: ". . . and let's see if we can't do without the philosophy. . . ."

One of the problems which prevents an unambiguous interpretation of this potent, dramatic story of ideas, is that Yudke, as he himself states, indeed never reaches his main point. A variety of interpretive approaches is necessary, including perceptions gained from Hazaz's confrontation stories (such as "Ashir varash nifgashu" [Rich man and poor man meet], 1928), some of his symbolic stories (such as "Hagilgul" [Transmigration], 1933), or other of his stories of ideas (such as "Harat olam" [The world reborn], 1936), "Havit akhura" [Murky barrel], 1937, and "Drabkin," 1938). Each genre, with its inner dynamics and its concomitant methods of analysis and interpretation, bears some importance for an understanding of "Hadrasha." The most effective tool of interpretation, however, is a pointed analysis of the relentless emotive contrast between Yudke and the group. That is to say, the key to the story again lies in the very conventions of realistic depiction which give the work its dramatic vitality.

The main dramatic effect in "Hadrasha" is Yudke's overwrought sensitivity, his emotionality with regard to Jewish history. His feelings, gestures, and overflowing thoughts contrast and clash unremittingly with the group's apathy and unwillingness to listen to or to understand him. The council members' indifference and hostility reflect a total lack of interest in history and its dynamics. Yudke is maximally involved, even agitated; they are minimally, if at all, concerned. His views on exile, suffering, martyrdom, and the spurning of redemptive beliefs, the break in Jewish history between the Diaspora, and the idea of the Jewish State -- all these notions leave them cold. Yudke's historical interpretations meet only with the chairman's cutting remark: "Have you finished?" And finally, by leaving the "main thing" unexpressed, Yudke (and Hazaz) leave the reader in a purposeful state of interpretive limbo. But the ludicrous closing remark of the chairman shows the way. The reader realizes that the remark cannot be taken seriously, that the "main thing" must already have been expressed in the story, in its dramatic action of confrontation, in the expression, agitated and frustrated as it may be, of Yudke's ideas, in the indifference toward them evinced by the council members.

My interpretation of "Hadrasha" is that it embodies Hazaz's first literary response to the Holocaust. That is how I understand the ideas of a historical "break" and "another people" and the "new beginning" Yudke so agonizingly expresses. Aside from the analysis of the story itself, and in the face of such obvious ambiguity, one is often forced to look outside the individual work. I base my interpretation on three factors: (1) the development in Hazaz's oeuvres of the story of ideas, from "Harat olam" to "Hadrasha," most of which have the rise of Nazism as their main subject;[12] (2) the *Sitz im Leben* of "Hadrasha," written in late 1942, after word of the Final Solution and the horrors of its implementation had reached Palestine;[13] and (3) the ongoing tradition in Hazaz's short stories, especially from "Rahamim hasabal" to "Hadrasha," of the one-scene story of dramatic confrontation. In both a chronological and textual analysis of these stories, the perception that proves most convincing is that Hazaz's fictive realism is the primary key to an interpretation of the historical and philosophical myths expressed by his characters.

Jewish Book Annual, 1983-1984: 140-148

Chapter 8:

1 See my study, *Ideas in Fiction: The Works of Hayim Hazaz* (Brown Judaic Studies Series, No. 31, Scholars Press, 1982), pp. 9-14.

2 Original publication: *Musaf Davar*, (May 30, 1933). Collected in *Rehayim Shevurim* (1942).

3 Original publication: *Lu'ah Ha'aretz*, 2 (1943): 82-96. Collected in *Avanim rothot* (1946).

4 See *Ideas in Fiction*, pp. 65-68, and 74f.

5 Original publications: "Kevo hashemesh," (signed "H. Tsevi"): *Hashiloah*, 34, 199-204 (Jan.-June, 1918): 274-284. "Marie": *Hashiloah*, 43, 2 (Nov., 1925): 123-133; 3 (Dec. 1925): 200-209. *Beyishuv shel ya'ar*: Stybel Press, Berlin-Tel Aviv (Part 1, 1930; Part 2, 1931). The Reb Pinhas story referred to here is "Ashir varash nifgashu": *Hatekufa*, 24 (1928): 70-96. The three short stories noted here were never collected.

6 *Rehayim shevurim* (1942), p. 215. All references are to this version of the story. The translation, by I.M. Lask, is found in L.W. Schwartz, ed., *The Jewish Caravan* (Schocken Books: New York, 1976), pp. 785-791.

7 Cf. D. Sadan, *Bein din leheshbon* (1963), pp. 246-247. I am indebted to Sadan for his insightful comments on these contrasted characters. On other aspects of the story see B.Y. Mikhali, *Hayim Hazaz: iyunim bitsirato* (1968), pp. 95-107.

8 For a full discussion of the story in the context of Hazaz's works of the late twenties and early thirties, see *Ideas in Fiction*, pp. 60-64.

9 See my complete analysis of "Hadrasha" in *Ideas in Fiction*, pp. 82-88. See also the introductory remarks on Hazaz's "stories of ideas," *ibid.*, pp. 65-68.

10 *Avanim rothot* (1946), pp. 234-235. All references are to this version of the story. The translation, by Ben Halpern, is found in J. Blocker, ed., *Israeli Stories* (Schocken Books: New York, 1962), pp. 65-86.

11 Though I differ with this interpretation of "Hadrasha," I am indebted to Y. Bahat for his analysis of the Yudke-group relationship. See his study, *Shai Agnon veHayim Hazaz* (Haifa, 1962), pp. 189-203.

12 See *Ideas in Fiction*, pp. 68-79, 86-88.

13 A microfilm perusal of *Ha'aretz* and *Davar* show that the news of the Nazi slaughter of European Jewry gradually found its way into the daily press in the summer and autumn of 1942.

Binary Oppositions in the Poetry of Amir Gilboa

The examination of "binary oppositions" (semantic structures of equivalence or opposition) in poetic texts has proved helpful in decoding messages which seem at first to be difficult to comprehend.[1] Since the text often creates its own semantic system, which may appear to be "ungrammatical" (i.e., not in consonance with generally accepted extratextual meanings), the reader may profit considerably by decoding the text's system of oppositions and interpreting their semantic value.[2]

Binary semantic structures are found throughout Amir Gilboa's poetry, from his early works (*La'ot* [For the sign], 1942) to his last, posthumous collection (*Hakol holekh* [Everything is going], 1985). In the earlier works, dualistic images and themes predominate: darkness and light, curse and blessing, sunrise and evening, pain and pleasure, joy and mourning, death and rebirth. Oxymoron -- a kind of microstructure of opposition -- is a central rhetorical figure; ironic rhyme and other structural and linguistic features (grammar, syntax, neologisms, and archaisms) are also used effectively in creating semantic oppositions.

In the works written after Gilboa learned of the Holocaust and his family's murder, probably late in 1942,[3] the oppositional structure becomes more complex; the glossary is more neutral and less conforming to extratextual meanings. The poet strives to express the inexpressible: a response to the full knowledge of the Holocaust horror. Here an examination of binary oppositions plays a greater role in clarifying the poetry's often ambiguous, unexpectedly dualistic figures.

The later poems, from the mid-sixties to the eighties, rely mainly on both structural and linguistic ambiguities. Here, too, thematic decoding is aided considerably by uncovering the system of binary oppositions operative in these works. An overview of Gilboa's poetry shows abundant evidence of an abiding and intensifying system of binary oppositions.

Several characteristics distinguish Gilboa's poetry from that of his older contemporaries. In contrast to Natan

Alterman (1910-1970) Gilboa focuses tenaciously on the emotional life of the individual, often himself, not on the creation of surrealistic imagery, folkloristic beings, or animated symbolic objects; his is an intimate, emotive lyricism, not a distanced, symbolistic one. Unlike Avraham Shlonsky (1900-1973) -- though indebted to him for his lush depictions of nature and his use of traditional religious language -- Gilboa avoids playful puns, euphemisms and rhymes, ideological themes, and the bombast of futuristic rhetoric; his is a more serious, internalized tone which reflects poignancy and pain far more than playfulness and verbal virtuosity.

In comparison with his younger contemporaries, Gilboa opts mostly for abstract tropes and mythological imagery, not for the concrete images and similes that abound in the writings of Yehuda Amichai (1924-). There is also little affinity with the Western (i.e., British and American) style of writing seen in the works of the late Dan Pagis (1930-1986) and Natan Zach (1930-). These poets respectively concern themselves with poetry either as an embodiment of charm, intellect, and clever perceptiveness, in the case of Pagis, or as a vehicle of dramatic immediacy and ironic, antiromantic import, in the case of Zach. Gilboa is occupied mainly with lyrical, ecstatic, and elegiac voices, with the poet as dreamer and rememberer, with emotional immediacy and unabashed romantic expressivity. His is a poetry of inner feelings, private associations, profuse metaphors, and enduring sorrow and wonderment.

These and other distinctive elements of his poetry demonstrate Gilboa's artistic affinity to Hayim Nahman Bialik (1873-1934), the leading poet in the Hebrew Renaissance at the turn of the century. Most of all, it is Gilboa's language, diction, and tone which are reminiscent of Bialik's poetry. Through the first half of his career (from the early forties to the early sixties) Gilboa, like Bialik, utilized mainly a vocabulary taken from the biblical books of the prophets, Psalms, Job, the Song of Songs, and from classical rabbinic literature, the *siddur* and the *mahzor*. The diction is archaized and heightened, the tone lyrical, frustrated, enthralled, or pained. At the center of the works of both poets is an individual, often a moral voice, manifestly the voice of the persona of the poet himself, speaking from the depths of emotion and sensibility about nature, memories, love, the Jewish fate, the place of the poet, transitions, loneliness, and losses. Like Bialik's, Gilboa's poetry is also energized by a blend of the mythic and the real, by a predominance of personal associations, and by a dedication to the spirit of natural beauty.

Most relevant for this analysis of binary oppositions in Gilboa's works are the contrasts and thematic dissonances found throughout Bialik's poetry. In such works as "Biteshuvati" (Upon my return), "Eineha" (Her eyes), "Al saf beit hamidrash" (At the threshold of the studyhouse), "Zohar" (Splendor), "Rak kav shemesh ehad" (Only one ray of sun), and "Ve'im yish'al hamal'akh" (Should the angel ask), Bialik's romanticism, the *Sturm und Drang* of contrasting motifs and feelings, are quite blatant. Gilboa's works, following in this romantic tradition, are similarly dissonant, replete with the contrasting emotions of love and anger, loss and fulfillment, happiness and sorrow. A significant source of Gilboa's use of binary semantic structures undoubtedly is Bialik's impassioned, dissonant, romantic style of composition.

In this discussion I focus on three poems, "Shir kemigdalekh hagavo'ah" (A poem like your high tower, 1946); "Uvekhen, tafasti et haparpar" (And so, I caught the butterfly, 1968); and "Bein ze laze. Kivenadneda" (Between this and that. As on a swing, 1973).

These particular poems were selected for reasons of both chronology and representativeness. Each was written at a different juncture in Gilboa's career -- the mid-forties, the mid-sixties, and the early seventies -- and collected in volumes which reflect different thematics. And yet Gilboa's basic poetics, his view of the world and his idiosyncratic way of expressing that view, remain the same. These poems and their use of binary structures represent not only the particular groups of poems of which they are a part but also the abiding poetic impulse Gilboa demonstrates in his artistic compositional form. This stylistic constant, the oppositional structuring of motifs, images, and feelings, identifies Gilboa as a romantic poet, one who often idealizes or mythologizes or rhapsodizes the world, especially the natural world, and who just as often depicts the inadequacies, agonies, and terrors of the world, especially the human world.

"Shir kemigdalekh hagavo'ah" is the lead poem of "Shti hayagon ve'erev hasimha" (The warp of sorrow and the weft of joy), a section of the volume *Sheva reshuyot* (Seven domains, 1949) which comprises twelve elegies written after the close of World War II. Much of the emphasis in these poems is on recovery: the poet, crushed by the loss of his loved ones, seeks consolation, a way somehow to keep on, to maintain an emotional equilibrium. The poem, therefore, with its open expression of agonized memory, anger, and call to vengeance, is more representative of the poems written during the war, immediately after Gilboa learned of his family's murder.

These works include "Kezimrat ma'asav shel avi" (Like the melody of my father's doings), "Zikhron devarim" (Memory of things"), "Nishmat Yossi ben-ahoti Bronia" (The soul of Yossi, my sister Bronia's son), and "Shir holekh-sovev" (A cyclical poem), which contain motifs of memory, redolent depictions of family members, childhood scenes, and the shock of disbelief. In addition, "Signonot shonim" (Different styles) features an anaphoric structure using the word *ze* ("this") which is parallel to the anaphora used in "Shir kemigdalekh hagavo'ah." Gilboa's placement of "Shir kemigdalekh hagavo'ah" in the *Sheva reshuyot* volume, therefore, shows it to be both a summary of all the pain and loss expressed in poems written during 1943-46 and a lead-in to the poems of psychological and emotional reconciliation of 1947-49.[4]

> A poem like your high tower filling with
>   sounds of a bell
> and sending their dimness in the fog upon the
>   earth
> to cover over the heads with a canopy of sky.
> A poem like a curtain of dreams, transparent,
>   glass-like, spread
> over eyelids and eyes
> and muzzles the mouth to let forth the scream
> which over the mouth of the abyss is
>   screamed.
> A poem like a boiling cauldron over against
>   your look
> and the awareness of the terror which is sighed
>   behind your back

A poem like your face which I kneaded with
     my fingers
 and like the weavings of the threads of my eyes
   that were interwoven with your eyes.
Like the tongues that stammered their word in the dross of a
fire conspiring destruction
       to beginning.
And like my cold and tired reckoning -- afterward -- as you
stood
one facing *three*
and together you were --
four.
(All the girls were born to give birth --
the ugly one and the reader,
the one of the gentle eye
and the one with the belted waist.
My beloved, I envy you!)

This is a poem of the rain on the tin roofs
(the sweet excitement of the child).
Its drizzle in the open field
(sucking the breasts of the world).

This is a poem of the embracer of the mossy trunk of a tree
in a dense forest
like the closing of the hands on the sculptured stomach
of the one maiden
(in her season!)
in the world.

Now we knew all the floods of visions
sparkling in lusts on fingernails.
And before fear came we loved to tremble
like the trembling of Death for its life.
And [with] drops of gold we decorated the sky
so they'd be high unto death.

This is a poem on nights high unto death
and at dawn a stillborn [child] screams
     on earth.
(No matter! Another day and he'll roar like a
     lion at the rusting of heaven,
"Barren," "barren" he'll revile in his lie the name of his
creating mother.)

This is a poem for which all introductions
            have been prepared,
deaths at the terrors of the roads.
And departures without explanation for chaos
to dance in a chorus of weepers
with the hope that merry musicians
soon will come.

This is a poem of shepherds who soon
            will come
to the pen to gather and to count the sheep.
And a pipe that's been cracked will yet gather
            its tunes
from the bleating of memories of the sheep
of gold of
blood that was spilled in the fields
between the green and the moss
and life which will arise and come
like the light in the fields.

This is a poem of all the lies that we wanted
            to hear
with a full belly and a key in one's pocket.
This is a poem of all the sorrows by a fireplace we lusted after
and our child's laughing to his angels from
            the cradle
and the shutter is closed.

But there is a God of deed -- base and cruel! --
He's shown us the lies alive
and imagination turns to truth
and everything's secure and firm and strange
and *terrible*
with the lie dying
at the openings of the eyelid.[5]

"Shir kemigdalekh hagavo'ah" was probably written
while Gilboa was still in Europe, after having served in the
Jewish Brigade of the British Army since 1942. It embodies one
of his most poignant and volatile responses to the Holocaust,
in which he lost his entire family, his parents, two brothers, and
four sisters.

The poem is structured on a varying sequence of static
and dynamic elements. The static elements consist of a list of

definitions which denote, or attempt to denote, the poem's parameters: its genre, contents, motivation, and other aspects of its sources or aims of expressiveness. (The dynamic or more narrative elements are mentioned later in this discussion.)

At the outset these definitions are given in the form of similes, as if the speaker is groping toward a cogent delineation of the poem being created. Lines 1-3 seem to refer to an idyllic place, a town perhaps, with a tower whose ringing but muffled bells "cover over heads with a canopy of sky." *Kemigdalekh* (like your tower) and *hupa shel shamayim* (a canopy of sky) evoke a Song-of-Songs, romantic, pastoral sort of situation; the tone is one of love, quietude, security, with the place personified as a beloved, female auditor. In lines 4-5 the next definition seems to continue the evocative, sentimental tone, as well as the theme of muffledness or dimness: "A poem like a curtain [or membrane] of dreams, transparent, glass-like, spread over eyelids and eyes." The atmosphere of dreaminess or seeing through a curtain adds a nostalgic note of looking backward, remembering the hometown, envisioning it dimly. The poem is denoted here as the instrument of this act of translucent dream-memory. The images are dualistic to a degree: the tower is filled with the ringing of bells, but the canopy created by their ringing consists of a muffledness or darkness (*im'um*) and fog (*arafel*). The dream-curtain covers the lids and eyes, yet it is transparent and allows the speaker to see.

The dualism strikes the reader with full force in line 6. The curtain not only covers and yet allows for sight, it also "muzzles the mouth to bring forth the scream that's screamed over the mouth of the abyss." The idyll, certainly, is destroyed; the memory-scene turns to abject terror. The reversal is marked by the blatantly ironic juxtaposition of *uvolem et hape* (and muzzles the mouth) and *lemalet haze'aka* (to let forth the scream). The immediate effect of this radically dualistic -- and impossible -- act of a closed-mouth scream highlights the speaker's agony at the awareness of the magnitude of the Holocaust horror.

The dualism or irony of this image effects at least three reading strategies. First, it forces us to begin to read the poem backwards[6] and to confront the parallelism in lines 2-3 and 6.

The rereading may lead us to perceive the bell tower's "darkness" and the act of covering as less-than-security or sentimentality-shaping acts. The ringing of bells may even call to mind other familiar poems ("Pa'amonim" [Bells] by Saul Tchernichovsky, for example) which link the ringing of bells in church towers with anti-Jewish violence.

Second, this initial instance of ironic dualism, the closed-mouth scream, may serve as an imagistic anchor, an abiding reference point, or "matrix,"[7] continually brought to mind as the reader moves through the poem and discovers situations, images, or tropes which are similarly dualistic and blatantly self-contradictory. Such would be the case in lines 46-47 with the juxtaposed images *mikhelet bokhim* (a chorus of weepers) and *nognim alizim* (merry musicians); in lines 37-38 with the apparently paradoxical combination of innocence and accompanying ominousness of *unetifot shel zahav anadnu lashamayim* (and [with] drops of gold we decorated the sky) followed by *sheyihyu gevohim ad mavet* (so they'd be high unto death); in lines 23-25 with the nostalgic images of "the rain on the tin roofs" and "its drizzle in the open field," which are counterposed with *mabulei mar'ot* (floods of visions) in line 33. The contradictoriness persists, too, in other mixed images, such as lines 53-54: the "gold of blood that was spilled in the fields"; line 60: "all the sorrows by a fireplace which we desired"; and line 61: "our child laughing to his angels from the cradle," an image included, ironically, within the framework of harsh truths, stillborn children, barren women, and "deaths at the terrors of the roads."

Although these reading options are valid and necessary, a third reading strategy, that of tracing and analyzing the binary oppositions in the poem, is more cogent in helping the reader perceive the work's semantic apparatus. Indeed, the initial contradictory image, *uvolem et hape lemalet haze'aka* (and muzzles the mouth to let forth the scream, line 6) leads to the discovery in this poem of an entire structure of binary oppositions. In the repeated listing of poem definitions, for example, *shir kedok halomot shakuf* (a poem like a curtain of dreams, transparent, line 4), an image, though fleeting, of somnolent quietude, is counterposed with *shir kayora kolha* (a poem like a boiling cauldron, line 8), a vision of dire prospects;

and *shir kefanayikh* (a poem like your face, line 10), which evokes a loving scene, is contrasted by *kaleshonot she'il'u devaram besigei esh zomemet kilayon* (like the tongues that stammered their word in the dross of a fire conspiring destruction, line 12), a scene of fiery destructiveness.

The various groupings of poem definitions themselves are presented in a structure of opposition: *shir kemigdalekh* (a poem like your tower), *shir kefanayikh* (a poem like your face) and *ukherikmot sivei einai* (and like the woven threads of my eyes" -- all love similes -- are contraposed by *shir kayora kolha* (a poem like a boiling cauldron) and *shir kaleshonot* (a poem like the tongues) -- similes of destruction.

In a syntactic vein, all the elliptical phrases in the first two stanzas beginning with the word *shir* (a poem) are contrasted with phrases entered later in the poem that begin with the words *ZE shir* (*this is* a poem): *ZE shir hageshem* (*this is* a poem of the rain, line 23), *ZE shir hahovek* (*this is* a poem of the embracer, line 27), *ZE shir beleilot gevohim* (*this is* a poem on nights high, line 39), and *ZE shir shekol hakdamot lo nakhonu* (*this is* a poem for which all introductions have been prepared, line 43).

The change itself, from *shir* to *ZE shir* (from "a poem" to "*this is* a poem"), is dualistic. It either denotes metaphors which are more specifically romantic (such as "This is a poem of the rain on the tin roofs," and the ecstatic "This is a poem of the embracer of the mossy trunk of a tree in a dense forest") or evokes their more specifically dire contrasts: "This is a poem on nights high unto death," and "This is a poem for which all introductions have been prepared."

In these contrasting *ze* (this is) definitions, their specificity represents the equivalence factor of the metaphors, while their semantic content reflects their opposition.

The list nears its end in the third- and second-last stanzas with the ironically rhymed and diametrically opposed final attempts at definition in lines 49 and 58: *ze shir haro'im* (this is a poem of the shepherds) and *ze shir kol hashekarim* (this is a poem of all the lies), though it is arguable that the shepherds' role in the gathering and counting of the sheep is in itself a dualistic image of end-of-day security and of end-of-life divine severity.[8]

At the center of the poem lies the point of non-definition, the point where metaphorical definitions cease, for the moment, where the speaker interjects his explicit response to all these possible responses: *Ata yada'nu* (Now we knew all the floods of visions sparkling in lusts upon fingernails, line 33). Just what is now known is not entirely clear. What *is* clear is that structurally this stanza divides the poem into two nearly equal parts. Semantically, too, the stanza, laden with a purposeful, multilayered ambiguity of images, metaphors, and tenses, dramatizes the poem's sustained structure of binary oppositions. In lines 33-36, the sparkling "visions" that come to mind are qualified by *mabulei*, uncontrollable "floods" of these visions; and the "lusts upon fingernails," which, after all, may be a memory of passionate loving -- a theme continued by *ahavnu lir'od* (we loved to tremble) in the following line -- are qualified by the purposefully ironic, Alterman-like simile *kir'od lehayav hamavet* (like the trembling of Death for its life). The image leaves the reader with a fearsome shiver, not a passionate love tremble.

The last two lines in the stanza (lines 37-38) seem to describe a childlike, innocent act of decorating the sky with *netifot shel zahav*, "drops of gold," play-stars, perhaps, which make the sky look pretty and "high." But the metaphor *gevohim ad mavet* ("high unto death") destroys the innocence and turns the playfulness into a horrible, Gothic nightmare. The death image returns the poem to its primary task of seeking self-definition, of searching for purpose and response in the inner and outer worlds, both of which have gone awry.

To return to the poem's structure and to the notion of static and dynamic elements, this central stanza (*ata yada'nu*, now we knew) is paired with the poem's closing stanza (*akh yesh Eloha shel ma'as*, but there's a God of deed, line 63). Both do not begin with an attempt at definition, but evince directly the speaker's voice; both depict the speaker's feelings of loss, anger, terror, and betrayal. Instead of the metaphorical expressions "a poem like" or "this is a poem of," which aim blindly at defining the poem, these stanzas are metonymic passages which describe what the speaker's world feels like after the Holocaust. Another significant binary opposition in the poem, therefore, is this interplay between metaphorical and metonymic passages, between passages of definition and the more narrative passages of the poem.

Binary oppositions pervade the poem at all levels of semantic activity: in similarly structured verb phrases: *lirkod bemikhelet bokhim* (to dance in a chorus of weepers, line 46) vs. *lifkod et hatson* (to count the sheep, line 50); in counterposed construct phrases (featuring an inverted alliteration which accentuates the contrast between the two images): *hakarat ha'eima* (awareness of the terror, line 9) vs. *rakat ha'ayin* (the one of the gentle eye, line 20); *shedei ha'olam* (the breasts of the world, line 26) vs. *eimei haderakhim* (the terrors of the roads, line 44); in phrases with one common part: *hupa shel shamayim* (a canopy of sky, line 3) vs. *haludat shamayim* (the rusting of heaven, line 41), *arafel al pnei eretz* (fog upon the earth, line 2) vs. *nefel al arets* (a stillborn [child] on the earth, line 40).

Individual word groupings are also counterposed: *zikhronot, rikmot, ne'arot, halomot* ("memories," "weavings," "girls," "dreams") vs. *ta'avot, mitot, yetsi'ot, ra ot* (lusts, deaths, leavings, sorrows). The same may be seen in contrasting thematic motifs: *uvolem et hape* (and muzzles the mouth, line 6) vs. *hu yish'ag ke'arye* (he will roar like a lion, line 41); *bitnah hamegulaf shel ha'alma* (the sculptured stomach of the maiden, lines 29-30) vs. *keres mele'a* (a full belly, line 59); *nakhon veyatsiv* (sound and firm,' line 66) vs. *muzar ve'ayom* (strange and terrible, lines 66-67); *tsore'ah nefel* (a stillborn [child] screams, line 40) vs. *veyaldenu tsohek* (and our child laughing, line 61); *kilayon* (destruction) vs. *reshit* (beginning, lines 12-13); *dimyon* (imagination) vs. *emet* (truth, line 65).

As is usually the case in works in which binary oppositions play a significant role, there are several words or images that have a dual semantic function; that is, they embody *both* meanings of the oppositional structure. For example, *sadeh* or *sadot* (field, fields) is the setting of both a soft, gentle rainfall and a stream of blood; *einayim* (or *shemurot, risim,* or *sivim*) -- eyes (eyebrows, eyelids, or eyelashes) -- are the instruments of both unmitigated pleasure and ultimate pain; *yeled* (or *yonek* or *nefel*) -- "child" (or "infant" or "stillborn") -- is the symbol both of innocence and new life, and of betrayal and death; *shekarim* (lies) connotes both a blissful state of prior innocence and a devastating reversal of God's trust. And *shir* (poem) itself, the most semantically laden word in the poem, reflects at once the sweet vision of the past and the terrible truth of the present. *Shir* embodies both a fervid, pathetic celebration of memory, and a bitter, unappeasable exclamation of agony and loss.

The larger images and themes in "Shir kemigdalekh hagavo'ah" loom in their oppositionism. The newborn vs. the stillborn, the young pregnant woman vs. the barren mother, lies vs. the truth, innocence (of children or lovers) vs. betrayal (most disturbingly, by God). In sum, love and death are the two central categories of opposition into which all other aspects of opposition in the poem may be placed: love, with all its ramifications of birth and life, and death, with all the loving and life it precludes. The horrible truth of Holocaust death brings to the poem its contraposed memories of the persons and things most beloved. All the poem's images, tropes, and structures fall into this subsuming love-death dichotomy.

As noted at the outset of this discussion, the structure of binary oppositions is evident as well in Gilboa's later collections. This is especially true of the volumes *Ratsiti likhtov siftei yeshenim* (I Wanted To Write the Lips of Sleepers, 1968) and *Ayala eshlah otakh* (Gazelle I'll Send You, 1973). In these collections the general style is manifestly different from the poetry in *Kehulim va'adumim* (Blues and Reds, 1963), Gilboa's major volume of collected works of the 1942-63 period, though obvious changes had occurred in "Shelosha she'arim hozrim" (Three recurring gates [or chapters],) the later and last section of that collection.

The basic alteration in these later collections is one of structure. In *Ratsiti likhtov siftei yeshenim*, the poems take the shape of introspective pensées; they ponder things beyond human control: life's swift passing, the impersonality of time, the dispensability of poetry, the poet's social and artistic isolation. At the center of these poems is the dream, that ironic moment of insight which cannot be relived or adequately transmitted once the dreamer awakens. The poet himself is the dreamer, the one asleep; he is caught in thought-limbo between knowing and fear, insight and helplessness, affirmation and negation. Many poems have no firm ending; verses are constituted of intermingled phrases that flow into one another without any clarifying punctuation. In *Ayala eshlah otakh* the structural changes persist: unpunctuated verse, ambiguous phrasing, a measured, pensive voice.

Despite these shifts in poetic expression, Gilboa's works still reflect the structure of binary oppositions which pervades the earlier works of the forties and fifties.[9] Two poems, "Uvekhen, tafasti et haparpar" (And so, I caught the butterfly) and "Bein ze laze. Kivenadneda" (Between this and that. As on a swing), both of which employ the image of the butterfly, elicit a strong sense of dualism and show clearly Gilboa's continued predilection for binary oppositions.

The first poem, the more playful of the two -- at least at its outset -- contraposes a dualistic situation against a ghostly, tertiary presence. This presence, in turn, stands in opposition to the duality of the butterfly and its would-be captor, the poem's speaker. The second work, more serious, even wearisome in tone, posits an existential dualism which depends for its forcefulness on the close repetition of binary oppositions.

> And so, l caught the butterfly. For a moment I was silly.
> But what's with it, before it and behind it, meantime it went
>   by
> and slipped out of my hand.
> I saw the butterfly. The butterfly possibly saw me.
> But who's this, or perhaps what's this, that both of us did not
>   see.
> I call the butterfly butterfly. I don't know   what if indeed
>   the butterfly also calls me by name.
> But who's this, or maybe what's this, that both of us do not
>   contain.
> The butterfly was very slippery and I, this time, quicker than
>   it.
> What's the name of the one who's immeasurably quicker
>   than both of us.
> Flutter flutter the butterfly from flower to flower.
> At its center, this time, my hand was sent forth and it
>   captured.
> How slow we both were in contrast to the one
>   quicker than both of us.
> I saw the butterfly. The butterfly possibly saw me.
> Whose eye hunted us both before.

> I sense him watching us
> from every side at once
> with a quickness always burning and creating.
>
> I don't know what name to call him.[10]

The poem's opening lines (1-3) describe the experience of catching a butterfly. In the opening sentence, *uvekhen, tafasti et haparpar* (and so, I caught the butterfly), the voice sounds victorious but understated, certainly less than euphoric; the sentence is short and nonexclamatory. The introductory word, *uvekhen* (and so), evokes a dramatic sense of being in the middle or at the end, but not at the beginning, of a narrative. In the same vein, the "and so" beginning also reflects an ambiguous reaction to the feat on the part of the speaker: he seems more surprised or ambivalent than triumphant.

The ambiguity is confirmed by the sentence that follows, *shelerega nishtateti* (for a moment I was silly), which emphasizes the impromptu nature of the catch. The speaker notes, apologetically, the silliness of the act. But then, as the captor begins to describe the catch and his response to it, the butterfly apparently escapes and flies off, despite the catcher's attempt to prevent it from doing so. The reader is confronted with a "live" situation, featuring a caught-but-not-quite-caught butterfly and a speaker-catcher who has spoken too soon.

Thus situation itself is dualistic. It is somewhat lamely explained by the speaker-catcher in a pair of oppositional sentences in line 4: "I saw the butterfly. Perhaps the butterfly saw me." The battlelines are drawn; the duality of hunter and hunted is reflected in their respective sights, in their mutual awareness of the fray.

In line 5, however, a third, rather ambiguous entity joins the scene. This ghostly figure, unseen by both hunter and butterfly, haunts the speaker throughout the poem. Its presence creates less a triangle of forces than a disruptive duality, a force of opposition as against the relatively harmonious unity, as it develops, between the hunter and the butterfly. In his confrontation with the butterfly the speaker knows exactly what he is dealing with: a butterfly. In complete, simple, paired declarative sentences (lines 6-7), he names it precisely: *parpar* (butterfly); and he wonders, in proper binary fashion, whether the butterfly has a name for him as well. In contrast, both the prior and the following sentences regarding the "something" or "someone" (lines 5 and 8) are elliptical, emphasizing both the confusion on the part of the speaker and the formation of a second binary opposition: the catcher-and-butterfly vis-à-vis the spooky figure, "which both of us do not contain." The syntactic differentiation in itself creates an added dimension of opposition.

The remainder of the poem features a number of overlapping images in the catcher-butterfly-specter groupings. In line 9, the established oppositional pattern is continued: the butterfly is "slippery" (i.e., evasive), but the catcher is "quicker." In line 10, the adjective *zariz* (quick) is used for the unseen specter, who is "immeasurably quicker than both of us," says the speaker. The overlapping use of *zariz* creates a number of different configurations. On the one hand, the catcher-and-specter are now united in quickness vis-à-vis the poor butterfly; the reader may well assume that the butterfly will not have to fend off two prospective hunters, one even faster and therefore more threatening than the other. On the other hand, the catcher-and-butterfly are still united by the specter's surpassing both of them in quickness. Indeed, in line 10 the catcher seems to convey a certain tone of fearfulness; namely, that the unknown, lurking spirit, who is "immeasurably quicker than both of us," may be hunting both of them. The dual ambiguity fortifies the general oppositional structure to this point in the poem.

Another elliptical sentence, line 11, replete with repetitions, alliterations, and binary divisions (*rifruf/rifruf, perah/perah*), returns the reader to the poem's initial, and continual, situation. The hunter, in line 11, is apparently successful in his capture of the butterfly, probably because he has struck with his hand precisely at the halfway point (*mahatsit*, "middle" or "center," line 12) of the butterfly's fluttering (*rifruf*) -- yet another image of evenly divisible duality. But there lingers still a feeling of inadequate quickness, in comparison with "the one quicker than both of us" (line 13). The butterfly's capture has not succeeded in warding off this stronger, foreboding presence. The catcher and his captive butterfly are now united, figuratively, in the hands of the unknown specter.

By repeating line 4 verbatim, line 14 ironically rearranges the hunter-vs.-hunted dichotomy; and line 15 realigns the binary opposition even further: it strikes the speaker that all along (*lifnei khen*, before) both catcher and butterfly have been observed (literally, hunted, *tsada*) by the eye of the spectral observer. In lines 16-18, the only place in the poem which features three consecutive verses comprising one sentence, the tone grows more serious. The casual, playful game of butterfly hunting is not so innocent or "silly" as it seems. The specter-observer-hunter is felt all about; his gaze, inescapable, comes across "with a quickness always burning and creating" -- quite a change from line 13, where the quickness of the specter merely stands in opposition to the relative slowness of the catcher and butterfly. The coda line, "I do know what name to call him," not only deepens the mystery of this pervasive spirit, it also counterposes the process of naming (or possible naming) in lines 6-7 with the impossibility of naming the specter.

Naming and non-naming, hunter(s) and hunted, seeing and not seeing, seen and unseen, catching and not catching, captured and uncaptured, quick and slow, life and death -- these are the thematic dichotomies which reflect the pervasiveness of binary oppositions in the poem. The parallels and differences in syntax, structure, and semantic repetitions and transitions reinforce these thematic oppositions.

Of course, one could venture an interpretation of the mystery figure: it is God, perhaps, the nameless or unnamed One (as in the Burning Bush scene, Exodus 3:13-14); the unseen One who constantly watches us in all our frivolity; whose presence is always felt; who constantly invades our thoughts; who has the power of destroying (lit., burning) and creating; who quickly, in the wink of an eye, can bring to life and cause to die; who is much quicker than a would-be butterfly catcher or a butterfly's escape.

The thin line between creation and destruction, life and death, hunter and hunted, freedom and escape, frivolity and significance, is the central subject of "Uvekhen, tafasti et haparpar." The dramatized situation, with its inner, active voice, continually projects a back-and-forth pattern which is fraught with binary oppositions in action, personae, theme, syntax, and structure. The turn at the end of the poem from the pairing of a butterfly hunter and hunted butterfly to the mystery of the unnamed specter -- the poem's dramatic climax -- leaves the reader with an added sense of opposition: the shift from the trivial and playful to the serious and spiritual. Much like those of "Shir kemigdalekh hagavo'ah," the closing lines also signal a shift from the metaphoric -- the triangle of central images -- to the metonymic. Gilboa ends the poem with a dualistic vision of the fragility of life, of life as an existence controlled by some ineffable force, which has the power, in a flash, to give life and to take it away. To surrender ultimately to this controlling force is the common fate of both butterfly and hunter.

Though written in the late sixties, the poem, with its multifaceted binary system of expression, reverberates with echoes of Gilboa's earlier works of the forties. The way the poems are syntactically structured and the modes of experience rendered have changed radically in these twenty years. However, as this synchronic, semantic view demonstrates, Gilboa's poetics, his essential style -- especially the evocation of oppositional patterns -- still abides.

*   *   *

> Between this and that. As in a swing. When
>   there's no longer
> either strength or any interest to continue to swing.
> It's also possible still even to fall. To the ground.
> But out of this great weakness,
> but out of this lack of interest,
> still the reason, like a limb that lives from the strength of its
>   strength,
> exists strong as a sea of boiling lime
> ready to burn and to be burned. To destroy and to cease.
> And this, in fact, is [what] the butterfly achieves in the
>   daylong portion of its life
> it sucks and is sucked till the end.[11]

The *Ayala eshlah otakh* volume, in which "Bein ze laze. Kivenadneda" is included, consists of poems written in the late sixties and early seventies, before the outbreak of the Yom

Kippur War in October, 1973. Some of the poems in this
volume reflect aspects of the poet's response to the Six-Day
War of 1967 and to the "War of Attrition" which followed.
"Bein ze laze. Kivenadneda" appears to have a philosophical,
existential import, and yet a worldly, political interpretation
seems plausible as well.

The main theme of this poem is dualism per se, an
existential feeling of being between things, an ambivalence
toward life, toward moving through it with a humdrum
regularity. The speaker is life-weary and weakened; he feels as
if he is swinging in a swing but has neither the strength nor the
interest to continue swinging. In line 3, the voice points out a
looming possibility: he may fall to earth, probably to die. The
tone is apprehensive: the speaker's mouth is full of adverbs
(*efshar, od, akh*), full of the fear of imminent demise. The
elliptical, one-word sentence *la'arets* (to the ground)
ominously stresses the inevitability and finality of the fall. It is
apparent, suddenly, that death, the abrupt end of the ride, is
uncontrollable, unpredictable, fatal. From the very beginning
of the poem, therefore, there is a doubling of ambivalence:
toward life as an unwanted existence and, in the typical
formula of a dichotomous existential dilemma, toward death
as an unwilled event.

In the central section (lines 4-7) of the poem, however,
there appears to be an abiding passion to persevere in living.
Out of the speaker's very weakness and indifference there
arises a "strong reason" (*hata'am. . . harif*) to continue one's
life. This motivation is as "strong as a sea of boiling lime [or
mortar]"; it lives on "like a limb that lives from the strength of
its strength." The context seems negative, there is no interest
or strength to go on. Yet the will, perhaps mainly a
physiological persistence, still exists, running on its own
power. This will is a force which in and of itself, outside the
actual human will, has the power of life and death: "to burn
and to be burned. To destroy and to cease."

From a different perspective, one might conclude that the
simile "as a sea of boiling lime" connotes a negative image, that
this kind of recalcitrant, physical persistence represents an
unhappy, depressing situation. The existential dilemma
possibly is exacerbated by the absolute will of the body to

function even when the individual will has stopped functioning. To use a contemporary social and moral parallel: much like a terminally ill patient who wishes to be rid of the suffering through euthanasia, the will to die is thwarted by others who point to the persistent heartbeat or still active brain waves. The patient-existentialist in "Bein ze laze. Kivenadneda" is indeed in limbo, hovering between a pervasive feeling of discouragement toward life and an impervious inability to abandon it.

What complicates the revolving and overlapping dualisms in this poem is the highly ambiguous and allusive nature of the vocabulary used in the poem's middle section. Gilboa is playing on words here: *harif,* translated as "strong," also means hot, bitter, or sharp, that is, spicy to the taste. The word *ta'am* in line 6, manifestly connoting reason or motivation, has as its first meaning "taste." *Ta'am harif,* therefore, may seems to be a spicy-hot or bitter taste. Moreover, the term *ever hahai* in line 6 refers unambiguously to the rabbinic prohibition to eat meat which has been cut from a live animal, or, in the rabbinic interpretation of Leviticus 17:10-14, to eat uncooked or blood-soaked meat.[12] Therefore, *ta'am,* in this context, could mean actual "taste"; and the phrase *hata'am. . . harif* may connote the "bitter taste" felt by the speaker at this point in life. The "living limb," by way of its reference to a food and ritual taboo, makes more explicit and unnerving the speaker's disgust with the body's recalcitrance in the face of the mind or feeling.[13]

The poem's final image, that of the butterfly, which the reader recognizes from "Uvekhen, tafasti et haparpar" is, in this context of imposed duality, an image indeed apropos. Following the erroneous but accepted notion that butterflies live only for a day, Gilboa, in the closing lines of the poem, uses the figure of the butterfly to resolve the dilemma. Like the "sea of boiling lime," which has within it the forces of both destruction and self-destruction, and like the weary person who feels suspended in the limbo of a morbid life, the butterfly exists in a wholly dualistic condition. However, unlike these parallel images, the butterfly "attains" this condition naturally. As it "sucks" the nectar of the flowers upon which it alights, the butterfly, with its limited life span, is at once "sucked till the end."

At least two interpretations of the poem seem possible. On the one hand, it may be that the butterfly indeed is a symbol of an existential "achievement"; it lives fully and dies fully within one and the same act. This rapid but complete life-death experience happens naturally and simultaneously, without the sense of suspension or dilemma, which is posed by the conscious dissonance between feeling and physical being. The butterfly, therefore, has attained a kind of nirvana, a state of being-dying which may be a consummate wish on the part of this poetic speaker. On the other hand, the butterfly may be a symbol of life itself as a simultaneous state of living-dying. As one lives, in other words, the closer one moves toward death. In this sense, life, like the butterfly's day, is a combination of these two opposite forces.

The possibility of a third interpretation persists: "Bein ze laze. Kivenadneda" may have a political or moral message, embodying Gilboa's response to the constant cycle of war in the Arab-lsraeli conflict. The poet has composed such "realistic" poems before; for example, "Malkhut demama" (Kingdom of Silence, *Ha'aretz*, April 3, 1953) was written in response to the first large-scale atomic bomb testing in November, 1952.[14] Another such example is the title poem of the *Ayala eshlah otakh* collection, which has the speaker guiltily sending off the lovely antelope -- a symbol of the beloved in the Song of Songs -- to die a violent, bloody death in battle.

In this realistic interpretation, "Bein ze laze. Kivenadneda" describes a situation of being caught between things, of swinging uncontrollably from one war to another. Even though there is apparently little interest in continuing the cycle, the bloody "limb" seems to have a life of its own. Like "a sea of boiling lime," war creates a situation of being at once the destroyer and the destroyed; no one is the winner. And this is the lesson of the butterfly: it lives dichotomously, vibrant in life, yet simultaneously dying. Such is the fate of those who exist in a war-to-war syndrome.

Like "Uvekhen, tafasti et haparpar," "Bein ze laze. Kivenadneda" displays a number of syntactic, structural, and other poetic features which reinforce the binary oppositionism of its semantic and thematic elements. Perhaps most obvious are the dualistic, complementary pairings of verbs: *lisrof ulehisaref* (to burn and to be burned, line 8), *lekhalot velikhlot* ('to destroy and to [be destroyed], line 8), and *hamotsets venimtsats* (it sucks and is sucked, line 10). Added to these duplicative pairings are word repetitions, which echo, in their very repetition, the oppositions elicited in the poem's semantic units. These include *bein ze laze* (between *this* and *that*, line 1), which in turn is echoed by *veze* (and *this*, line 10); the former opens the poetic discourse on the existential dilemma, the latter, in a closing echo, introduces the poetic resolution. (*Hazot* and *haze* are also placed in the same positions at the ends of lines 4 and 5.) The word *ko'ah* (strength) is also repeated: it appears first in line 2 as *lo ko'ah* (no strength), which is reinforced by its equivalent *hahulsha* (weakness) in line 4, and it reappears in juxtaposed repetition in the phrase *ke'ever hahai miko'ah koho* (like a limb that lives from the strength of its strength") in line 6. The first use of *ko'ah* delineates the speaker's weakness; the later, close repetition accentuates the uncontrolledness of the physical body, the "living limb," as opposed to the speaker's confessed feeling of being emotionally sapped.

Syntactic units which reflect the poem's structure of binary oppositions include the repetition of phrases structured in parallel, such as *lo ko'ah. . . lo inyan* (no strength. . . no interest, line 2), *aval mitokh* (but out of, lines 4-5), and *hahulsha hegedola hazot. . . hoser ha'inyan haze* (this great weaknessthis lack of interest, lines 4-5); the repeated use of elliptical sentences, varying from one-word sentences (lines 1 and 3), to short phrases (lines 1 and 8), to longer, dependent clauses (lines 1-2); and the contrast of the elliptical sentences both with the long, middle sentence (*aval . . . ulehisaref;* but. . . and to be burned, lines 4-8) and, especially, with the complete, unambiguously declarative and fully structured closing sentence (lines 9-10), in which the speaker states his understanding of the dilemma. Once again, as in both of the other works discussed here, this poem shifts from a metaphoric to a metonymic mode of expression, reflecting Gilboa's view of the nature of life.

From the point of view of the reader, this sort of closing plays a dual role: not only does it bring the poem to an end, but it also puts an end to the dissonance, ambiguity, confusion, duality, and mixed emotions caused by the pervasive play of binary oppositions in the body of the poems. It is as if Gilboa, at the ends of these poems, sets aside the oppositional structures, shifts away from the emotional conflict altogether, and ends, decidedly, with "facts" or "truth." Metaphor, the figurative language through which the feelings-in-the-poem are expressed poetically, gives way to metonomy, the concrete language through which the feelings-of-the-poet are expressed directly and passed directly on to the reader.[15]

More subtle elements of opposition and parallelism are evident in the nearly homophonous, rhymed pairing of *kayam* ("exists") and *keyam* (like a sea) in line 7; the rhyming of *ta'am* (reason, line 6) with this pair, though the accent is different *(ka-YAM* and *ke-YAM vs. TA-am);* the doubled consonant in the word "to suck," *m-ts-ts* (line 10); and perhaps the most important of these secondary dualistic features; the verbal affinity of consonantal doubling found in the roots of the words for "swing" and "butterfly," *nd-nd* and *pr-pr.* Embodied in the poem's central images, in other words, is a phonetic duality which, among other structural elements, radiates the binary mode that is so pervasive in this work.

The three works by Amir Gilboa discussed here were written over a span of more than twenty-five years. Despite many changes in Gilboa's general style, each of these poems demonstrates a persistent stylistic trait; namely, the expressive implementation of binary oppositions. Rooted in the romantic tendencies of Bialik's poetry, this equivalent structuring of semantic materials provides the reader with continuous clues to "the basic paradigm of the system"[16] found in many individual works, even in entire cycles and volumes of poetry by Gilboa.

In great measure, Gilboa's poetics -- his perception of the world around him and the way he shapes his poetic vocabulary to express this perception -- relies upon the utilization of this structure of binary oppositions. While it displays an essentially romantic impulse on the part of Gilboa, the use of semantic equivalence structures also provides the reader with a sense of

Gilboa's inventiveness, of the beauty and affectivity of his poetic expression.

Association for Jewish Studies Review,
Spring-Summer, 1988: 103-127.

Chapter 9:

[1] See Nomi Tamir-Ghez, "Binary Oppositions and Thematic Decoding in E.E. Cummings and Eudora Welty," *PTL* 3 (1978): 235-248. For a discussion of "equivalence" and "opposition," see Jurij [Yuri] Lotman, *The Structure of the Artistic Text* (Ann Arbor, 1977), pp. 78-93.

[2] On "ungrammaticality" see, for example, Michael Riffaterre, *Semiotics of Poetry* (Bloomington, 1978), chap. 1 et passim.

[3] The first poem Gilboa wrote in direct response to the loss of his family seems to have been "Ani yatom" (I'm an orphan), published in the Jewish Brigade's mimeographed Hebrew journal *Lahayal* (For the soldier) in Italy, May 7, 1943. The poem was later collected in *Sheva reshuyot* (Seven domains, 1949) under the title "Yetom" (Orphanhood).

[4] It is virtually impossible to determine from the original dates of publication of the 1943-1949 poems when exactly most of these works were written. Having published only a small number of his wartime poems in *Lahayal* (also entitled *Hahayal ha'ivri* [The hebrew soldier]), Gilboa, in the postwar 1946-49 period, set about publishing dozens of poems written during the war in Israeli newspapers and journals, including *Ha'aretz, Davar, Al hamishmar,* and *Gazit.* The poems appeared in a helter-skelter fashion, with no hint of the chronological order of their composition. Moreover, when Gilboa collected the poems for *Sheva reshuyot,* for the most part he grouped them topically rather than chronologically, thus further obscuring their actual chronology.

[5] Although written in 1946, as annotated by Gilboa, the poem's publication was put off more than two years. Moreover, the original publication is unclear. The Genazim Literary Archives' index of Gilboa's works in Tel Aviv shows a publication entitled "Petiha lishti hayagon ve'erev hasimha," *Al hamishmar,* December 17, 1948, "Shir kemigdalekh hagavo'ah" was first collected in *Sheva reshuyot* and does appear as the opening poem to the section "Shti hayagon ve'erev hasimha," but I have not been able to verify that this poem is indeed the *petiha* (opening poem) published in *Al hamishmar.* The translations herein are done purposely in a rather literal style, so that the reader might refer more easily to the Hebrew and English texts.

6 The concept seems to have originated with Riffaterre. See his essay, "Stylistic Context," in *Essays on the Language of Literature*, ed. Seymour Chatman and Samuel L. Levin (Boston, 1967), pp. 431-444. See also Menahem Perry, *Hamivne hasemanti shel shirei Bialik* (Tel Aviv, 1977), pp. 42-51.

7 The term is Riffaterre's. See *Semiotics of Poetry*.

8 The motif itself is ironic, in that it is reminiscent of the famous High Holy Day liturgical poem "Unetane tokef," in which God counts each individual for judgment as a shepherd counts the sheep in his flock.

9 In his review of *Ratsiti likhtov siftei yeshenim*, Boaz Arpali notes that the volume is filled with "word combinations, phrases, sentences, lines and topics which contradict one another, balance one another, nullify one another, or evade one another." See "Ledovev siftei yeshenim," *Davar*, December 24, 1971.

10 "Uvekhen, tafasti et haparpar" is one group of four poems which appeared as a prepublication selection from *Ratsiti likhtov siftei yeshenim* in *Al hamishmar*, May 5, 1968. In the *Ratsiti* volume it appears on p. 89.

11 Original publication: *Molad* 28, 25-26 (Aug.-Sept., 1972). In the *Ayala* volume it appears on p. 25.

12 The rabbinic discussion is found in Pesahim 22b.

13 In the talmudic literature, *sid rote'ah* (boiling lime or mortar) is also associated with food taboos. In the *Yerushalmi* (Shabbat 3:3) the rabbis allowed the rolling of a raw egg on a roof of hot mortar on the Sabbath (to warm it before eating) but not the rolling of an egg on hot dirt. The same discussion is recorded in the *Tosefta* 2:22. (The Babylonian Talmud [Shabbat 39a] uses the phrase *gag rote'ah*, "a boiling roof.")

14 Told to me and Stanley F. Chyet in a conversation at Gilboa's home in December, 1982.

15 Particularly relevant here, in reference to Gilboa's closings, are comments by Barbara Herrnstein Smith on the "substantial. . .force" of closure and the "sense of truth" and "unqualified assertion" often brought in the closing lines of poems. See her *Poetic Closure: A Study of How Poems End* (Chicago, 1968), pp. 96-150 and 182-195.

16 The phrase is from Nomi Tamir-Ghez, "Binary Oppositions and Thematic Decoding," p. 238. See also the chapter "Romanticism Revisited" in Yael Feldman's study, *Modernism and Cultural Transfer: Gabriel Preil and the Tradition of Jewish Literary Bilingualism* (Cincinnati, 1986), pp. 73-88, and especially pp. 75-77, which contain several comments pertinent to Gilboa's "romantic" free verse poetry.

Poems of Saul: A Semiotic Approach

Of all the Biblical figures that have been the more frequent subjects of modern Hebrew poem -- Isaac, Jacob, Moses, Samson, David and Absalom, among others -- the figure of King Saul predominates. Indeed, poems on the subject of Saul are curiously prominent in the modern Hebrew poetic canon. The progenitor of the "Poems of Saul" genre is the Hebrew Renaissance poet Saul Tchernichovsky (1875-1943). Two early works, "Be'Ein-Dor" (At Ein-Dor) and "Al horvot Beit She'an" (At the ruins of Beit She'an) were written in 1893 and 1898 respectively. But it was Tchernichowsky's classic ballad, "Al harei Gilboa" (On Mt. Gilboa, 1929) which ultimately canonized the genre.

Since the publication of "Al harei Gilboa" the subject of Saul has been selected by Hebrew poets with some consistency. Several poems of Saul were penned by the older generation of twentieth-century Hebrew poets, including Yocheved Bat-Miriam (1901-1980), Natan Alterman (1910-1970), and Alexander Pen (1906-1972).[1] Later, over the course of about a dozen years in the fifties and early sixties, there is a veritable outburst of Saul poems written by four prominent contemporary Israeli poets: Amir Gilboa (1917-1984), Yehuda Amichai (1924-), Nathan Zach (1930-), and Meir Wieseltier (1941-). This group of poems of Saul and the proximity of their production deserve to be examined from various perspectives.

The primary aim of this paper is to probe these four poems from the point of view of the semiotics of culture. The purpose of this approach is to discover the cultural implications which might arise from the texts individually and as a group. Toward this goal I examine the intracanonic relationships of these poems, offer interpretations of each work by way of intrinsic analysis, and discuss the various similarities and differences which bind these works together as a subsystem of Israeli literature and culture.

This combined methodology is informed by three sources. (1) Several of Yuri Lotman's studies, especially *The Semiotics of Russian Cultural History*, in which he details his ideas on "cultural semiotics"; (2) Jonathan Culler's work on semiotics in *The Pursuit of Signs*; and (3) an unpublished paper by Chana

Kronfeld which focuses on the "double dynamic" of modern Hebrew poetry: the "inner dynamic" of Hebrew linguistic development, and the "outer dynamic" of the advent of European Modernism in Hebrew poetry.[2]

Yuri Lotman suggests the notion that reading "becomes an exercise in cultural 'translation' from. . . the appropriate language of cultural signs."[3] He speaks of culture as "a system of collective memory and collective consciousness" which reflects "a unified value system for the group."[4] In Saussurian terms, Lotman comes to view "the real life of a society as a text (*parole*) organized according to a specific cultural code (its language) [Saussure's *langue*]."[5] He argues, therefore, that a society's character and dynamics may be understood by means of a "synchronic study" of selected texts. The text, he claims, is always in a "communicative situation"; it reflects the writer's consciousness, the world that is embodied in the work, and "a real or potential audience."[6]

Jonathan Culler presents a Saussurian semiotic checklist similar to Lotman's. He accepts the idea of literature as a system, emphasizes the distinctions between texts, and suggests that the analyst reconstruct the "cultural norms and conventions which operate subconsciously" and "show how the phenomena become [cultural] signs."[7]

Taken together the concepts suggested by Lotman, Culler and Kronfeld emphasize not the interpretation of individual texts but the semiotic search "to discover the conventions which make meaning possible" in the larger contexts of society and culture. My own position is that the intrinsic analysis and interpretation of texts are a necessary first step in determining the basic conventions, distinctions and dynamics which may lead to the broader cultural conclusions.

Amir Gilboa: "Saul" (1950)[9]

Saul! Saul!
I don't know whether it was shame
or fear of a disembodied head—
But as I passed by the wall of Beit She'an
I turned my head away.

Then, when your boy refused to hand you the sword

as you had commanded
I stood mute, speechless
and my blood flowed from my heart.
I really don't know to say what I in his place
had I been your boy.

And you are the King.
And you are His Majesty the King with your command.

And I really don't know to say what I in his place.

Saul Saul come!
At Beit She'an the Children of Israel live.

Of the four works, the Gilboa poem presents the most authentic, or at least biblically derived, dramatic situation, i.e., Saul's death at Gilboa. The speaker, while passing by the walls of Beit She'an and glimpsing the King's bodyless head, recalls the tragic-heroic scene and ponders what he might have done had he been in the place of Saul's young arms bearer. The other poems also allude (or seem to allude) to salient parts of the Saul story, but they do so in a passing, ironic, or nondramatic manner. Because of this primary distinction, Gilboa's poem has a metaphorical connotation, while each of the other three constitutes a metonomy, a message derived from the story of Saul yet essentially unrelated to it.[10]

At the outset of the poem the speaker is shouting to Saul, or to his ghost, trying to get his attention. The speaker seems distressed or embarrassed and wants to share his feelings with the King. He tells the King quite plainly that he cannot bear to look at the King's "bodiless head" on the wall of Beit She'an. The first stanza, then, places the speaker at the ancient scene, after the death of Saul at Gilboa, when the Philistines, vengeful in victory, display the head of the King on the walls of their city. It is possible, too, that the scene is a dream, an imaginary, personal vision of being present at or near the time of Saul's death. Whether dream or recreated scene, the first stanza emphasizes the distress the speaker feels at seeing Saul so hideously dead. He is horrified at the barbaric exhibition of the King's decapitated head and calls out to Saul to tell of his pain.

The second stanza focuses on another source of grief for the speaker. He has great difficulty with the behavior of the King's young arms bearer, who did not obey the King's command to kill him with the sword before being set upon by the enemy. Once again the speaker is thrust (or injects himself) into the scene, a re-creation of the dramatic death scene on Mt. Gilboa. In this scene the speaker seems even more upset. He says that he was struck dumb -- twice: *ilem*, "mute," and *netul hadiber* (speechless, line 7); and he adds that "[his] blood flowed from [his] heart," obviously connoting that he was in a state of shock as a result of the arms bearer's inaction. Furthermore, the speaker confesses to a psychological dilemma: what would he have done were he in the boy's shoes? The pain and guilt he feels at this question are so excrutiating that he can express his feelings only by an elliptical stutter.

> I really don't know to say what I in his place
> had I been your boy. (Lines 9-10)

This sense of helplessness on the speaker's part causes him such immense anguish that he repeats the plaint in nearly the same words again in line 13.

The speaker's trepidation at the thought of not obeying the King implies that for the speaker Saul is still a symbol of royal power and authority, that he still possesses an aura of majesty which commands obeisance. This understanding seems to gain support in the fourth stanza, as the speaker ponders the commanding presence of the King (lines 11-12). The King is the dominant figure here; the speaker is continuously upset by the way Saul has been treated, both by his arms bearer and by the Philistine mutilators. The speaker's response reflects the lingering tradition of Saul-as-tragic-hero as recorded in the Tchernichovsky ballad.[11]

With line 15, however, another interpretation is possible. By restating the speaker's dilemma as to what he might have done had he been in the position of the arms bearer, the poem is refocused on the figure of the speaker himself. This is the dramatic center of the poem: What would the speaker have done at the moment of impending, inevitable slaughter? At this point the dilemma of the speaker's helplessness in the face of impending disaster replaces the King as the dominant image in the poem.

As we "read the poem backwards"[12] we note that the speaker and his intense emotions indeed have had an equal measure of emphasis on the poetic structure. In the first stanza he mentions his "shame" and "fright" at the King's mutilated body; in the second, he notes both his numbing shock at the boy's refusal to obey the King's command and his uncertainty as to his own response to the King's command. In addition, there is the repetition of his dismay at the lack of obeisance, now coupled with an insistent sense of personal dilemma (lines 11-13).

There are also a few subliminal aspects of the poem which serve to focus our attention on the figure of the speaker. One such aspect is the speaker's apparent confusion; he seems to get the story of Saul wrong. For example, the speaker says that he had to turn his head away from the sight of Saul's "disembodied head" (*rosh netul-guf*) nailed to the wall of Beit She'an; but the story of Saul's death states that the king's body was beheaded and that his "body" (*geviyato*) was nailed to the wall of Beit She'an (1 Samuel 31:10). Of course, it is possible that Gilboa may have been alluding to the other version of Saul's death, in Chronicles, where it is stated that the Philistines indeed nailed Saul's head to the wall; but in that version the head is nailed to the wall of Beit Dagon, not Beit She'an (1 Chronicles, 10:10).

Furthermore, the speaker, in addressing the ghost of Saul, notes that the King's arms bearer "refused to hand you the sword as you had commanded"; however, there is no such command by Saul in either version of the story. In both versions the King says, "Draw your sword and stab me with it."[13] It is only after the boy fails to do the King's bidding that Saul "took the sword and fell upon it." Saul never asks the boy to "hand" him the sword, nor does the text state that the boy "refused" to do so. (Gilboa uses the verb *me'en*, refuse, while both biblical versions use the phrase *lo ava*, "did not wish to.") The speaker seems to be partly confusing the texts and partly conveying his own version of the story.

Finally, as already noted, the speaker adds to his sense of shame, fright and confusion by injecting himself into the death scene and noting how dumbfounded he was when the arms bearer did not perform as the King had asked. In all these details the reader is drawn less to the already familiar figure of King Saul and more to the psychological portrait of the speaker shaped by Gilboa.[14]

A pronounced duality of themes clearly predominates this poem. On the one hand, with its oblique acknowledgment of the King's majesty and tragic death, the poem embodies the earlier heroic canonic and cultural model. On the other hand, with its colloquial direct speech, its dual dramatic situation, and especially its focus on the perplexed speaker, the poem forges a new cultural model of the traumatized, helpless witness.

This inner dynamic of thematic duality and traumatic tragedy leads me to understand Gilboa's "Sha'ul" as a metaphorical Holocaust poem. For Gilboa, Saul is only one of the victims at Gilboa, perhaps even the minor one. The speaker is the main victim. He is completely traumatized, befuddled, utterly helpless. It was impossible to save the King. Death was upon him; only death with dignity was still possible. Yet even a mercy killing was not to be; the speaker arrived on the scene too late. He enters at Beit She'an, with the King's disembodied head on display. He is a witness to the tragedy, but not an eyewitness. And what would -- or could -- he have done, had he been present at the death scene? Probably nothing is the implication.

The only thing the speaker can do at this point of shame, shock and pain is to look beyond the tragedy to the larger scene: "Saul Saul come!" he calls out at the end of the poem to the King's ghost; "at Beit She'an the Children of Israel live." The scene is now contemporary; Jewish settlers have returned to Beit She'an. Only this, the evidence of the people's survival and continuity, can provide any solace.

Gilboa's text broadens the symbolic projections of Saul as a historic figure. In its inner dynamic the poem diminishes Saul as the tragic hero of classic balladry; the King's death is replaced by a new, contemporary tragedy: the total sense of helplessness to prevent the tragedy from happening. The tragic hero is the witness-survivor who finds himself in the dualistic condition of despair and hope. By turning the theme of tragic hero on its head -- the anticanonic act -- Gilboa creates a cultural sign which reflects the national trauma of the Holocaust from a different perspective. This is the poem's outer dynamic. "Sha'ul" is the *parole* which presents a new tragic hero through the medium of the *langue* of the survivor.

From the point of view of cultural semiotics, Gilboa's poem signifies, at the very least, an ongoing sense of the immediacy of the Holocaust trauma.[15] However, what primarily connects "Sha'ul" to the following three poems is the pervasive theme of power and powerlessness. Each of the poems in the century-long tradition of poems of Saul focusses either on the myth of Saul's power and heroic death or on a breakdown of the myth.

The poems that follow involve issues of force and impotence, war and war-tiredness, strength and weakness, heroism and cowardice, risk-taking and folly, physicality and emotionality, grandiosity and the commonplace. These themes, like those evident in Gilboa's "Sha'ul," continue to reflect cultural patterns prevalent in the first decade and a half of the nascent Israeli culture.

*   *   *

Yehuda Amichai: "King Saul and I" (1956)[16]

1

They gave him a finger, but he took the whole hand.
They gave me a hand, but I didn't even take the little finger.
While my heart was weight-lifting first feelings,
he trained by ripping oxen apart.

My pulsebeats were like drips from a tap.
His pulsebeats pounded like hammers on a new building.

He was my big brother
I got his used clothes.

2

His head's like a compass, always leading to the precise pole
    of his goal.
Like an alarm clock
his heart is set for the hour of his reign.
When everyone's asleep, he cries out
till all the quarries are hoarse.
No one can stop him!
Only the asses bare their yellow teeth.
At the end of his road.

3

Dead judges turned the wheels of time,
when he went out searching for asses,
which I, now, have found.
But I don't know how to handle them,
they kick me.

I was lifted with the chaff
and fell with the heavy seeds.

But he breathed into the winds of his history.
He was annointed with royal oil
as with wrestlers' grease.
He struggled with olive trees,
forcing them to kneel.

Roots bulged on the earth's forehead
    from the strain.
The judges escaped from the ring,
Only God remained, counting:
Seven. . . eight. . . nine. . . ten. . .
From their shoulders down, the people rejoiced.
Not a man stood up. He won.

4

I'm tired,
My bed is my kingdom.

My sleep is my justice,

My dream, the verdict.

I hung my clothes on a chair
for tomorrow.

He hung his kingdom
in a frame of golden wrath
on the wall of heaven.

My arms are short, like a string too short
to tie a parcel.

His arms are the chains in the harbor,
cargo sent beyond time.

He's a dead king.
I'm a tired man.

Amichai's poem alludes to several details from the
biblical story of Saul, for example, the mules Saul was
searching for, his being annointed with oil as King, but these
are rather spare, unweighty, details. Amichai is less interested
in King Saul as a historic, heroic-tragic figure than he is in the
royal aura of power, assertiveness and achievement. Most of
all, Amichai is interested in affirming the opposites of these
attributes, the benign powerlessness, passivity and humdrum
life of the common person.

The distinguishing feature of "Hamelekh Sha'ul va'ani"
is its running comparison between "Sha'ul," the King, and "I,"
the speaker. The nature of the comparison is a process of
measuring up. The method of comparison is a series of
analogies, a listing or "catalog" between the King and the
speaker.[17] The King is adroit, strong, favored, resolute,
authoritative, victorious; the speaker is just the opposite: a
wimp, a schlimazel, and a schlemiel rolled into one. His life is
one of the usual ups and downs, while the King has made
something of himself and shaped his own royal destiny.

One might say that there is no comparison between the
two personages. Who would want to be like the downtrodden
schlemiel? On its surface, therefore, the poem seems to
embody an aggrandizement of the aggressive, powerful,
majestic, superior attributes of the King. However, through the

subtle use of sarcasm, irony, and absurdist figurative phrases and images, Amichai is really celebrating the unheroic non-exploits of unmythical humanity.[18]

The basis for this reading is the semantic system of culture-bound language and description utilized by Amichai in the poem. All is either cliché, conventional proverb and schlemiel-like characterization or their opposites. Imitating the familiar image of the faltering fool -- the pathetic personae of Charlie Chaplin, the Sad Sack, or Woody Allen -- Amichai presents comparisons which are based on overstated grandness and plainness, heroics and shortcomings, all of which are permeated by the absurd.

Part 1 sets the pattern for the rest of the poem. First Amichai plays with the saying: "They gave him a finger but he took the whole hand." The case of the speaker-schlemiel is just the opposite: "They gave me a hand, but I didn't even take the little finger" (lines 1-2). To give the reader an idea of Saul's strength, the speaker says, "He trained by ripping oxen apart," the ancient equivalent, apparently, of ripping apart telephone books. This contrasts with the weakly, immature speaker, whose heart was just beginning "weight-lifting first feelings" (lines 3-4). The King's pulse, too, is majestic; it compares to the pounding of "hammers on a new building," while the speaker's is "like drips from a tap" (lines 4-5). Obviously, the two are completely mismatched; Saul is aggressive; the speaker is withdrawn. Saul is physically fit, strong, a giant; the speaker is a weakling, a runt.

Even at this early point in the poem, the reader is struck, perhaps comically so, by the outrageousness of the contrast between the two personages. One cannot help be impressed positively by Saul and unimpressed by the schlemiel-like speaker. But what puzzles the reader is the blatant tone of utter self-denigration on the part of the speaker. The only source of possible empathy for the speaker is his position as the recipient of hand-me-downs, a position which engenders the image of a neglected, unfavored child. At best, the speaker's act of self-denigration is ambiguous. Clear beyond any doubt, however, is Saul's strength and physical dominance; the speaker, at least at the start, is impressed. In the main, parts 2 and 3 discontinue the unbalanced contrast and focus on another catalog of the King's manifestly heroic attributes. However, the pattern of comparative couplets established in part 1 is still resonant. In part 2, for example, the King's head is "like a compass always leading/to the precise Pole of his goal."   Moreover, his heart is set, "like an alarm clock . . . set for the hour of his reign" (lines 9-12). The first simile is akin to the phrase "straight as an arrow," meaning that the King always knew where he was headed in life, obviously right to the top. The second simile reinforces this directedness on the part of Saul, a directedness unconfirmed in the biblical story, it should be noted, even though the alarm-clock metaphor, by way of anachronism, seems rather sardonic. To each of these figurative depictions of Saul the conditioned reader mentally adds the binary opposite as it pertains to the speaker. The obvious conclusion is that in contrast to Saul, the speaker-schlemiel is completely directionless and has his eyes set on no particular goal.

The speaker is also quiet, unassuming, vocally withdrawn, as opposed to the King, who shrieks violently at night "till all the quarries are hoarse" (line 14), an image which makes Saul's screaming voice even louder and more powerful and persistent than the sounds of hammers in the quarries. Whether this is complimentary to Saul or not is unclear, but the reader undoubtedly will find this last image inconsistent with the first two.

At first, then, Saul appears in complete control, paving a clear path to the kingship. However, his screams in the middle of the night remind the reader of the darker side of Saul, the melancholic and violent sides of the King. "No one can stop him [i.e., shut him up]!" says the speaker (line 15); but here again the image of power is not very flattering. When "the asses bare their yellow teeth" at Saul (line 16), one has the feeling they are mocking Saul, as if sticking out their tongues at him. By the close of part 2 there appears to be a crack or two in the image of the omnipotent King.

In part 3, the poem returns to the comparative-analogy pattern of part 1. While the speaker-schlemiel, a wimpy lightweight, "rose with the chaff and fell with the heavy seeds" (lines 23-24) -- borne with the breeze, so to say. Saul takes charge of the wind itself and "breathed into the winds of his history" (line 25). In consonance with his upward-bound mentality, Saul is then annointed with kingly oil "as with wrestlers' grease" (lines 26-27), which again enhances his physicality. Saul is the beach bully; the speaker is the binary-oppositional ninety-pound weakling.

There is a measure of irony here, however. The King's lowly, and unlikely, wrestling opponents are olive trees. which he easily beats. In addition, the framework of the fight also becomes suspect. The "judges" (a play on *shoftim*) have all fled, and God, downgraded to the position of part-time wrestling referee, counts the opponents out. The match is not only one-sided, it is patently absurd. Saul's , as God's, mythical power is sardonically diminished by Amichai's ludicrous images. This is Amichai's subtle way of denigrating the power of the mythic hero. First he aggrandizes the hero, and then he sets about demythologizing him through hyperbole, cliché, and absurdist depictions.

Amichai climaxes the process of demythologization in part 4. The speaker continues to expand the list of contrasts between the King and himself, the conventional person: "I hung my clothes on a chair/for tomorrow," says the speaker in Amichai's laconic style of everyday behavior (lines 41-42); while the King, in grand metaphorical style, "hung his kingdom/in a frame of golden wrath/on the wall of heaven." (lines 43-45). In like manner, the speaker has trouble tying up a package with string, while the King's "arms are like chains in a harbor/cargo to be carried beyond time" (lines 48-49). The image of the King projects ever larger mythical, even cosmic, dimensions. His portrait shows that he has gone down in history as a larger-than-life raging warrior, whose physicality and megalomania have become his most memorable characteristics.

While Saul is being pictorially and historically ensconced by Amichai in this unflattering way, part 4 fixes the fate of the common, conventional person by setting him in the concrete of daily existence. He gets tired, he goes to bed, he sleeps, he dreams. "My bed is my kingdom," he posits. "My sleep is my justice,/my dream, the verdict" (lines 37-40). These are his daily achievements, his rewards or punishments, the routine, of an actual, normal, earthly life.

The poem's ending is anticlimactic.

He's a dead king.
I'm a tired person.

As the equivalent of the phrase, "Better a live coward than a dead hero," the closing comparative couplet pithily sums up the undoing of Saul's grandiosity. The "live schlemiel" is the antiheroic survivor. Throughout the poem Amichai confronts the reader with an utterly engaging but ultimately jarring combination of classical mythmaking, contemporary clichés, sardonic oppositions, and absurd images. By subtly celebrating the unheroic through the contrasting imagery and language of the mythic and the mundane, the schlemiel becomes hero.

Amichai's use of sarcasm, cliché and absurdist farce constitutes the inner dynamic of the poem, which effectively scorns the King in favor of the common person. The poem's outer dynamic is its anticanonic overturning of the traditional image of Saul as a classic hero. Beyond these dynamics, the poem functions as a cultural sign in its prepossessionary theme of the weak and the strong. Like Gilboa, Amichai counterposes images of the powerful and the helpless (or hapless). Gilboa's image of Saul is demythologized by the King's lack of power to command his death with honor. The arms bearer and the speaker-observer are also enmeshed in a powerlessness which prevents any action they may have done to help (kill or save) the King.

What unifies the Gilboa and Amichai poems is the ironic transfer of focus from the heroic tradition of Saul to the secondary, ambiguous position of the speaker. Compared to the King's mythic majesty and physical grandiosity, the speakers, on the one hand, are devoid of action and power; on the other, they are far more real and are permeated with human emotion. Although they are characterized quite differently -- one is traumatized by tragedy, the other ironically resolute in commonplaceness -- both figures respond directly to the question of power vis-à-vis powerlessness.

As stated above in the analysis of "Sha'ul", Gilboa's frame of reference regarding the sense of powerlessness is the Holocaust. With Amichai the derivation of the theme is more ambiguous. In general, Amichai's early poetry is infused with sarcasm toward or disdain for sacred cows.[19] This is true of his war poetry with regard to images of the heroic and victorious, his theological poetry with regard to God, his poetry of holy places such as Jerusalem, and his biblical poetry with regard to King David, Jacob, the Queen of Sheba, and other great and royal personages, including Saul. In "Hamelekh Sha'ul va'ani," however, Amichai poses a personal comparison between "himself," in the guise of a schlemiel-like speaker, and Saul, a comparison which is palpably oppositional.

The poem's disdainfulness is aimed directly at the adoration of power. Amichai may have been responding to a lingering devotion to heroic acts engendered by Israel's War of Independence, or he may have been expressing reservations toward the hero-worship directed at the Palmach, the elite corps of commandoes (of which he was a member) who were lionized in song and story. He may also have been affected by his own philosophical perspectives on issues of power vs. normalcy in Israeli society.

Semiotically speaking, the questions of derivation or motivation are less significant. The poems themselves are read as cultural signs; they signify the ideational atmosphere of a culture over a particular period of time; they reflect the "collective memory" of the body popular, its central issues and values. In this sense the Gilboa and Amichai poems together project for the early fifties the continuing aesthetic value of using classical or mythic personalities to express contemporary thoughts. Early Israeli culture understands and accepts this method of artistic communication. In addition, the tentative "trend" seen in these first two poems of Saul is toward a comparative mode of expression, with the nonheroic figure taking the place of the canonized hero as the poem's main character. This polarized dualism leads the reader to understand that the culture is not unanimous in its worship of cultural heroes, that there are voices which rise to the contrary, voices which use the framework of mythic heroism either to highlight the trauma of abject helplessness or to accentuate the need for regained normalcy.

Finally, with the breakdown in the fifties of the Tchernichovskian canon, Israeli literature, a major cultural system, is beginning to produce artifacts which reflect less on the canon itself than on the cultural background from which they arise.   That is to say, these two poems are less directly about Saul than they are semiotically about the inner life of Israeli society and culture.   They present the culture as enmeshed in continuing nightmares of Holocaust trauma and permeated by heretofore antithetical or unmentionable or views of power and powerlessness.   They record the wish to forget, to set aside the national traumas, to put an end to grief, tragedy and heroics.   They evince an Israel willing to move toward a state of normalcy, perhaps even to create a new collective memory.

The following poems bring additional dimensions of semiotic signification.

*   *   *

Nathan Zach: "A precise description of the
music that Saul heard in the Bible" (1953)[20]

Saul hears music.
Saul hears.
What sort of music does Saul hear?
Saul hears music that gives him a cure.
Saul hears music.
Music Saul hears.
And the people around him are not there, as if
they've disappeared, the entire nation's become mute.
For Saul hears music.
Is this the music
that Saul should be hearing
at a time like this?
Yes, this is the music that Saul
should be hearing at a time like this
for there is no other now
and perhaps there will be none
until Gilboa.

Zach's poem is distinct from the others mainly in its structure and in the nearly non-narrative nature of its contents.   The structure is essentially one of repetition.   The phrase "Saul hears music" is repeated in several variations from the title throughout the entire poem. There are only two breaks from the pervasive refrain, i.e., from any mention of either "hears" or "music" or any description of either. (The hiatuses occur in lines 8-9 at the middle of the poem, a kind of caesura, and in lines 16-18, at the closing.) Even these breaks, however, allude in some way to the music. Line 9 states that "the entire nation's become mute" (*ne'elam kol ha'am*), i.e., they make no sound as does the music; and line 16 refers directly to the music with the phrase *ki ein aheret*, "for there is no other," to which the reader adds the elliptical antecedent, "music."

The pervasiveness of the phrase "Saul hears music" is extended to two seemingly artificial question-and-answer segments concerning the type of music Saul hears. "What sort of music does Saul hear?/Saul hears music that gives him a cure" (lines 3-5); "Is this the music/that Saul should be hearing/at a time like this?/Yes, this is the music that Saul/should be hearing at a time like this." (lines 11-15). The injected dialogues add dimensions of narrative and a quasi-dramatic situation; they create the illusion of presence and immediacy, as if a querulous bystander or reporter is asking the royal press secretary for more information about how things are faring in the palace. In the concrete structure of the poem, however, the dialogue sections create opportunites to repeat the recurring phrase four additional times, with very little added by way of "information." This usage, in Jakobsonian terms, denotes the "poetic" function of the poem's language, i.e., the way the language is used to "focus on the message [of "hearing music"] for its own sake."[21]

That is to say, the "precise description of the music that Saul heard in the Bible" is an imprecise description at best. Indeed the music may be totally indescribable, or so it appears in this poem, which feigns description but remains, at least verbally, undescriptive. And yet, by the very repetition of the phrase, the reader becomes familiar with the music, or if not with the music per se then with the musicality of the music-like repetition.[22] Meir Wieseltier points out that in the mid- to late fifties Zach was intent upon breaking the Alterman-Shlonsky hegemony in Hebrew poetry by creating a new "cautious modern poetic synthesis." One of his central poetic concepts was the idea of the musicality of poetry, in the T.S. Eliot sense of reflecting in poetry a "music which is latent in the prevalent speech of its time."[23] The musicality in the poem is expressed by a varied repetition of the title phrase, an extended melodic line of theme and variations, in language which shows few characteristics beyond its being fairly colloquial and self-generating. The poem seems rather playful throughout, until the ominous ending, "until Gilboa." The playfulness is anticanonic; the ending, however, is canonic, in that it unambiguously foretells Saul's tragic end.

Because the poem consists of both canonic and anticanonic dimensions, the message that emerges is that of a dualistic perspective on both the tradition of poetic form and the theme of the tragic hero. The casual, repetitive, musical nature of the poem conflicts incrementally with the expected but thwarted narrative aspects of the work. Zach tells abundantly of the music "Saul hears," but then, having purposely skipped over the entire biblical narrative of Saul, refers at the very end of the poem to a different, ominous sort of music at Mt. Gilboa. To paraphrase the poem's progress: Saul hears music; it's actually therapy; it's timely, too; for soon it will be time. Zach's liberation from both form and content goes hand in hand with the existential theme of death, a theme which closes the poem and predominates Zach's entire 1960 collection, *Shirim shonim* (Different poems).

Zach's quest in "Te'ur meduyak shel hamusika sheshama Sha'ul batanakh" is primarily to break down the narrative component of the poem. He has done this in other poems collected in *Shirim shonim*, such as "Keshetsiltsalt ra'ad kolekh" (When you called your voice trembled), "Hashir 'al ahi Jonathan" (The poem about my brother Jonathan), "Shum davar" (Nothing), and "Ve'od lo amarti hakol" (I haven't finished yet). It may be that Zach wrote some of these poems as song lyrics, but this would only strengthen the idea of the importance of poetic musicality for Zach. And although it seems ironic that such an overwhelmingly dramatic poet as Zach would also constrict the narrative dimension in other of his works, the duality may be understood as Zach's inveterate experimental bent in the early years of his career.

Zach surely was driven to make his poetry different. His tapping of the poetic resources engendered by T.S. Eliot, Pound, Marianne Moore, e.e. cummings, and others in the British and American traditions also demonstrates his intent to change the face -- or at least broaden the horizons -- of Israeli poetry. This is the outer dynamic of the poem. The inner dynamic is constituted by his playful repetitions and static structure. He repeats certain phrases, changes the declarative sentences to interrogative ones, inverts the order of subject and predicate, plays with rhymes and homophonic words (*ne'elmu*, they disappeared, and *ne'elam*, was mute). Then, in a masterful anticlimax, he brings all the playfulness to a close with the brutally unsubtle ending.

Zach overturns the poetic tradition in this poem by making the poem's structure into its inner dynamic and by relegating the tragic story of Saul to the very end. This is a structural ploy which has great impact. Primarily the ploy is used to set the figure of Saul -- his entire story, in fact -- in the concrete structure of the poem. There is no drama to the story, no scene of heroic-tragic death, except for the opening and lingering, melancholy portrait of Saul listening to music.

The semiotic message here combines aesthetic change and cultural transition. The new canonic model engenders a new cultural sign. With Zach's "Te'ur meduyak shel hamusika sheshama Sha'ul batanakh" it is permissible, if not obligatory, to blend the subject matter of the poem with the structure of modernist poetics. It is also fashionable, even obligatory, to write a poem about King Saul which is only peripherally about King Saul, thereby continuing the anticanonic mode of Gilboa's "Sha'ul" and Amichai's "Hamelekh Sha'ul va'ani." Zach's poem is a dual metonym for the creation of a new style of Hebrew poetry and for new cultural values. As such, it reflects a continuing search in the fifties for values, both aesthetic and cultural, which blend a distinctive Hebrew or Israeli particularism with a poetic universalism.

*   *   *

Meir Wieseltier: "Saul Reenthroned" (1967)[24]

Fresh oil pours through your curls,
do you feel the subtle difference, Saul?
What's one oil from another, the look on the spectators' faces
is not much like spring anymore, the time that's elapsed
between enthronements
like a blackout forcing a pause in the music
has salted hearts,
has seasoned derision,
has sullied innocence.
The "Who needs it!" is already being said
(in whispers at first)
The "Each man to his tent!" bubbles up,
waiting wearies
the mind,
hearts flower but fleetingly
such is the nature of things, things
novel yet unhoped for
already course through your veins, you're given
a new sword, soon to play a role,
a gift
from the military which betokens its
confidence anew on this solemn occasion, Saul.

In its dramatic dimension, Wieseltier's poem bears a resemblance to Gilboa's "Sha'ul." It features a speaker who is an eyewitness to a Saul event and who addresses the King directly, in thought if not in actual voice. In fact, "Sha'ul momlakh bashniya" goes beyond the Gilboa poem in its immediacy, because Gilboa's speaker becomes entangled in his own emotions vis-à-vis the question of what he would have done had he been in the shoes of the young arms bearer, while Wieseltier's speaker remains on the periphery of the scene and maintains his sardonic sang-froid throughout the poem.

The speaker focuses entirely on Saul at the moment of an apparent resurgence to royal power. It should be noted at the outset that this is a fictional moment created by Wieseltier; there is no such event in the biblical story. However, the general story of Saul is so familiar that the reader actually may be taken in and accepts the scene's historicity. Yuri Lotman states that "memory is reconstructed by the [poet]" and the readers, knowing the general allusiveness of the text, "imagine themselves in a position of familiarity." In this way the poet actually "changes the extent of the reader's memory, since the reader . . . is able to recall what his memory did not know."[25] The theory may be debatable, but Wieseltier clearly succeeds in recreating a plausible historical scene, mainly through his dramatic verve and his deft use of an authentic-sounding archaic language.

Apparently an onlooker at the coronation ceremony, the speaker possesses a keen, pragmatic sense of the pressures of continued military activity. Though Saul is being recoronated, the speaker, whose tone is blatantly sarcastic, intones: "What's one oil from another" (line 3) and goes on to describe how war-weary and disgruntled the soldiers feel after all the battles they have fought alongside the King. And, at the end of the poem, while the military outwardly professes "its/confidence anew on this solemn occasion, Saul" (lines 22-23), the soldiers present the King with a gift of "a new sword [which is] soon to play a role" (lines 19-20). Saul himself feels a distinct chill; "things/novel yet unhoped for / already course through your veins," notes the speaker (lines 16-18). Instead of a celebration and a recognition of Saul's bold leadership, the ceremony evokes a sense of betrayal, the beginning of the King's inexorable path to doom.

Aside from its reenactment of a creatively imagined event, the poem's main distinction -- and its inner dynamic -- is to be found in Wieseltier's masterful linguistic constructions. Resembling a refashioned Ein-Dor prophecy, the archaic vocabulary and diction engender the work's authenticity as a historical poem. The words *beinot* (I. 1), *bahasha'in* (I. 12), *mal'a* (I. 14), *mohin* (I. 15), *hidli'ah* (I. 10), *hehel* (I. 11), *matat* (I. 21), the phrases *ma shemen mishemen* (I. 4) and *ish le'ohalekha* (I. 13), and *momlakh* (in the title) are all purposeful archaisms in the poem's semantic design. The usage functions centrally as a "mock-archaic" language, akin to the mock-heroic mode of satire, which overthrows Saul's heroic image from within its own "historic," cultural-linguistic milieu.

Precisely in the center of the poem, however, stands the modern colloquialism, *ma pit'om* ("Who needs it"), which suddenly and unexpectedly contemporizes the entire poem. The anachronism forces us to read the poem dualistically, so that from this point on, past and present are linked inextricably together. The reader now understands that Wieseltier's message is a contemporary one; his method is to distance the message in time, much like the method of some historical fiction. In this sense the reconstruction of historic events allows for the imaginative description of possible events. Thus the quasi-mutinous tenor of the soldier-observer's thoughts is perfectly acceptable as a poetic extension of Saul's biography.

Like the poem of Saul by Zach, Wieseltier's work is simultaneously canonic and anticanonic. It is canonic in its "authentic" depiction of a Saul event, in its use of appropriate archaic language, and in its depiction of Saul as a victim of his own thirst for power, symbolized by the recoronation and the taking up of the new sword.

But all these dimensions of canonic authenticity fall before the breakdown supplied by *ma pit'om* and its implicitly anticanonic, unsubtle hint of a contemporary message. The poem's outer dynamic is based on the transmission of an ominous warning, not to Saul within the poem but to the contemporary Israeli reader: the relentless pursuit of a militaristic agenda will lead to calamitous results.

From the mid-sixties through the seventies Wieseltier was the leading political poet on the Israeli literary scene. The author of scathing editorial commentaries presented as the "opening statement" (*petiha*) of several issues of *Siman kri'a*, a literary journal founded in the early seventies, Wieseltier has been a feisty antiestablishment spokesman for equal rights, Arab and peace issues, and aesthetic and cultural renewal. A good number of his early poems combine the backdrop, characters, and speech of ancient scenes,[26] but his critical messages have been consistently contemporary.

"Sha'ul momlakh bashniya" is linked to the other three poems of Saul in several similar and different ways. Like Wieseltier, Gilboa uses a blend of archaic and contemporary diction; his speaker is also injected into the ancient scene and functions as an observer who ponders the meaning of what he sees. Amichai's absurdism is completely different from Wieseltier's mode of scenic authentication, yet the speaker's "revenge" on Saul is just as sweet; and Amichai's implied critique of power-mongering is parallel to Wieseltier's message that militarism must be contained. Zach's poem offers aesthetic newness, but Wieseltier's opts for ideological and moral engagement.

At the core of each of these four poems of Saul are two basic similarities: the diminution of Saul as a classic hero, and a dualistic blend, both thematic and semantic, of the ancient and the contemporary worlds. The Gilboa poem dramatizes an ancient, tragic scene but does so to reflect on the Holocaust; it ends with the speaker, who was just at the walls of ancient Beit She'an, calling for Saul's ghost to visit the contemporary Jewish settlement there. Amichai's poem alludes to ancient scenes but gives them a satiric, contemporary nuance; Saul's image is used sardonically as the mock-measure of the modern Everyman and vice versa. Zach, while weaving the music Saul hears into a new modern poetic style, still conjures up the canon of Saul's tragic end. Wieseltier reenacts a fictional historic scene, but his poem of betrayal and downfall metonymically suggests a disdain for unmitigated militarism and brute power.

The four "Poems of Saul" in this discussion should be seen as a unified, synchronic subsystem of Israeli culture. Sharing a variety of similarities and differences, they evince a number of cultural signs which transmit broader meanings pertinent to contemporary Israeli culture and society.[27] These signs include an abiding preoccupation with classical roots and images; a relentless redolence of past national glories and tragedies; a predilection for relaying contemporary messages through classical figures; a preoccupation with the images of power and powerlessness; a pervasive linguistic interplay of archaic and colloquial phraseology and diction.

Most of all, the poems reflect a proclivity toward pondering the national ethos by way of national myths. It is especially the confrontation between hero and anti-hero which pervades the culture. In the terms of cultural semiotics, the four poems presented here shape a cultural code which reflects "the dynamics of [that] culture's self-consciousness."[28]

Prooftexts 10, 1990: 313-334.

Chapter 10:

1 See Gershon Shaked, "Five Poems on King Saul" [Hebrew], *Lamerhav,* May 16 and 23, 1958. Shaked discusses the poems by Tchernichovsky, Alterman and Pen, as well as the poems of Saul by Amir Gilboa and Yehuda Amichai, whose works are analyzed here from a different perspective.

2 Kronfeld's paper was presented at the Annual Conference of the Association for Jewish Studies, Boston, December, 1986.

3 *The Semiotics of Russian Cultural History* (Ithaca, 1985), p. 22.

4 Ibid., p. 30f.

5 Ibid., p. 21.

6 Ann Shukman, *Literature and Semiotics: A Study of the Writings of Yu.M. Lotman* (Amsterdam, New York, Oxford, 1977), p. 21 ff.

7 See *The Pursuit of Signs* (Ithaca, Chapter 2. There are several interesting convergences between Culler's and Lotman's perspectives. Culler's view of literature as a system or "functioning totality" is parallel to Lotman's view of the structure of culture or society. His comment on the paradigmatic relationshp between texts parallels Lotman's emphasis on binary oppositions. Lotman discsusses the idea of "cultural codes," while Culler refers to "the deeply rooted set of cultural norms and conventions which operate subconsciously." And Culler's suggestion to "show how the phenomena become signs" is similar to Lotman's idea that the results of these semiotic studies should be expressed is a "symbolic notation," as Levi-Strauss had done for myths.

8 Ibid., p. 3

9 First published in *Al Hamishmar,* May 12, 1950; collected in *Kehulim va'adumim* [Blues and Reds] (Am Oved, 1963), p. 216. The translation, purposely done in a rather literal style , is my own. Throughout this article the line numbers refer to the Hebrew texts.

10 This is the case especially with the Amichai and Wieseltier poems discussed below. The Zach poem may be seen as a combination of metaphor and metonomy, since it contains both an extrinsic meaning and, by implication, the intrinsic drama of the Saul-David rivalry and Saul's eventual death.

11 In this sense the poem falls into the semiotic category described by Lotman as a culture which "reveals a dependence upon the cultural model that existed earlier." See *The Semiotics of Russian Cultural History,* p. 30.

12 The term and suggested procedure are Michael Riffaterre's. See "Semantic Overdetermination in Poetry," *PTL* 2 (1977): 19.

13 The textual references are 1 Samuel 31:4 and 1 Chronicles 10:4.

[14] In "Five Poems on King Saul" Shaked states that the poem represents "a formal break [with] collective literary forms." He bases his assessment mainly on the colloquial language used in the poem and on the quasi-personal relationship with the King that is engendered by the speaker. However, toward the end of his discussion Shaked also notes that the poem reflects the "heroic, collective image" typical of the War-of-Independence generation of writers.

[15] Additional support for this interpretation is the fact that Gilboa published two other biblical poems, "Yitzhak" (Isaac) and "Moshe" (Moses) alongside of "Sha'ul." Both these poems evoke either a World War II or a Holocaust context.

[16] First published in *Lamerhav*, August 3, 1956; collected in *Shirim* [Poems] *1948-1962.*, pp. 101-104.

[17] See Boaz Arpali, *Haperahim veha'agartal - shirat Amichai 1948-1968: mivne, mashma'ut, poetika* [The flowers and the urn -- Amichai's Poetry 1948-1968: structure, meaning, poetics] (Hakibbutz Hameuchad, 1986), pp. 32-37. Within his definition of the "catalog" in poetry, note especially the section on "Structures of Composition and Structures of Meaning" (p. 35f) and his comments on "common denominators" and "semantic equivalence" (p. 37).

[18] See *Haperahim veha'agartal*, pp. 52-53, on poems in which the poet characterizes himself in comparison to other personalities, with specific reference to the life of the common person.

[19] See, for example, the following poems in *Shirim 1948-1962*: *El male rahamim* (God full of mercy), *Ani rotse lamut al mitati* (I want to die in my bed), *Hora'ot linsi'a* (Directions for a trip), *Ya'akov vehamal'akh* (Jacob and the angel), and *Nimusim* (Manners).

[20] First published in *Likrat*, 1 (1953): 5; collected in *Shirim shonim* [Different poems] (Hakibbutz Hameuchad, 1974), p. 33. The translation, done in a literal style, is my own.

[21] Roman Jakobson, "Linguistics and Poetics," in *Style in Language*, T. Sebeok, ed., (Cambridge, Mass., 1960), p. 356.

[22] "A Vertical Cut Into Natan Zach's Poetry" [Hebrew], *Siman kri'a* 10 (1980): 415.

[23] Ibid., p. 418.

[24] Collected in Wieseltier's first volume, *Perek alef perek bet* [Chapter 1 chapter 2] (Akhshav Publishing, 1967), p. 45. The translation is taken from Warren Bargad and Stanley F. Chyet, *Israeli Poetry: A Contemporary Anthology* (Bloomington and Indianapolis: Indiana Univeristy Press, 1986, p. 219.)

[25] Y. Lotman, "The Text and the Structure of Its Audience," *New Literary History*, 14 (1982): 81, 85.

[26] See, for example, the poems *Bo tir'e et hamordim sheli* (Come see my rebels) and *Itot ba'amora* (Times in Gomorrah) in *Perek alef perek bet*.

27 In his introductory commentary to *The Semiotics of Russian Cultural History*, pp. 16-17, Boris Gasparov writes the following: "Cultural codes are systems of more or less conventional signs that a member of a given society must internalize in order to participate in that society's life. . . Any system with a heightened and deliberate internal organization will tend to play an important role in this process of internalization."

28 *The Semiotics of Russian Cultural History*, p. 30.

Reviews

Ruth R. Wisse: *A Shtetl and
Other Yiddish Novellas*
Robert Alter: *Modern Hebrew Literature*
Yehuda Friedlander: *Bein havaya
lehavaya* (Existence and Experience in the
Hebrew Writings of Y.L. Peretz)

Taken together, these three volumes present interesting insights into the growth of Hebrew and Yiddish literatures in the modern period. Though distinct in content and in mode of presentation, the books have much in common: they discuss, either centrally or by way of introduction, the transition in both Hebrew and Yiddish literatures from a Haskalah-dominated set of literary values to a more artistic sense of literary expression; they examine the nature of various writers' renderings of Jewish life since the 1890's; and they aim to shed light on several aspects of these literatures which have been for the most part obscure, whether out of inaccessibility or undue neglect. There are obvious differences as well, since the volumes in the Behrman House series are readers meant for a more general, English-speaking audience, while the book on Peretz is a critical study meant in the main for the professional academic. This basic difference in genre prompts the separate treatment of the Peretz volume as well as the juxtaposition of the two readers.

In their respective volumes Robert Alter and Ruth Wisse have set divergent paths for themselves. Professor Alter has selected a wide range of translated Hebrew works, from the 1890's through the1960's, including stories by Mendele, Peretz, Feierberg, Bialik, Brenner, Barash, Agnon (four), Hazaz (two), Yizhar, Amichai, Oz, and Yehoshua. (There are also two essays, by Ahad Ha-am and Bialik.) this broad spectrum clearly aims at a selective representation of an entire field. Professor Wisse, in contrast, has opted for a much more limited selection of five longer works -- novellas by I.M. Weissenberg, David Bergelson, Opatoshu, Ansky, and Mendele -- all from the classical, turn-of-the-century period of Yiddish literature. The choice of a specific genre from a circumscribed historical period

146

aims at conveying to the reader glimpses of the *shtetl*'s transition to modernity prior to the disintegrating force of World War I and the Russian Revolution.

The Yiddish volume is particularly distinguished by the fact that these five novellas appear here in English for the first time, a fact which not only attests to Professor Wisse's skills at editing and translating but also evinces her substantial historical role in preserving and disseminating valuable works of a literature which has become, alas, an endangered cultural species. The Hebrew volume is distinguished by Professor Alter's deft introductions to the individual works he has collected. His main role is that of the literary analyst, whose perceptive, cogently structured interpretations provide the reader with a keen sense of the particular artistic configuration and meaning of each work as well as its contribution to the modern Hebrew literary tradition.

Each of these two volumes also bears a lucid outline history of modern Hebrew and Yiddish literature since the Enlightenment. In their respective discussions the authors point out two central factors which reflect an apparent common ground for the development of both literatures: the collapse of the "Haskalah" and its values of acculturation, and the struggle to fashion authentic literary languages out of Hebrew and Yiddish respectively. However, for each author Haskalah has a somewhat different connotation. Alter stresses a broad shift in cultural attitudes. With the relaxation of the Haskalah's ideological aims in the 1880's, he notes, Hebrew writers were able "to balance programmatic criticism with intimate insight and affection in rendering the world of East-European Jewry." Linguistic development -- by which the Haskalah writers' overwhelmingly biblical style of Hebrew became more rabbinic and hence more flexible -- was born of this new artistic freedom. The key figure was Mendele Mocher Sforim, who seemingly "waved a magic wand and made modern Hebrew prose possible" by virtue of his single-handed transformation of Hebrew into a multi-faceted literary medium.

Ruth Wisse, on the other hand, stresses the more specifically linguistic aspects of change which allowed Yiddish literature to emerge and flower. Her view of the Haskalah is primarily that of the modernizing movement which held up German as its cultural model and scorned Yiddish as a lowly "jargon." Once the Haskalah was "discredited" (during and after the reign of Alexander II, a period which Alter also marks as seminal for the emergence of modern Hebrew literature), Yiddish was judged to be legitimate and "the literature became freed to occupy its own ground." One of the key figures in the founding of this literature, due to his success in "projecting a believable and authentic folk style," was -- Mendele.

This overlapping of perspectives, with regard to the respective rise of expressive languages and modern literatures, is highly instructive; and so is the dual reference to Mendele. The inadvertent overview shows that the Jews of Eastern Europe actually lived in a bilingual or bicultural framework (or perhaps tricultural, if one takes into account the Germanic or Slavic parameters), a framework which allowed several important writers to move back and forth, in a time-span of thirty years or so, between Hebrew and Yiddish creativity.

Mendele, Peretz, and Sholom Aleichem all began their careers as Hebrew "Maskilim," and all three eventually turned to Yiddish as the central focus of their creative activity. Only Mendele returned in full force to Hebrew literature; and it was most likely his own reworking of his Yiddish writings into Hebrew which contributed so greatly to the development of an unstilted literary Hebrew. Whether modern Yiddish was similarly influenced by its founders' prior or simultaneous use of Hebrew is a more complex question.

Dov Sadan in several of his writings has mentioned just such a mutual influence: Yiddish "lowered" Hebrew to a "quasi-vernacular," hence, it became a more fluid literary language, and Hebrew fed into Yiddish and raised its status from an abject vernacular to a literary medium. (Sholom Aleichem's *Tuvye*, with its blend of colloquial Yiddish and biblical phrases, may be instructive here.) In any case, it would be erroneous to see the modern developments of these literatures as growing from widely disparate roots, and a broadly conceived study of *both* Hebrew and Yiddish literatures -- or even a scientific cultural history of Jewish life in Eastern Europe -- from about 1870 to World War I is very much a desideratum.

Two additional mutualities are evident in these lucid, informative introductions. The first involves the explanations as to why these writers chose to write in these respective languages, and the second, the unifying principles noted in each anthology's selection of texts. What motivated the Hebrew writers in the post-Haskalah period, according to Professor Alter, was "a new quest for connection with the Jewish people," a quest which took first the form of proto-Zionism and later Zionism itself. Interestingly enough, Professor Wisse intimates a similar motivating force for the Yiddish writers: their choice of Yiddish "was felt as an obligation [which reflected] an uncommon sense of national responsibility." Later, Yiddish became associated with the Jewish Labor Movement and Jewish Socialism. Both editors are surely correct in pointing to a certain sense of national dedication and cultural allegiance; but these ideals do not explain the option taken for one language or the other.

What Alter omits (it is mentioned in passing by Wisse) is that most of the younger Hebrew writers who formed the Odessa circle around Mendele and Ahad Ha-am in the 1890's -- Bialik, Tchernichovsky, S. Ben Zion, and Klausner, to name a few -- were either renegade *yeshiva-bochurs* or already "enlightened" secularists whose attachment to Hebrew, their "language of learning" (*leshon limudim*), was probably more a result of their striving to join an intellectual elite rather than a wish to share in a political ideology or in a romantic "bond with the people." By all accounts Sholom Aleichem abandoned Hebrew for Yiddish not out of a sense of "sacrifice" or condescension, but out of a desire to reach as large an audience as possible through writing in that audience's own expressive idiom.

In the statements regarding their selection of writings each editor points to a central theme which brings these literary pieces together. Alter states his attempt "to follow a central line of historical development within modern Hebrew literature," a line depicting "the gap between the old and the new, between the world of Jewish tradition and the realm of upheaval and confusion" of modern times. Several of Alter's selections, however, do not bear out this sentiment; and it is unfortunate that Alter's generally excellent introduction should end with this rather forced appraisal.

In like manner, Wisse writes in her preface that each of the novellas she presents "deals in a different way with a single topic: the Jewish confrontation with modernity." Though the shtetl is indeed "the setting or the subject of all the works in this volume," it is clear that two of the five novellas do not, in fact, portray a confrontation with modernity. Opatoshu's "Romance of a Horse Thief" is an adolescent love story reminiscent of Gorky's naturalism, Bialik's "Aryeh Baal-Guf" and Babel's later Odessa stories; and Mendele's "Of Bygone Days" -- far and away the best story in this volume -- is a fictional memoir of coming of age within the shtetl, a memoir portrayed with considerable artistry through deft portraiture and poignant understatement. Both editors may have been a bit too concerned that their selected texts indeed be viewed as authentic reflectors of Jewish civilization, and not merely as eminent samplings of two great literatures. The lesser goal, at least, has been accomplished without question, and both editors and their publisher should be heartily congratulated.

In his study of Y.L. Peretz's Hebrew works, Yehuda Friedlander's aim is threefold: to show the basic "unity," especially in theme and technique, in all of Peretz's works, Yiddish and Hebrew; to demonstrate how his Hebrew writings, though often neglected, reflect Peretz's aesthetic concepts; and to revise what has heretofore been a negative critical view of these Hebrew writings. The first half of the volume is devoted to analytical articles which discuss Peretz's aesthetic theories, evaluate his Hebrew poetry and dramatic works, and give close readings of two prose texts which exemplify Peretz's talent for commingling Jewish "existence and experience." This section also includes a selected bibliography of Peretz's Hebrew poetry and plays, and a list of critical articles on these works. The second half of the volume contains a selection of the Hebrew works themselves -- about a dozen poems and one short play (originally written in Yiddish) -- collected here for the first time. The editor also appends a few pages of notes and commentary.

One interesting aspect of the book is Professor Friedlander's bringing the original Yiddish into the notes. (In the body of the book, he has translated into Hebrew all quotations from Peretz's Yiddish articles.) In this way the reader may check the original for a particular nuance or for accuracy, and he is thus given the opportunity to be a living witness to the bilingualism which characterized the times in which the articles were written. One can learn much about the contemporary evolution of Jewish culture from this sort of reverse *ivry-teitsch* alone!

A disappointing aspect of the book is Friedlander's lack of utilization (with little exception) of the very texts he has appended to the volume. The lapse, however, is understandable in view of the author's own inference that for the most part these works are not among Peretz's best, that he is simply making them available to the interested reader. Hence, it is clearly not upon these works in particular that Friedlander wishes to base his revision of Peretz criticism. And when one compares the interpretive comments in the chapters on the prose works with those in the chapter on the poetry, one concludes that it is by virtue of his prose, indeed, that Peretz's literary reputation is assured.

With regard to Peretz's aesthetic notions, Friedlander makes it quite clear at the very outset that much of what Peretz had to say was said in a polemic vein, with Hebrew literature as the target of degradation. Friedlander's apparatus, too, makes this argumentative factor quite unambiguous, since most of the opinions quoted are taken from Yiddish articles Peretz published after the Czernowitz Conference (1908), which marked the final, bitter rift between the Yiddish and Hebrew camps. Less involved in this polemic, it seems, are the various sources of inspiration which Professor Friedlander has culled from these writings (and some letters) by Peretz: suffering, remorse felt toward a valueless world, humankind's destiny, alienation and loneliness. These pathetic (and somewhat romantic) categories shape Friedlander's view of the later Peretz as a writer of despair.

The central theme in this study is that Peretz's works as a whole evince his artistic ability to seek out and portray the emotive inner experience (havaya) of external Jewish existence (havaya); and this knack, in turn, has synthesized Peretz's works -- whether Yiddish or Hebrew, prose, poetry, or drama

-- into a fundamental unity. Personally, I feel this interpretation is somewhat overstated; but whether a fully accurate appraisal or not, it shows that Friedlander is aligned with a broadly humanistic, culture-oriented school of literary criticism. This delineation notwithstanding, there seem to be two issues which need further clarification; first, the definition of "inner experience," which is sometimes vague in Friedlander's exposition, ranging from "symbolic" or "allegorical" to "mythic" and "impressionistic;" and second, the methodological problems of utilizing both literary and essayistic materials of different periods and of different genres in the formulation of an all-encompassing theory of composition. Beyond these points, Professor Friedlander is to be credited with bringing to our attention these long overlooked areas of literary research.

Association for Jewish Studies Newsletter, June, 1976: 27-28, and 12.

Amos Oz: *Unto Death*

English readers have been introduced to the works of the Israeli author Amos Oz in a haphazard fashion which prevents a coherent chronological appreciation of either the writer's concerns or his art. *Micha'el sheli* (My Michael), Oz's first work to appear in English (1972), was actually his third published volume (1968), following the short story collection, *Artsot hatan* (Lands of the jackal, 1965) and the novel, *Makom aher* (lit., An other place, 1966; published as *Elsewhere perhaps* in 1973). This problem of chronology is not unusual in the publication of works by foreign authors, but the English reader should be aware of the actual sequence of original publications, so as to achieve a proper perspective on the author's creative development as well as an appropriate interpretation of his works.

Ad mavet (Unto death) consists of two novellas originally published in the fall, 1969, and fall, 1970, issues of the Israeli literary journal, *Keshet*. Both works signaled a definite shift in artistic direction for Oz, especially in terms of genre, yet both develop in different ways certain stylistic and structural characteristics found in Oz's previous writings. The mater of chronology looms largest, however, in the very *Sitz im Leben* of these two novellas: written in the late sixties, each in its own way embodies Oz's artistic response to the 1967 Six-Day War. The time factor is crucial in interpreting these works, since the reader may confront the stories for the first time two or three years after the 1973 Yom Kippur War.

The novella "Ad mavet" (translated as "Crusade") first appeared in English in *Commentary* in August, 1971. It is the story of a group of medieval Crusaders, led by one Count Guillaume of Touron, traveling across Europe toward the Holy Land. For non-Jews or non-Arabs to be at the center of a work by an Israeli writer is in itself quite extraordinary, but the particular genre Oz has utilized here, historical fiction, is also new to his works. Nearly all of Oz's writings before "Crusade," from the short stories of the early sixties to *Elsewhere Perhaps* and *My Michael* (completed just prior to the 1967 War) had been of the "engaged" variety. His style of writing reflected a moralistic critique in fictional guise, aimed

in particular at the kibbutz and in general at what Oz's view of
Israel's growing militaristic bent.

In "Crusade," however, Oz is not really so very
inconsistent. In the stock tradition of historical fiction, Oz
utilizes time-distancing to comment on the contemporary
scene. The story is presented as if it were an actual chronicle of
a Crusade journey, recorded by the Count's cousin and cohort,
Claude Crookback; however, the story's central import,
rendered obliquely through psycho-symbolic elements, relates
directly to the very real fears of survival engendered by the
traumas of May-June, 1967.

Two of the work's dramatic focal points depict in
excruciating detail the cruel, gratuitous murders of Jews at the
hands of the roaming Crusaders. In the first scene, a Jewish
peddler is divested of all his goods, told he is to die, and is
felled by arrows as he attempts to escape. The second is more
gruesome: a Jewish community spokesman, left behind to make
a deal with the Count, concedes all and is betrayed. His death
is described in torturous detail, purposely rendered with
graphic visual effect. ("Crusade" seems much influenced, in
both visual and conceptual terms, by Bergman's *The Seventh
Seal*.) From beginning to end, the Jews in the story are the
unambiguous victims of a whimsical, sadistic scapegoatism.
The characters and the plot exist only to exemplify and
animate this syndrome of prejudicial hatred.

The story's third dramatic focal point reveals the tale's
major theme.

> Surely a Jew had mingled with the Christians in disguise,
> was walking along the way with us, and cursing us. And
> what is Jewish in a Jew -- surely not any outward shape or
> form but some abstract quality. . . . Simply this: a terrible, a
> malignant presence. . . . There is a Jew in our midst.
> (Pp. 27, 30)

The notion of a "secret Jew," a phantom, accompanied by
the motif of "signs," grows in intensity until the entire cast of
characters becomes obsessed with identifying the hidden Jew.
For the Jew is responsible (so goes the extrinsic anti-Semitic
libel, and the inner implication of "Crusade" as well) for all the

ills in the world: suffering, fear, insanity, "unto death" itself. The search-and-destroy mission sharpens as the Crusaders, forced to spend the winter in an abandoned ruin, go mad and wander off to die.

At the story's dramatic climax the Count concludes that his piper, Andres, is the "dearly beloved Jew." But as he takes up his spear to kill Andres, the Count himself leans on the spear and dies. The mystery of the "secret Jew" is Oz's way of depicting the madness of the Judeophobia underlying much of the civilized world, a madness so ingrained as to be inexplicable, uncontrollable, and ultimately self -destructive.

The shaping of "Crusade" casts Oz, in the role of a social historian in fiction-writer guise. The narrator's musings on the nature of Jerusalem as an abstraction display the blatant but intriguing symbolism.

> Does Jerusalem really exist. . . or is she perhaps nothing but pure idea. . . ? [And, in fact, for these Crusaders] Jerusalem ceased to be regarded as a destination, as the arena of glorious deeds. . . the Jerusalem they were seeking was not a city but the last hope of a guttering vitality. (Pp. 45, 48)

This "Crusade" represents Oz's historical thinking rather than any fictional reality. The minimal plot, the character typology, even the style -- a kind of "Gothic lyricism" marked by Oz's verbal virtuosity in static background description -- are subservient to the story's central idea: Judeophobia is to this day a powerful, mysterious mania. In its continual attempts to cleanse itself of the Jews, to make it *Judenrein*, the world will stop at nothing, not even at abject lunacy and self-destruction.

*   *   *

"Ahava me'uheret" (Late love), the second novella in the volume, differs from "Crusade" in technical construction but not in theme. The story is energized by the rambling diatribes of Shraga Unger, an old, self-taught bureaucrat-intellectual who obsessively lectures (usually to sparse audiences in Israel's rural settlements) on one pervasive issue: the Bolshevik terror. The Bolsheviks, he claims, aim to destroy the Jews. Their anti-Semitism, however, is merely the first stage of a Hitlerian scheme of world conquest which threatens to overturn and take control of the entire cosmic order. The extreme political viewpoint (or paranoia) is matched in hyperbole by Shraga's recommended solution: an all-out preemptive war against Bolshevism to be led by the Israeli Defense Forces, beginning with a blitzkrieg of Eastern Europe (including the fantasized liberation of the still extant Warsaw Ghetto) and ending with the conquest of Moscow! The obvious irony is inflated by Shraga's repeated insistence (in mock tribute to Bellow's Herzogian depiction of intellectual frustration) that he will soon communicate this solution to Israel's Defense Minister, Moshe Dayan.

Both Shraga and his plans are ludicrious, yet the story effectively expresses the heightened feelings of anger, frustration and alienation which beset Israel's populace during the Six-Day War. The appalling actualities of late spring, 1967, are transformed in Shraga Unger's monologues into an overwrought philosophy of doom. As a political activist linked to leftish-dovish platforms, Oz himself surely does not hold to this philosophy. His aim is not a willful didacticism; it is to pose assertions and project emotions which challenge the reader.

Reminiscent of several monologue-oriented stories of ideas by the late Hayim Hazaz, "Late Love" depicts a haranguing, exasperated character whose emotive reactions are even more important than his stated notions. Though neither a tirade nor an apologia, Oz transmits his own political perspectives through Unger. Similar to Hayim Hazaz's "stories of ideas," the oblique communication occurs during the character's quieter, more meditative moments, when the feverish pitch is toned down and the reader is less reactive and more calmly attentive. It is Oz, then, who is speaking near the end of the story in Shraga's letter to Hugo, the husband of an old actress friend.

> The Jewish people, Hugo, are totally unable to withdraw from the game once and for all. Did we really hope to take refuge here and build a new land and pretend to be a Bulgaria or a New Zealand? Think it over, Hugo: Are we really capable of sitting here quietly for the next thousand years, plowing all day or buying and selling horses, drinking in

taverns or dancing with peasant girls in the evening, sleeping peacefully all night long. . . . Na! It would be utter nonsense even to entertain such an idea. . . . Let me tell you something Hugo: All the anger, all the misery, all the enthusiasm, all the hysteria, all the madness in the world, all the revolutions and ideologies and complexes and suffering and horror, everywhere, are all directed against us. . . . There is a terrible passion, Hugo, a mad, murderous passion in the heart of every people and at the root of every ideology. . . this sinister passion. . . is directed against us day and night, threatening us, radiating toward us all the time. Even here. Even on a balcony facing the sea in Tel Aviv. (Pp. 161-162)

Oz is not simply ridiculing jingoist war fever in this story, nor is he presenting fantasies of super-Sabraism or senile chauvinism. He is expressing the breakdown of the myth of normalcy which has been at the center of Zionist longing for decades: the envisioned State of Israel, with its promise of autoemancipation, which would make of the Jewish people a nation among nations. For Oz it is still an impossible dream.

As in "Crusade," broad contemporary problems are seen through the fictional narrative in "Late Love." Similar, too, is the use of a recurring motif of mysterious forces at work beneath the surface of events and ideas. Parallel to the "secret Jew" theme in "Crusade" is Shraga Unger's reflection on the world beyond visual perception, the outer, cosmic world of "eternal flux," which threatens perpetually to demolish the lower orb of human activity. Shraga is the only one able to perceive this "circling grip of strong bands, the forces of Earth and Sun, planets and comets, the galaxies, blindly erupting forces." He is the watchman who has taken on the responsibility to warn all who will listen of the impending danger.

It is Shraga Unger's central role in "Late Love" which makes this story the more interesting of the two. His frustration is born of failure in the Russian Revolution and in youthful love; his dramatized obstreperousness is at once repulsive and engaging. The scene in which Shraga visits the old actress, Liuba, his former partner on the lecture-dramatic reading circuit, also contributes much, through its varied narrative perspective and comic relief, to the story's appeal. Both Shraga and Hugo, Liuba's husband, are amusingly trapped in her strong-willed grasp and constant chatter. In his role as a shunned, obedient robot, Hugo reflects the futility and helplessness of Shraga's frustrated monologues. Attempting to have Liuba use her influence for an audience with Dayan, Shraga finds himself suddenly out of character, so to speak. He becomes singularly uncommunicative and no longer in control of the story's verbal action. Only the effete Hugo listens to him. Despite the passion of Shraga's notions, manner and purpose, for him it is too late. Now it is Liuba's more mundane complaints about the polluted atmosphere of Tel Aviv -- a cleverly ironic parallel to Shraga's cosmic-political vision of collapse -- which occupies center stage. The dichotomous sense of perdition heightens Oz's moralistic message of the post-1967 doldrums. Beyond the fictive silence of alienation, he implies: where do we go from here?

Midstream, November, 1976: 61-64.

A.B. Yehoshua: *Early in the Summer of 1970*

In his fifteen-odd years of prose writing, Avraham B. Yehoshua has moved through three distinct phases. His first stories were brief, allegorical narratives, absurdist in tone and structure, and existential in import. Later, in the mid-sixties, he wrote longer stories, more psychologically dependent upon strong doses of interpretation. And in the seventies, especially with his most recent Hebrew publication, *Hame'ahev* (The lover), Yehoshua has turned still further away from symbolism. Instead, his works have become rooted unambiguously in one, all-encompassing reality: war and its accompanying stresses on the human psyche.

The three stories collected in *Tehilat kayitz, 1970* (Early in the summer of 1970) span the three stages of A.B. Yehoshua's writing career. Thus they reflect in full measure both the range and the development of the author's particular methods of literary expression. "Hamefaked ha'aharon" (The last commander), collected in Yehoshua's first volume of stories (*Mot hazaken*, The death of the old man, 1963), is a heavily symbolic work with socio-psychological implications. "Early in the Summer of 1970," first published in *Ha'aretz* in the spring of 1971, is structured along the lines of the French *nouveau roman*, blending reality and fantasy -- the fall of a son and the father's wishful dream of his survival -- with an abrogated sense of time. And "Basis tilim 612" (Missile base 612), which appeared in the Spring, 1974, issue of *Keshet*, is a realistic but ironic work about ennui and futility in the life of an intellectual, both at home and at the front. The theme of war unites the three stories; but their particular chronology and varied modes of depiction and narration make the collection an interesting one indeed.

The key to the symbolism in "The Last Commander" may be found in the story's epigraph, an excerpt from Gershom Scholem's essay entitled "Redemption Through Sin," concerning the distinction in Gnosticism between "a good but hidden God" and a Demiurge or Creator of the physical universe. The story deploys two contrasting commanders. One, named Yagnon, who seems to have no active plans for the training mission, spends most of the time sleeping and orders his men continually to rest. The other, unnamed, whips the men into shape, assigns constant drilling and, before leaving, orders an arduous seven-day trek through the desert wilderness. As soon as he departs -- lifted by helicopter (as he had come) from the midst of the by now rebellious soldiers -- the men throw down their packs and guns and revert, happily and wearily, "to the tender mercies of Yagnon's bony hands."

The dichotomous leadership represents two diverse attitudes toward war and military achievement. Yagnon (the name may be a pun on the Hebrew *yagon*, "sorrow" or "grief") is the embodiment of indefatigable peacefulness, the antithesis of military action and efficiency. In contrast, the other commander symbolizes activity and accomplishment. He unfurls "the forgotten war flag," engages in constant war pep-talks, and plans even more demanding exercises.

The contraposition of two seven-day periods bespeaks a dialectical scheme of things, a symbolic, dichotomous world of two extreme gods, one of total rest/peace and one of total action/war. The reservists complain of post-war ennui, of being imprisoned "in murky offices, pushing pencils. . . ." They are victims of normalcy, Yehoshua implies, in a country which is continually buffeted by spasms of war and peace. The "last commander," The Great God of War, comes out of the sky to rescue these people from their useless lethargy, but he is rebuffed, banished by Yagnon, himself a symbolic victim of warfare. The men lie about in "a sleepy, paralyzed camp," watching sporadically for the helicopter's return. The Israelis are caught in constant limbo, says Yehoshua, between these two ambivalent modes of existence.

                    *   *   *

"Missile Base 612" concerns itself with a youngish philosophy professor who is going through a difficult time. He faces an impending divorce; he is academically "adrift," having published nothing for several years; and his sabbatical is slowly coming to an end with little sense of accomplishment. Tired of the tedium of regular reserve duty, the teacher volunteers for the army's lecturers pool. At the center of this story is his brief, frustrating encounter, somewhere in the Sinai desert, with a small group of soldiers, four to be exact, who are totally uninterested in him or his lecture. The encounter, however, is actually with himself. Unsure of his topics ("The Israeli as Jew," "The Face of Israeli Society Under Drawn-Out Struggle"), ambivalent toward its usefulness, troubled by his personal problems, the lecturer leaves the scene without giving his lecture and heads for home with its promise of further irresolution, "prepared to give battle."

The list of equivocations and frustrations is long. Too long, in fact; for the main character ultimately becomes merely a conglomerate facsimile of a number of social and psychological problems. Enmeshed in a web of implications, he embodies a pastiche of motifs already familiar from other works by Yehoshua ("Mul haye'arot" [Facing the forest], "Shtika holekhet venimshekhet shel meshorer" [The continuous silence of a poet] and by other authors, especially Aharon Megged and Oz. Yehoshua has attempted to delve into the dilemmas confronting Israelis today, but the overdone characterization makes more for melodrama than for cogency.

*   *   *

By far the best selection in the volume is the title story. It tells of an old high school Bible teacher, also unnamed, who, though beyond retirement age, refuses to relinquish his classes; he feels a sense of duty to his students in the critical, post-'67 War of Attrition period. One day, as he routinely enters his senior class, he is pursued by the school principal (who hasn't spoken to him in three years) and told that his son has been killed in the Jordan Valley.

What follows is a mixed series of episodes and flashbacks. We learn about the old man's son. He had lived many years in the United States, became a professor, married and had a son, and finally returned, though he seemed so alien, during Israel's time of crisis. The episodes depict the father's reaction to his son's death: his ramblings to the son's university office, to his home, to his wife, to the military morgue, and to the front. The ordering of these flashbacks and scenes is not fixed chronologically. At one and the same time the reader is thrust into the past and impelled through the present. The abrogated time scheme, probably modeled after the French novelist Claude Mauriac's technique of the "immobilization of time," provides the structure which allows Yehoshua to blend real and imagined occurrences. The deft blending of time elements results in a magnificently wrought study of shock and bereavement. Confronting a questionable present, the reader is all the more willing to suspend his disbelief; he accepts even entirely implausible situations. For example, when shown his son's body, the old teacher claims they've made a mistake: the body is not his son's. Already prepared by the "truth" of past information and by knowledge of the father's stubbornness, the reader perceives the situation as indeed conveying a possible error in identification. Later, when the father "actually" locates the son at the front and speaks to him, the reader is taken in once again, both by his own wistfulness and by the dual-time structuring.

What becomes increasingly evident in the story, however, is the recurring leitmotif of the son's death. Just prior to the morgue scene, the old teacher is depicted giving the school's graduation address -- a most poignant speech, worthy of special attention -- in which he refers to himself repeatedly as a bereaved father. The principal's tragic message recurs several times in the course of the narrative. Like a litany, the story closes with the very words of traumatic beginning.

> Five or six hours ago --
> In the Jordan Valley --
> Killed on the spot --

In this technically dazzling work, it soon becomes clear that the entire action of the story has taken place in the mind of the bereaved father. The "time of narration" seems to encompass several days; but the story's "narrated time" is only a few minutes duration. Informed of his son's sudden death, the old teacher faints dead away. The rest of the story is composed of a kind of dream sequence or inner depiction of the father's mind and feelings as he copes with the awesome truth. The story is a tour de force in structure and psychological portraiture. Though marred in some ways by awkward translation (the original tone and syntactic rhythm are often lacking), "Early in the Summer of 1970" stands as one of A.B. Yehoshua's finest achievements to date.

Midstream, October, 1978: 76-78.

A.B. Yehoshua: *The Lover*

Renowned as a writer of short fiction, A.B. Yehoshua, at 40, has authored his first novel, and an experimental novel at that. The experiment is the key to its aesthetic vitality as well as its eventual disappointment. Yehoshua's artistic ploy is to have each character "speak" his or her own part, in Pirandello-like fashion. Each part is introduced by the character's name and has an average duration of two to three pages. The format, then, is a continuous series of monologues which in themselves constitute the fabric of the novel's narrative.

Though somewhat reminiscent of Virginia Woolf's *The Waves*, Yehoshua's work is not really a sequence of soliloquies. As "self-narrators," the characters present some personal perspectives, but they shed less light on their inner lives than on the novel's internal development. That is not to say that Dafi, the young daughter of Adam and Asya, does not tell us how she feels about loving the Arab boy, Na'im; and Na'im ("pleasant") conveys his own confusion concerning the difficult situation. The emotional responses, however, do not go much beyond an expected perplexity. The shallowness of vision seems to bespeak the author's aims: to highlight the taboo itself, and to weave it into the novel's main themes of disfunctioning relationships and abortive love.

Hame'ahev (*The lover*)is not really about a lover at all. Gabriel, the "lover" of the title, is the work's *eminence grise*. He makes a brief appearance, disappears for most of the novel, and reappears only toward the end to tell his own bizarre story. In the book's longest monologue (35 pages) Gabriel finally solves the mystery, which has been *The Lover*'s recurring focus since its opening lines: "And in the last war we lost a lover. We used to have a lover, and since the war he is gone. Just disappeared."

The story, therefore, is about the lover's absence, about the people he's left behind during the Yom Kippur War, about the characters who replace him for the novel's duration. Adam, the main figure, a successful mechanic with a garage of his own; Asya, his wife, a serious, competent schoolteacher; Dafi, their daughter, sprouting into unsure adolescence; Na'im, an Arab boy who works for Adam; and Veducha,

Gabriel's grandmother. The storyline: Gabriel has returned from a long stay in Paris to claim his inheritance. Veducha, though on her deathbed, has not yet given up the ghost. Idle and aimless, Gabriel is taken in by Adam and soon becomes Asya's lover (a triangle reminiscent of another Israeli's story, Uri Orlev's "Like Salt on Birds' Tails"). When the 1973 War erupts, Gabriel disappears with Veducha's car, an old Morris. Suddenly, Veducha makes a miraculous recovery, moves into her own apartment, and waits for Gabriel's return. Adam sends Na'im to live with Veducha and spends most of his time searching for Gabriel. One night, on a towing job, he comes across the Morris and eventually tracks Gabriel down. He had been living in the ultra-religious quarter of Jerusalem, clad in Hasidic garb, absorbed into the Orthodox community, in hiding.

Though complicated, the plot does not capture the novel's central preoccupation, which involves several complex sets of relationships and various social issues. The Jew-Arab love taboo (prominent in earlier Hebrew fiction by, among others, Yehuda Burla and Benjamin Tammuz) is clearly an issue, but the theme is only symptomatic of deeper contexts. For example, Na'im, the Arab, provides in his monologues several subliminal perspectives of the "Arab problem": how Jews see Arabs ("No, they don't hate us . . . .We're beyond hatred, for them we're shadows"); how he dreams of studying at the university; how Veducha finds him fearsome but ultimately worthy of love.

> He may be an Arab, but he's somebody at least. . . . But when evening came. . . panic seized me. . . . Then the idea occurred to me of asking him to kiss me. Once he'd kissed me he couldn't use violence against me. . . my first kiss in fifteen years.

The multilithic view of the Arab -- enemy-victim, foe-lover, being-nonbeing -- demonstrates Yehoshua's concern for Arab issues, which, after the 1973 War, developed fully in his increasingly engaged social consciousness. Though obliquely expressed, the central topic of *The Lover*, is war and its effect on the Israeli mind and behavior.

Love and losers are the novel's central symbols and as such convey the work's primary meaning. Why does Adam bring Gabriel home in the first place? Why does he need a lover for Asya, "someone who would fall in love with her for my sake, too," as he puts it? And why is Gabriel absent for so long (a situation reminiscent of Agnon's novel *Shira*)? Piecemeal, the motivation becomes clear: Adam suffers from a growing sense of impotence, a feeling caused, perhaps, by the tragic death of their deaf son, Yigal, which leaves him unable to relate to Asya. Even more debilitating is his inability to define Asya clearly, to delineate the devastating dilemma. By making Gabriel his surrogate, Adam induces a twisted sense of normalcy; but once the lover is missing, his world again becomes unsettling, insecure. The pursuit of Gabriel, therefore, is not at all the search for an "MIA"; it is an all-encompassing obsession with the recovery of normalcy, bizarre as it may seem. By the same token, Gabriel's desertion and concealment reflect a similar need for normalcy and peace, for a life insulated from the disastrous, recurring shocks of battle.

These subtleties of characterization and plot reflect an abiding dualism in the novel. The reader is confronted continually with overlapping dimensions of psychological and socio-political realities. Adam's needs are thwarted by the war; Gabriel's detachment from Asya becomes an escape into anonymity; Na'im's love for Dafi occurs when the taboo would seem to be the strongest. Thus, the War is at the center of each circle of personal action. The inherent dualism suggests an interweaving of the individual and history, of feelings and facts, of family and fable. And in this dualistic framework, the continuous sequence of monologues functions admirably in creating an aura of naturalness, an authenticity which, in turn, blends effectively the characters' lives and their historical setting. By means of interpolating testimonies, Yehoshua has shaped a cogent illusion of personal dilemma while telling a tale of social, national stress.

The suspension of disbelief fails, however, as the structure of self-told narratives contains flaws which ultimately vitiate the illusion of reality. Two problems persist: the "instant replay" effect of juxtaposed monologues, and the tendency toward a mannered self-questioning. By echoing the same "lines" in consecutive speeches, Yehoshua effects the novel's basic pattern of dual perspectives. For example, after reciting by heart part of a Bialik poem, Na'im notes that Dafi and her parents "nearly fell off their chairs"; and in the following section Dafi remarks, "I nearly fell off my chair" (pp. 166-167). More than an act of contrapuntal confirmation, the replays give the reader-viewer a second look, an opportunity to perceive nuances which may have been missed the first time around. The new information takes on greater significance and elicits a more emphatic reader response. The recapitulations, however, appear artificial and forced, and the ploy eventually works against itself.

Self-questioning also lends the characters a certain genuineness. But the main purpose of these inner dialogues seems again to be an unrelenting emphasis on Yehoshua's concerns rather than self-revelation. "What's he thinking to himself? What does he think of me . . . ?" says Adam of Na'im. "So what if he was an Arab . . . what's the difference?" says Dafi. Taken together, then, the use of repetition and voiced questions ultimately vitiates the intended effects of authenticity, continuity, depth, and engagement. Obtrusiveness and artificiality uncover only too glaringly the hidden "plot of issues" which *The Lover* tries so subtly to express.

The novel's dualism of personality and setting is revealed most obviously in the characterization of Veducha, the grandmother. Consequently, Veducha's passages demonstrate the work's main achievements and highlight its weaknesses. As the most lyrical of narratives, the old woman's monologues are deft dramatizations of inner awareness and feeling. Her unpunctuated lines flow with metaphorical states of being -- a stone, a plant, an animal -- portraying her miraculous resurrection. But as her vitality is renewed, Veducha waxes more obtrusively symbolic. Born in 1881 ("when the first "Bilu" settlers arrived in the country"), "a lady of history," she struggles both to remember her own name and to rediscover the name "Jerusalem."

Veducha represents both a renewed consciousness of self and an embodiment of the land and its history. Since nothing is resolved by her return to life, and nothing is resolved by

Gabriel's return, Veducha dies. Her death tells us that memory and loss are the lessons of war. As a symbolic character Veducha connotes Israel's recurrent fits of strife and remembrance, renewal and forgetting, defeat, deliverance, and despair. The old past is gone, says Yehoshua, and Israel is caught in the grasp of an endless search for social values and a normalized self-identity. As Adam remarks, "But what to do now? Where to?. . . I shall have to start from the beginning." In its novelistic configuration, the message is often poignant, artful, and engaging, but it is just as often irresolute, schematized and tendentious.

Midstream, August/September, 1979: 55-56.

Avoth Yeshurun:*The Syrian-African Rift and Other Poems*

In the afterword to his *Pegimot* (Flaws), a collection of translations and adaptations (Tel Aviv, 1979), the Israeli poet Meir Wieseltier states that "transforming [poetry from one language] into another language is. . . a process in which one should and must combine a total faithfulness with a total, unabashed unfaithfulness. . . .The translated poem, therefore, is considered first of all as to how it stands in its new, translated version, and as to the interest and enjoyment it engenders in this version. At the same time, there is no doubt that we have before us a flawed version; as good as it is, there is always something lacking in it. . . ." Translating poetry is, to be sure, a difficult, often hazardous, always trying task. The difficulties are there under "normal" circumstances: how to achieve a reexpression of someone else's art; how to transform the particular poetic language into a poetic reproduction which is not overly flawed; how to convey a sense of the original. When the poetry is especially difficult, abstruse or complex in and of itself, the difficulties of translation are enormously compounded.

Avoth Yeshurun's poetry is indeed complex. The poetic voice is at once that of an observer, commentator, stream-of-consciousness rememberer. The vision is quite graphic, down to earth, focusing on a multitude of everyday objects and occurrences: birds, plants, a bookcase, a watch, a woman, daily errands and chores. Often the images combine in metonymic association: a child and the moon, a bookcase and poetry, a bird's nest and Old Tel Aviv. The themes are mainly the vulnerability and fragility of existence, the all-inclusiveness of poetry and poetic materials, reminiscences of childhood, parents, and pioneering days which flow plangently into the present. Memories of milking cows combine with Kol Nidre *taleisim* that blend in turn with the rain of Tel Aviv which, in its ironic everydayness, elicits all memory and other primordial forces. The poet's own identity, experience, and growth, his perceptions of the land and its essence, its and his frustrations, are all combined in an evocative, often fitful spewing out of

words, images, disjointed sentences and abrupt disruptions of
sequence.

The essential ingredient in Yeshurun's poetic style is its
low diction, its abject colloquialness. (Harold Schimmel, the
translator, calls it "the accent, the gesture in the voice.") The
voice often seems "primitive," crude or peasant-like (*prost*, as
the Yiddish has it); it seems even to border on the inarticulate.
The purposeful, simulated style creates a tone of naturalness
and artlessness, much akin to the situations and images
Yeshurun employs throughout the poetry.   The illusion
engendered has two purposes: to evoke the lowly yet vigorous
origins of significant experience (the *shtetl*, the physical labor
world of early Tel Aviv, the flea market, the flowerpot); and to
shape a poetic voice which reflects a verbal struggling toward
articulation.   The words and phrases appear to flow too
quickly, to be unrestrained and unfiltered; the poet grasps
spasmodically at the expression of inner worlds of memory,
feeling, and association.

Any translation of this kind of poetry must effectively
reproduce aspects of its peculiar, "inarticulate" style. Though
he seems to identify the general stylistic problem, Schimmel
does not deal with it very successfully. Instead of recasting the
twisted syntax and colloquially wrought phrases into a parallel
English version of *prost* diction, he opts for an extreme
"faithfulness" to the text, narrowing his vision to individual
words and syntactic phrases. The attempt to reflect the poet's
usage with such literalness and precision unfortunately creates
the impression that the translator has made little effort to
perceive the poetry and its style as a total, expressive unity.
The poems appear less than inarticulate, as they ironically
should, and often they seem incomprehensible.

The problem in the translations is not imprecision, it is
precision gone awry; *ka'asher ish lo ro'e* is given as "when a
man doesn't see," when it should be "when no one's looking";
yare'ah mukhan omed is "a ready moon stands" instead of "the
moon stands ready"; and *ledaber bah tsarikh* is "to speak to her
you need" instead of "you should talk to her." The overdone
literalness often leads to mistranslations; but pure
mistranslations, the results of misreadings, also abound:
hashuv kamet is given as "important as dead"; *hashekhuna al*

shemo as "the neighborhood on his name"; *shikheha* as "forgetfulness," when it refers to the biblical law of grain left behind in the field; *shenat pah* as "quick pace on Pesach" instead of "the year of '28" (?!).

The outright errors are troubling -- they should have been detected at the editorial level -- but the more annoying lapses, since they purport to reflect Yeshurun's style, are the constant dropping or misuse of articles and personal pronouns: "Coat/he wore/ shoe" instead of "a coat" and "a shoe"; *ha'eynayim* should be "his eyes" not "the eyes"; *hibita* is "she looked" not just "looked." And sentences like "This [book]case has more than man/can assume Energy" (p. 25), "Big in riding he is in her eyes" (p. 57), and "Goes round in my head/this name several days" (p. 97) may faithfully reproduce Yeshurun's syntax, but they are essentially unfaithful to his tone and diction. His language is *prost*, not a pidgin.

The essential error the translator makes in this volume is to confuse Yeshurun's special poetic language (his *parole*, in Saussure's terminology) with deviations from standard Hebrew usage (Saussure's *langue*). In identifying the poet's diction and syntax as deviations from *langue*, Schimmel has opted for a kind of deviate English, a pidgin which follows too carefully the "rules" of the language he finds in the text. Had he recognized Yeshurun's language as an idiolect, a one-of-a-kind *parole*, he might have sought parallel means -- less "precise," perhaps, but also far less awkward -- to transmit the poet's particular style. The new version might have been "flawed" or less "faithful," but, as Wieseltier notes, it also might have engaged the reader with a greater, more enjoyable sense of Yeshurun's complex but compelling poetry.

Association for Jewish Studies Newsletter, Summer, 1982: 6.

S.Y. Agnon: *A Simple Story*

In the Afterword to his translation of *Sippur pashut* (A simple story, 1935), Hillel Halkin grapples forthrightly with the novel's paradoxes. If the work is an antiromantic comedy, he poses, why does it involve so much pain? And if it projects a serious message about traditional values and social order, why do we, the readers, feel that Agnon, a confirmed *Galitsianer*, is constantly pulling our leg? As the novel's own narrative voice might put it, the truth is that the meaning of this delightful yet perplexing little novel lies somewhere in between these two perspectives. Its purposeful ambiguity is precisely what makes the work so classic, so timeless -- so *un*simple.

The victim/hero of *A Simple Story* is Hirshl Hurvitz, son of Tsirl and Boruch Meir, well-to-do shopkeepers in the Galician town of Szybusz (pronounced "SHE-bush," which meaning "muddle" or "mistake", a name Agnon often used as a fictional counterpart to his hometown of Buczacz).

In his late teens Hirshl falls in love with Blume, a poor, orphaned cousin, who comes to live with the Hurvitzes and becomes their housekeeper. Mother Tsirl sees and fears the worst. She quickly enjoins the local matchmaker, Yona Toyber (both names mean "dove," referring to his potential clientele), to bring Hirshl under the wedding canopy with Mina Ziemlich ("suitable"), the *right* girl, daughter of Bertha and Gedalia, prosperous farmers in nearby Malikrowik. Through a series of missteps, mishaps, and misrepresentations, Hirshl and Mina find themselves in the center of attention at a raucous Chanukah party, which, unbeknownst to them, had been arranged for their surprise engagement announcement. Not long after, they marry and live. . . and here is where the not-so-simple story begins.

Depressed and anxious, Hirshl deteriorates emotionally during the first year of marriage. At the dramatic center of the novel is a poignant portrait of Hirshl, standing in the rain at night outside the Mazal house, where Blume has taken refuge with friends, so as to catch a fleeting glimpse of his true love. Soon after, only several weeks before Mina gives birth to Meshulam ("completeness"), Hirshl suffers a nervous breakdown; he is found wandering in the fields outside

Szybusz, wearing a shoe on his head, variously crowing like a rooster and croaking like a frog. According to several critical interpretations, Hirshl has been emasculated and falls from his middle-class status as a Jewish Galician Prince to a lowly, but temporary, state of frogdom.

Instead of being rescued and transformed by a princess's kiss (presumably Blume's), Hirshl is carted off to Vienna and, after several months' treatment, cured by an innovative psychiatrist, Dr. Langsam ("slowly" or "gradually"), probably the first psychiatrist to appear as a full character in modern Hebrew literature. The therapeutic method is quite interesting: Langsam sits with Hirshl and tells him stories of his own (Langsam's) hometown experiences. (Halkin correctly identifies the technique as transference.) Hirshl returns to Szybusz, reconciles with Mina (and apparently with Szybusz), fathers another son, and lives. . . happily, we presume, for here the story is ended. "But," the narrator, ever playful and ambiguous, notes at the close.

> Blume's [story] is not [ended]. Everything that happened to Blume Nacht would fill another book. And were we to write about. . . all the other characters in our simple story, much ink would be spilled and many quills broken before we were done. God in Heaven knows when that will be.

Agnon goes to great lengths to highlight a sense of ambiguity and dualism in characterization, backdrop, motivation, narrative tone, plot, motifs, structure, even syntax. For example, when Hirshl has his breakdown, rumor has it that the whole affair was staged to help Hirshl evade the impending military draft. Even Bertha Ziemlich, Hirshl's mother-in-law, perceives the situation this way, and Tsirl does not deny it. Furthermore, in the background there lingers a curse of madness in Tsirl's family, which absolves Tsirl of the blame for Hirshl's collapse. The narrator, continually sarcastic and uncompromisingly elusive, plays to the hilt the role of Master of Ambiguity: why was Hirshl so pensive and preoccupied after Blume had given him her hand in the room? "[S]omething had happened. . . and yet. . . it seemed that nothing had happened after all."

Szybusz itself is being torn in two. Its conservative burgher class and the town's entire social order are threatened by strong Socialist unionizing. And with its turn-of-the-century image, Szybusz projects a dualistic character, traditional in manners and morals, it is also on the verge of modernity.

Far more than a simple storyteller, the narrator is a cultural historian, an artful raconteur, an ardent psychologizer, a knowledgeable source of the properties and prerogatives of Jewish law and custom, a gossiper, a conjecturer, a self-proclaimed truth-teller, an inventor of aphorisms, and an eyes-to-heaven, comic affirmer/denier of divine control over earthly events. (The reader may recognize aspects of Sholom Aleichem's narrators here, and indeed there is a great deal of Sholom Aleichem in this satirical comedy of manners.) The narrator functions as a glib master of ceremonies who sets the folksy tone of the novel with his homespun diction. He also presides over what the Israeli scholar and critic Gershon Shaked has termed the novel's "orchestration of motifs," a ceaseless barrage of motifs that weaves the characters and action inextricably into an ironic design.

Halkin properly identifies Szybusz as the novel's main presence, the innocent culprit, one might say, responsible for Hirshl's dilemma. It is through a painful but ultimately effective accommodation with Szybusz that Hirshl can eventually move away from Blume, begin to love his wife Mina, and readjust to an active existence as shopkeeper, citizen, father, and son. However, Halkin seems to be too quick to dismiss the narrator's "mock naive antimodernism," a stance he readily attributes to Agnon but discounts in favor of a more defensive, conservative perspective on the part of the author: "The enemy is social disorder," Halkin states in the Afterword. What he misses, however, is that the narrator of *A Simple Story* is himself a Szybuszian, a wry insider/outsider who unfailingly enjoys telling Hirshl's story out of both sides of his mouth. Neither fully a comic nor a realist, the narrative figure is a satirist who pokes fun (at Tsirl and her collaborators) and ponders the fate of the innocent victim (Blume). Had Halkin identified the novel more as a satire and its narrator, not just

Agnon, more as a crafty *Galitsianer*, the translation might have taken on a somewhat different mien.

A Simple Story is not so simple to translate. The language and diction intentionally evoke the shtetl milieu; and there are many allusions to somewhat esoteric (by current standards) holidays, prayers, customs, and rituals, as well as innumerable uses of holy-language phraseology. Halkin has done an outstanding translation. He has captured the intermittent comedy and pathos of scene and character; he has dealt judiciously, at times by paraphrase, and at other times by omission, with the less familiar references. (This strategy was the only sure way to avoid adding a cumbersome glossary.)

Some aspects of the translation could have reflected more authentically the particular "flavor" of the text: the narrator's rhythmic cadences, parallelism of syntax, the subtle nature of imitated speech, the aphoristic texture of bourgeois discourse, the artful recurrence of themes.

In shaping the central presence of the narrator, for example, Agnon often has him "speak" directly to the reader in his characteristic mimetic-parodic manner. When Hirshl and Toyber the matchmaker, meet for the first time after the engagement, the narrator goes round the room briefly describing each individual's thoughts. Turning to Toyber he offers coyly (in my very literal translation): "What was Toyber thinking of at that moment, who knows." The Halkin translation reads: "[Toyber] kept his eyes shut as though meditating on something of a highly private nature." Here the reader is deprived of the narrator's presence, his playfulness, his ironic demureness, not to mention Agnon's psychological insight into the matchmaker's totally guiltless, pragmatic mentality. The example may seem minor, but the phenomenon, a kind of squelching of the narrator's obtrusiveness, proliferates. In several instances, too, the narrator's asides to the reader, part and parcel of the narrative act, are set in parentheses as if given separately from the text, which is not the case in the original Hebrew.

Later in the novel another brief narrative passage is omitted altogether. "If we were to try to tell [all the conversations between Mina and her confidant, Sophia Gildenhorn]," says the narrator, "we'd never have enough time." The omission may seem insignificant; but it is especially peculiar, since the novel ends with the same sort of remark about Blume and her story. Again the careful design of the novel is muted.

Several religious phrases or folkish expressions need not have been deleted: Blume's mother, "May she rest in peace"; Hirshl's whispered prayer, "May it be Thy will"; the narrator's mock-heroic declaration, "A [divine] covenant has been forged with Szybusz"; even the not-so-esoteric Sabbath rituals of *Kiddush* and *Havdalah*. All these are omitted on seemingly arbitrary grounds.

One of the most significant components of the novel is the characters' use of aphorism. For example, when Tsirl tries to express her sympathy for the unmitigated financial failure of Blume's father she says, "*Lav kol adam zokhe*"; the translation, "Not everyone can be fortunate," falls flat; it misses Tsirl's snobbish self-righteousness. The well-known saying from Ecclesiastes, "To every thing there is a season," is given as "Right timing is all." Near the end of the novel, the narrator comments: "[Hirshl], it would seem, had made his peace with the world, which could not be expected to change because of him." The original reads something like: "The world moves in its own way, and such is the way of the world." The phrase may be read as an imitation of Hirshl's inner speech or as the narrator's comment on Hirshl's reconciliation with the unswerving ways of the Szybuszian universe.

Often the mannerisms of the narrator are replaced by those of the translator, who tends to be somewhat too conscious of movement, too solicitous toward the reader, too Dickensian. Nevertheless, the translation as a whole is well crafted according to a felicitous set of translation principles. At long last, *A Simple Story* has become available to English-reading audiences who will undoubtedly derive much pleasure from this delightfully entertaining, masterfully wrought novel.

Midstream, February, 1987: 61-63.

Esther Fuchs: *Israeli Mythogynies: Women in Contemporary Israeli Fiction*

Israeli Mythogynies (1987) explores the images of women portrayed in contemporary Israeli literature from the late 1940s to the early 1980s. After an introduction that proclaims her intent to redress the wrongs of neglect and marginalization brought upon Israeli literature by male literary critics and writers, Fuchs proceeds assertively to assess the women characters in major works by A.B. Yehoshua, Amos Oz, and Amalia Kahana-Carmon. Her readings and argumentation are grounded solidly in contemporary feminist theory and cultural ideology.

In evaluating a study such as *Israeli Mythogynies*, one confronts the fundamental questions of the legitimacy and utility of the feminist literary perspective. As with any ideologically based approach to the arts and culture, feminist analysis focuses on the specific parts of literary works which are deemed pertinent to the cause. Thus, the feminist critic concentrates on depiction of women (or "gyniconologies") and measures these perceived images against the movement's values. Following the feminist perspective, Fuchs in general demands a redressing of wrongs against women in Hebrew literature and in particular suggests rereadings or reevaluations of works which feature women as main characters.

Fuchs is generally correct in noting the lack of a conscious feminist tradition in both the creative and critical dimensions of Israeli literature. She rightfully asserts her path-making role in applying feminist critiques to contemporary Israeli fiction. However, the question remains as to the legitimacy of an approach that is purposely partial, both in its bias toward feminist concerns and in its nonholistic engagement with individual works. Once these partialities are understood, the reader will at least more clearly perceive the feminist effort, if not completely embrace it. The central issue in evaluating *Israeli Mythogynies*, therefore, is the extent to which the reader is subjectively attuned to or tolerant of feminist principles and perceptions. A traditional, "objective" approach

177

will not be very successful; however, disagreement is possible, especially when the rereadings seem blatantly forced.

Fuchs approaches her task passionately and immediately draws the ideologically lines: "It should be clear. . . that what I am interested in is not the extent to which Israeli mythogynies ("patriarchal myth[s] of womanhood," p. 9) prevaricate historical realities or authentic experiences of Israeli women. Rather, I read Israeli mythogynies as ideological expressivities" (p. 10). Utilizing a methodology that is in itself ideologically motivated, Fuchs reads the literature as simultaneous sources of concrete information about women, of implied attitudes toward womanhood in general, and of abstract meanings evoked by women characters in the various literary works. Her approach demonstrates both the blend of life and art and the perceived quality or value of that blend which are at the center of the feminist critique.

Fuchs confronts the literature with the overriding viewpoint that contemporary Hebrew fiction exhibits a "strange complicity. . . with one of the most oppressive ideologies of all times. . . patriarchy" (p. 12). True to the feminist motive, she finds that the images of women in Israeli literature are far from the desirable images that the literature could have portrayed were it not for the male-based prejudices of the authors, the critics, the literary tradition, and the broader culture. Following this line of thought, Fuchs condemns the writings of the Generation of Statehood in the 1960s and 1970s because of its blatantly negative portrayal of women. In a survey of these works (in Chapter 2), she sees mainly images of "mad, materialistic, and hedonistic women bent on the destruction of the male protagonist [who is identified with] the national Self" (p. 14). Fuchs attributes this objectionable portraiture to the male writers' "susceptibility to symbolic expression and social critique" which aims at excoriating "Israel's ideological disorientation [and] the increasing consumerism of a capitalistic economy" (p. 22ff). The problem with Fuch's survey is that she compiles a spectrum of damning evidence without subjecting it to a contextual analysis. Thus, her allegations seem to derive from selective, composite characterizations that conform to images deemed unsavory by recent feminist critics. The impression throughout is of an ideologically motivated confrontation that suspends the need for a thorough literary analysis.

In Chapters 3 and 4 neither Yehoshua nor Oz fares well under Fuch's critical feminist eye. In the case of Yehoshua, she brings a barrage of negative generalizations and overstatements, ignores female personae who do not fit her definition of "passive" or "domestic". . . Mrs. Ashtor in "The Death of the Old Man," for example . . . and claims incorrectly, I think, that "the difference between [Yehoshua's] later and earlier characters is not substantial" (p. 37). In fact, from the 1960s to the 1980s Yehoshua's works have gone through vast changes in style, narrative technique, and characterization. By ignoring Yehoshua's significant shift from metaphor (or allegory) to metonomy, Fuchs misconstrues his depictions of women and misinterprets numerous characters, scenes, and entire works.

For example, Dafi, the teenage daughter in *The Lover* (1977), though acknowledged as a "partially successful attempt to present [a woman] capable of feeling and thought" (p. 44), ultimately is judged a "flimsy teenager" whose "gyniconology does not permit even in this moment [of making love with Na'im, a teenage Arab] an ability to be emotionally or physically alert" (p. 44f). The opposite is the case: Dafi and Na'im are young lovers; a primary topic in the novel is the Jewish-Arab love taboo; the theme is connected to Asya's (Dafi's mother) affair with Gabriel, which is strangely sanctioned by Adam (Dafi's father); and the whole novel embodies Yehoshua's complex responses to the 1973 Yom Kippur War. Fuchs avoids the multiple complexities and chooses to see the teenage love scene as a rape. The forced rereading is symptomatic of the biased perspective which underlies *Israeli Mythogynies*.

In her discussion of Amos Oz, Fuchs takes the position that his female characters suffer "from the perennial inability... to distinguish right from wrong," and that only his male characters have the capacity to "change and develop" (p. 61). This is a gross overstatement. For example, the main male personae in *Elsewhere, Perhaps* (1966), Reuven Harish and Siegfried Berger, are deserving of the most scathing of characterizations; instead, Noga, Harish's wayward daughter becomes the focus of Fuch's anti-Oz vituperation. Ignoring Noga's role as a symbolic rebel against the hypocrisy of high-minded kibbutz standards, Fuchs sees only her unflattering surface. Even when Noga transparently divulges her role. . . "You always, always, always want everything to be good. Why should things be good? Why? Why shouldn't they be bad?". . . Fuch's stilted response is that finally "Noga is *faintly aware* that her behavior is 'bad'" (p. 73; my emphasis . . . WB).

In like manner, Fuchs identifies the male characters of *My Michael* (1967), Michael and Ya'ir Gonen, as positive characters, while their wife and mother, Hannah Gonen, is misshaped by Oz as a neurotic Jewish Israeli Princess, a "castrating mother," and "little more than the typical frustrated homemaker." At the same time Fuchs views "the hardworking Michael," and a "mature" Yair as the unfortunate victims of Hannah's "maternal dysfunctioning," her "bad case of penis envy," and her "nymphomaniacal callousness" (pp. 76-80). With these various interpretations Fuchs misreads both the metaphorical nature of Hannah and the satirical, symbolic depiction of her husband and son.

Fuchs fares much better in her discussion of Amalia Kahana-Carmon's writings in Chapters 5 and 6. She cogently defines Kahana-Carmon's narrative technique as a "focusing . . . on the drama of consciousness [utilizing] a loosely connected plot line consisting of epiphanic episodes," and rightly praises the author for allowing the reader "to perceive the uniqueness and even 'sacredness'," of her female personae (p. 90f). Unfortunately, the forceful analysis is permeated by Fuch's ideologically based ambivalence: perhaps the characters still are too vulnerable and dependent; perhaps "consciousness" vis-à-vis "body" implies an outdated Victorian sense of "propriety"; perhaps there is an idealization of woman as victim; perhaps the retreat to a world of inner consciousness signals "an escape into 'a prisonhouse of sensibility'" (p. 103). Here Fuch's overbearing feminist critique vitiates a well-deserved appreciation for Kahana-Carmon's sensitive characterizations.

The book's best chapter is its last, in which Fuchs focuses on Kahana-Carmon's 1971 masterpiece, *And Moon in the Vale of Aijalon. (Veyare'ah be'emek Ayalon)*. However, the discussion ends with a query regarding a later novella, "There in the Newsroom" (1978).

> I am not sure why Kahana-Carmon denied Wendy the protagonist status she gives to male-dependent women like Mrs. Talmor [the lead character in *And Moon in the Vale of Aijalon*]. . . . I also wonder why [she] preferred to give this character an American identity. . . . Did [she] feel that she might strain her Israeli readers' suspension of disbelief by offering us a sympathetic treatment of an ambitious and independent Israeli woman? (P. 122)

Fuch's ambivalent query is significant in itself. It reflects a questioning of motive, a disappointment with a woman writer who fails to satisfy a feminist critic apparently on an obsessive quest for "the story of the Israeli woman as a 'liberated' woman" (p. 122). In literature as in life, conflicting ideological positions may be too complex, perhaps too personal or subjective, to meet such idealized expectations.

International Journal of Middle East Studies,
May,1989: 281-283.

'48-ers, 5
1973 War, 163
Absurdism, 23, 128, 130 - 131, 139, 160
Agnon, S.Y., 3, 5, 23, 41, 49, 64 - 68, 82, 147, 167,
    173 - 177; 176; "Aggadat hasofer" (The tale of the scribe) 43, 66;
    allegory, 66; allusions, in 41 - 45, 49; ambiguity, 64; archaism, 42;
    art, 49, 50; "Betrothed,""65, 66, 67; *BereshitRabba*, 47; "Bidmi
    yameha" (In the prime of her life), 66; bourgeoisie 46, 48;
    Buczacz, 170; Canaan, 43; comedy, 173; cosmogony, 47; dualism
    46, 47, 175; "Edo ve'enam" (Edo and Enam), 66; Expressionism,
    68; folklore, 42; German Neo-Romanticism, 66; the Gothic, 43;
    Galicia, 44; Galitsianer, 173; "Givat hahol" (The hill of sand), 66;
    halakhic texts; 44; Hebrew Literary Tradition, 49; heroism, 173;
    Impressionism, 68; industrialism, 44; irony, 46, 66; "Jugendstil,"
    67 - 68; *Jugend,* 67; kashrut, 46; "Kedumot" (Antiquities), 42;
    literary history, 49 - 50; Modern Hebrew literature, 174;
    modernity, 175; modernism, elements of 46; myth, 42; narrative
    voice, 174; Neo-Romanticsm, 68; "Polin: Sippurei Aggadot"
    (Poland: stories and folktales), 42: parody, 46; psychotherapy, 46;
    psychiatry, 174; realism, 174; sarcasm, 174; semantics, 42;
    "Shevu'at emunim" (Betrothed), 65: *Shira*, 167; *Sippur pashut*
    (A simple story), 44, 173 -177; social novels, 44; socialism 44, 175;
    syntax, 176; "Tehilah," 66; *Tractate Hulin,* 45; traditionalism, 46
Ahad Ha-am, 147, 150
Akhsanya (Forum), 8
Akhshav (Now), 11
Aleichem, Sholom, 149 - 150, 175
Allegory, 34, 66, 153
Alienation, 38, 157
Allusions, 35, 41 - 49, 59, 176,
Alter, Robert, 147 - 151
Alterman, Natan, 21, 119, 134; *Seventh Column*, 21
American literature, 136
Americans, 182
Amichai, Yehuda, 14 - 27, 96; "A Body in the
    Battlefield," 19; "Achziv Poems," 25; and Arendt, Hannah, 26;
    and Auden, 26; "The Battle for the Hill," 23; *Behind All This is
    Happiness Hiding,* 25; Alterman, influence of, 22; archaisms, 21;
    and Auden, 22; diction, in, 22; *die dinge* (things), 16; dramatic
    elements in, 23; "Elegy on the Lost Child," 16; Existentialism, 16;
    and Gilboa, 21; figurative patterns in, 22; Germany, 24; "God Has
    Mercy on Kindergarten Children," 23;   "Hashir al ahi
    Yehonatan" (The poem about my brother Jonathan), 135;

Sadan, Dov, 149
Sanders, Roland, preface
Sarcasm 56, 60, 61, 174
Satire, 16, 18, 79, 175, 181
Saussure, 172
Second Generation, 5
Semantics, 42, 53, 55 - 56, 95
Semiotics, 119 - 140, 172
Semiotics of Russian Cultural History, The 119
Shami, Yitzhak, 29, 30
Shamir, Moshe, 5, 6, 69; activism in, 7; Ahad Ha-am, 7;
black ideology, 7; ideology, 7; Marxism, 7; nationalism, 7;
philosophy of literature, 7; "relevance," 7; socialist realism, 7;
Utilitarianism, 7; *"With my contemporaries"* (Im bnei dori), 6
Shlonsky, 12, 21
Six-Day War 1, 25, 154, 157
Siman kri'a (Exclamation Point), preface, 1 - 3;
aesthetic intentions 4, 5, 10; as "an indication of what to read," 8;
avant garde, 11; cultural studies, 10; departure from previous
patterns of allegory, 5; essentialism, 10; historical consciousness
of, 9; humanism, 10; journalistic model, 11; manifesto, 9;
political self-image, 2; realism, 8, 11; Siman Kri'a Publications,
12; translated works, 12; translation policy, 12; revoutionary
stance, 4
Slang, 21
Smilansky, Moshe, 29; *B'nei Arav* (Children of Arabia), 29
Smith, Carlene, preface
Social novels, 6
Socialism, 28, 44, 150, 175
Socrates 20
Steinberg, Ya'acov, 31; "Bat harav" (The rabbi's daughter), 31
Stream of consciousness, 37, 69, 73, 76, 170
Stybel Press, 3
Surrealism, 23, 96
Sussman, Ezra, 8
Symbolism, 15, 17, 35, 38, 52, 155 - 156
Syntax, 53, 54 171, 172, 174, 176

Taboo relations, 31, 34, 165 - 166
tabula rasa, 17
Talmud, 90
Tammuz, Benjamin, 5, 31, 33 - 34, 69, 166; allegory in,
34; Arabs, 33; fratricide, 34; *Hapardes* (The orchard), 34; paradox,
33; the State, 34; "Taharut sehiya" (The swimming race), 33;
Tchernichovsky, Saul, 102, 119, 122, 132, 150; "Al harei gilboa"

מעגנון עד עוז

עיונים בספרות העברית החדשה

מאת

זאב ברגד

פרופסור לספרות עברית באוניברסיטת
פלורידה
גיינסוויל, 1995

אזכרה לאחותי, סימה לאה

תוכן העניינים

שלושה מונולוגים על הציונות: עגנון, הזז, עוז

שלושת המונולוגים על הציונות שברצוני להציג ולנתח מובאים
מיצירות מופת של ספרותנו החדשה: א) 'אורח נטה ללון' לש"י עגנון
(1939); ב) "הדרשה" לחיים הזז (1943); ג) "אהבה מאוחרת" לעמוס
עוז (מתוך הכרך 'עד מות', 1971). לכל המונולוגים האלה יש מכנה
משותף כללי אחד: הדברים הנאמרים בהם, נדמה שהם מופלאים או
מפתיעים, או שהם סותרים דברים אחרים שנמסרו כבר בטקסט, או
שהם מהווים סטייה בולטת, בין שזה באיפיון הדמות, במוטיבים, או
במסר מסויים שעולה מן הטקסט. הווה אומר: המבנה המשותף שלהם
הוא מה שמכונה ע"י המבקר ג'ונתן קלר "אליגוריה של אי-קריאות"
(unreadability).[1] ז"א, בכל מונולוג נתקל הקורא לא רק בהבדלים
בין יחידות טקסטואליות מסויימות, אלא בתוך היחידות המסויימות
האלה, כך ש"היחידה מובדלת מעצמה",[2] ובכל מונולוג נוהג הכלל,
ש"אין להבדיל בין הפעולה וההערכה ובין שאלת הקריאה (עצמה)."[3]
תוך קריאת המונולוגים האלה מובלט לעיני הקורא איך הטקסט עצמו
"חותר תחת הפילוסופיה שעומדת במרכזו, ואפשר לזהות...את
האמצעים הריטוריים היוצרים את...מושג-המפתח המכוון."[4] בדיקה
כזאת, המעריכה את לשון הטקסט כאמת וכמסווה בבת אחת, עשוייה
לברר לא את הכוונה המוחלטת של הדברים, אלא את הערפול הבלתי
מוחלט שבהם. המטרה שלי היא לאו דווקא להסביר את הסתירות
הקיימות, אלא לציין את הסתירות כחלק בלתי-נפרד של הטקסטים
הנשארים עומדים בסתירתם הפנימית.[5]

א. ש.י. עגנון 'אורח נטה ללון'

המונולוג הראשון מתוך 'אורח נטה ללון' מופיע לקראת סיום
הרומאן, בסוף פרק 75 (מתוך 80 פרקים). ההקשר הדרמטי הוא
פגישת-הפרידה בין האורח ובין רב העיר שיבוש ימים מספר לפני
שהאורח יוצא מעיר מולדתו, לאחר שהות של שנה בערך, על מנת
לחזור לביתו בירושלים. הרב מוכיח אותו על שלא בא לראותו כבר זמן
רב, והאורח משיב שהיה קשה לו לסבול את התייחסותו השלילית של
הרב לא"י. הרב אומר: "הרי אני אוהב למר אהבת נפש". האורח
משיב: "מי אני ומה אני שיאהבני. הלוואי שאזכה להיות גרגיר קטן

בעפרה של א״י. אמר הרב, וכי בגנות אדמת הקודש אני מדבר, איני
מדבר אלא בגנות יושביה״. וכאן מתחיל המונולוג - דברים של רוגז
ושל התגוננות בצורת שאלות ריטוריות ואנקדוטות, ולבסוף, האשמה
עקיפה כלפי הרב, שהוא מוציא דיבה על הארץ.

אמרתי לו לאיזה מיושביה מתכוין מר, שמא לאותם שמוסרים
נפשם על אדמתה ומחיים אותה משממותה וחורשים וזורעים
ונוטעים חיים ליושביה. או שמא הוא מתכוין לשומריה,
שמפקירים עצמם על כל פיסה ופיסה שלה. או שמא לאותם
שלומדים תורה מעוני ואינם מרגישים ביסוריהם מאהבת השם
ותורתו הקדושה. או שמא לאותם שמניחים כבוד עצמם מפני
כבוד השכינה ועומדים כל ימיהם בתפילה. או שמא מתכוין מר
לעני ארץ לסבלים וכתפים וחייטים וסנדלרים, נגרים ובנאים,
טייחים וחוצבים ומצחצחי מנעלים ושאר כל בעלי המלאכה,
שמפרנסים את ביתם ביושר ומפארים את הארץ במלאכתם. פעם
אחת נזדמן לי חייט אחד לבוש קרעים ומצאתיו בקי בארבעה
טורים בעל פה. אמרתי לו, כל כך יש בידך ואתה מטליא טלאים.
הראני סנדלר אחד יחף, שיודע למצוא כל מקור ומקור לדברי
הרמב״ם, ועדיין אינו מגיע לקרסוליו של מצחצח נעליים אחד
שיושב בשוקי ירושלים ויודע לפסוק דין מן הזוהר. והוא אינו
אלא תלמיד קטן בישיבת הסבלים, שבקיאים בכל סודות הקבלה
מן הגמרא. אלא ודאי מתכוין כבודו לאותם שהארץ מניקתם
מחלבה והם מטילים בה ארס, כאשה שמניקה את בנה ובא נחש
וינק עמו והטיל בה ארס. אבי שבשמים, אם אתה סובל אותם אף
אנו נסבול אותם. לאחר שסיימתי את דברי קמתי מכסאי ואמרתי
לו שלום.[6]

דברים אחדים מתבלטים בטקסט:

1)   הרוגז מצידו של האורח הוא יוצא דופן. בדרך כלל הוא
משיב בנחת או בלשון לימודים או בשתיקה (כמו שעשה במפגש
הראשון עם הרב בפרק 30).

2)   ההתגוננות פה נשמעת מוגזמת. היא יוצאת כנראה מתוך
גישה אידיאליסטית או רומאנטית או אפילו מיתולוגית ביותר: שאפילו
בעלי המלאכה בארץ, ודווקא הפשוטים והירודים שבהם, הם תלמידי
חכמים מובהקים. הרומאנטיזציה המיוחדת הזאת של הלמדנות בידיהם
של בעלי מלאכה מזכירה את הרומאנטיזציה הכללית שיצר
האורח/הסופר בשיריו האידיליים המופרזים על א״י וירושלים - על כך

מאשים אותו ירוחם חופשי, הצעיר שעלה ונתאכזב ושוב ירד (פרק 17).
(מעניין שבאותה שיחה עם ירוחם הופך הסופר הרומאנטיקן *לריאליסט*
מובהק, ומאשים את ירוחם, שהוא וחבריו הצעירים היו להם ציפיות
מופרזות, וזה גרם לאכזבתם, ולא שירתו).

(3) מאידך, יש במונולוג סימנים אנטי-רומאנטיים; זוהי
התגוננות חלקית ולוקה בחסר. האורח מזכיר ומדבר לטובתם של
החקלאים, השומרים, המתפללים, ובעלי המלאכה - בעיקר חייטים,
סנדלרים ומצחצחי מנעלים - אבל הוא לא מזכיר בכלל את המנהיגים,
הפוליטיקאים, בעלי המקצוע, ואפילו לא את המתקוטטים - ז"א, כל
המעמד הבינוני החילוני והעירוני חסר פה לגמרי. (מעניין שוב שדווקא
ירוחם מזכיר את הפקידים, הסוחרים ובעלי החנויות והוא מוסיף גם את
אלה שעלו ושוב ירדו למקום מולדתם - כך, כמובן, הוא עוקץ
לאורח).[7]

החלקיות הזאת שברשימה פוגמת במיתיות שבה, והיא מפנה תשומת-
לב לדברים בלתי רומאנטיים, דברים *ראליסטיים*, שעולים בפי האורח
במקומות שונים ברומאן. למשל: (א) הוא ממאן למסור את דברי הגנאי
של ירוחם על הארץ, אבל הוא מודה לפני הרב שאין כל תושבי הארץ
צדיקים.[8] (ב) הוא מזכיר אחד שעלה לארץ וציפה לומר את כל תפילתו
בדבקות, אך אחרי עלייתו הוא חזר בו וציפה לומר אפילו מילה אחת
מתפילתו בדבקות.[9] (ג) א"י אינה ללא פגם, הוא מודה: היא בית ולא
היכל; לבניינה ניתנו לבנים ולא אבנים.[10] בכלל, הסתירות וההיפוכים
בין האידיאליזציה הרומאנטית ובין הקביעה הריאליסטית מהדהדים
בכל חלקי הרומאן. (אפשר לומר, שהרומאן משקף חופפות מסויימת
בין שני קטבים: בין התמונה הרומאנטית של העלייה וההתיישבות ובין
ההשקפה הברנרית הסבוכה יותר.)

(4) המונולוג כשלעצמו משקף ריאליזם פנימי: כשנפגש המספר
עם החייט לבוש הקרעים הוא אומר לו: "כל כך (תורה) יש בידך ואתה
מטליא טלאים". אפשר שאלה הם דברי רחמנות או דברי פליאה, אבל
אפשר גם להרגיש בהם שמץ של השפלה: כל כך למוד אתה ולזה
הגעת, להיות חייט לבוש קרעים או סנדלר יחף? דומה שהנתונים
הריטוריים מתנגשים פה.

(5) הצד האנקדוטאלי של המונולוג (המפגש המתואר עם החייט
ודבריו על הסנדלר ומצחצח המנעלים) גם הוא מציין דואליזם בטקסט
הרחב יותר: (א) חייטים וסנדלרים - ובגדים ומנעלים - מופיעים פעמים
רבות, לרוב בצוותא. (עיין, למשל, פרק 48.) (ב) החייט הראשי נקרא

"שוסטר", ז"א סנדלר. (ג) הדבר הראשון שעושה האורח בשיבוש הוא לקנות מעיל חדש. (ד) בפרק 58 הוא קונה בגדים ונעליים חדשים ומעיר איך "עניות גדולה ירדה לעיר" - וזה מייד לאחר שסיפר לילד רפאל את אגדת הסמבטיון. בסיום האגדה הוא מספר איך אבדו נעלי הקסם בנהר, ובזה נותק הקשר בין האב בגלות והבן בארץ הקודש. (ה) קניית בגדים ונעליים חדשים ולבישתם מכניסות את המספר לתוך מערבולת של זהות עצמית והגדרת מקומו בחברה המקומית. (ו) ולקראת סוף הרומאן (פרק 72, שלושה פרקים לפני מונולוג זה) האורח חושב לעצמו, שאין לו צורך לקנות בגדים ומנעלים חדשים "מפני מה אותו אדם מתיירא מפני בגד קרוע ומנעל מרופט...?" ומייד הוא מסביר לעצמו שני ההסברים המתנגשים על התייחסותם של עניים לבגדיהם של עשירים.11

הווה אומר: בגדים ומנעלים עומדים במרכז הבעייה הנפשית של האורח: שהוא אורח, שהוא במקומו ולא במקומו, שהוא עשיר בין עניים או סתם אדם בין שווים, שהוא קרוע בין הנאמנות לעיר מולדתו ובין המולדת וביתו בירושלים. הקרע הנפשי, שעומד במרכז הרומאן, מוצא את הבעתו פה, במוטיב הרב-גוני של חייטים-סנדלרים-בגדים-מנעלים, וגם בהתייחסותו של המספר אל עצמו ואל שני מקומותיו. *המסמן והמסומן משמשים פה בעירבוביה.*

לסיכום: ב'אורח נטה ללון' נתקל הקורא בגיבור שמוצא את עצמו שרוי בשני עולמות. קריאת המונולוג לפי נקודת המבט של תורת ה- Deconstruction מאפשרת לנו להבין, שאין חזרתו של הגיבור ארצה מייצגת פתרון. הקרע והערפול מושרשים בתודעתו של הקורא ע"י מבנים ריטוריים מתנגשים וסותרים - ואין זה מקרה שיש לרומאן שני סיומים: (א) "כאן נשלם סיפורו של אותו אדם...שחזר למקומו ויצא מכלל אורח" (עמ' 444): ו- (ב) "תם מעשה האורח ונשלמו ענייניו שבשיבוש" (עמ' 445). כמו אצל סיומו של הרומאן 'סיפור פשוט', הקורא מגיע למצב של ערפול ואמביוולנטיות.

ב. ח. הזז: "הדרשה"

על הסיפור "הדרשה" לחיים הזז כבר עמדתי במקומות שונים, וניתוח הסיפור ופירושו נמצאים בספרי *Ideas in Fiction: The Works of Hayim Hazaz*.12 אני חוזר אל הסיפור פה, כדי להבהיר את המושגים של "אי-החלטיות" ו"אי-קריאות".13

רוב הסיפור "הדרשה" עשוי מונולוג דרמטי אחד, ארוך וממושך.
יודקה פותח בהתנגדותו להיסטוריה היהודית, מפני ש"אין לנו
היסטוריה כלל". מפני "שלא אנחנו עשינו את ההיסטוריה שלנו, כי אם
הגויים עשו אותה לנו".[14] עיקר טענתו הוא שהיהודים היו פאסיביים,
שלא היו לנו גיבורים, שהיתה לנו "פסיכולוגיה מיוחדת...לילית" (עמ'
233). הראייה לכך היא שהיתה בנו נאמנות קיצונית לגלות, לקידוש
השם, ולביאת המשיח. אבל כל זה היה כזב, והוא מוסיף: היהודים
באמת לא האמינו במשיח. זו היתה רק אגדה מופלאה: היהודים אהבו
את הייסורים והגולה הרבה יותר מהגאולה. והדברים די ברורים -
אטומים ומסובכים אולי מבחינה רעיונית, אבל הגיוניים לפי הרצאת
הדברים בטקסט.

השאלה היא: איך מגיע יודקה לרעיון הציונית, לרעיון שיש קרע
בין היהדות והציונות: "לפי שלי, אם לפי שלי", הוא כאילו מגמגם,
"אין הציונות והיהדות דבר אחד, אלא שני דברים שונים זה
מזה...הציונות מתחילה ממקום הריסת היהדות, ממקום שתש כוחו של
העם. זו עובדה!" (עמ' 240). יודקה מגיע לטענה ראדיקלית זו מתוך
שהיהודים הדתיים מאמינים במשיח אך למראית עין, והם חובבי גלות
ולא חובבי ציון - ואין סיכוי לאיחוי הקרע לעולם.

אבל, מאידך, הקורא עומד ותוהה: הדברים נשמעים ראדיקליים
ושליליים מדי. ויודקה ממשיך בדברים אפילו יותר חריפים: הציונות
היא "עקירה והריסה", "תנועה לא עממית בהחלט". היא "חותרת (תחת
העם) ועוקרת אותו", היא "גרעין של עם אחר...לא חדש ולא מחודש,
אלא *אחר* ... (ו)א"י זה כבר לא יהדות...לא המשך, אלא קרע" (עמ'
242).

כאן הקורא משתומם עוד יותר - וכך גם המבקרים, שבאו לפרש
את הדברים וראו את יודקה כנושא לסאטירה, את הזז כאנטי-ציוני,
וכדומה.[15] מצד שני, הקורא שמכיר את הוויכוחים בתוך הציונות
בתחילתה יזכור את ברדיצ'בסקי ואת הערותיו הניטשיאניות על הרס
ובניין, על הצורך "להרוס מקדש כדי לבנות מקדש". אם כן, אולי דבריו
של יודקה אינם כל כך מפליאים, רק קצת אנכרוניסטיים. אבל קריאה
כזאת אינה תופסת: הרבה מדבריו של יודקה רק *מטעים* אותו לחשוב
שיש לפנינו המשך לאותו וויכוח ישן על בעיית "היהודיות" בתוך אומה
וחברה ותרבות חילוניות. ולא כן הדברים, לדעתי.

כאמור, איני בא כאן לפרש את הדברים, אלא לציין את אי-
ההחלטיות שבהם. שהרי בסוף החלק האחרון של המונולוג, נמצא

בבירור היפוך הדברים. הלא שמענו עד כה דברי גנאי או השמצה או,
לכל הפחות, ביקורת חריפה כלפי הציונות, שהיא "מסיחה דעתה מן
העם, מתנגדת לו, הולכת נגד רוחו ורצונו". אבל לקראת סיום המונולוג
כתוב ההיפך, ודווקא בהחלטיות בולטת.

זהו! זה הכל אחת לאחת. ברור, לא המשך, אלא קרע, ההיפך ממה
שהיה, התחלה מחדש...פרט קטן, בלתי חשוב, לא היה כדאי כל
כך להאריך בו, אבל הוא בא ללמד על הרבה...אני נטיתי הצידה.
לא אעכב עוד אתכם הרבה. אני גומר. במלה אחת, הכוונה: עם
אחר, ובראש ובראשונה עם היוצר לו את תולדות ימיו בעצמו,
בכוחו ורצונו, ולא שאחרים עושים אותם לו, הסטוריה ולא פינקס
של קהילה, ולא *פינקס*, הנה האיך הוא הדבר! כי עם שאינו חי
בארצו ואינו שולט על עצמו אין לו הסטוריה. זוהי האידיאה שלי.
אני כבר אמרתי לכם את זה והנני חוזר ואומר, ותמיד אחזור על זה,
יומם ולילה...מובן? מובן?...[16]

כאן הופך יודקה את היוצרות. מטיעון של שלילה וגנאי, הוא
עובר להצעת פתרון ציוני מובהק: עם שחי בארצו יעשה את ההיסטוריה
שלו. זוהי טענת ה"אוטואמנציפציה", תורת העצמאות הלאומית
הקונבנציונאלית!

הצרה היא - צרת הקורא והקריאה - איך אפשר לעכל את
הסתירה הבולטת הזאת? הזז מגדיל את הבעייה בצורת תרופה-למכה
אירונית ביותר - ושוב יש לפנינו סיום כפול: לאחר סיומו של מונולוג
אחרון זה, היושב-ראש שואל אותו "אתה גמרת?" ויודקה קופץ
ממקומו ועונה *לא*. שהוא עוד לא הגיע אל ה"תוך" אל "המטרה" שלו.
"כן! ועכשיו לעיקר. אני מבקש עוד רגעים אחדים סבלנות ושקט".
הסיפור מסתיים בלי שום "עיקר" - והיושב-ראש מוסיף: "טוב תמשיך,
אבל בלי הפילוסופיה..." (עמ' 244) - סיום אירוני ופתוח, סיום שמחזיר
את הקורא שוב אל ההתחלה.

דומה שניתן להחיל על הטקסט ההזזי את השקפתה הביקורתית
של ברברה ג'ונסון בכתבה על 'בילי בוד' של מלוויל: "הסיפור מתרחש
בין הנחת ההמשכיות שבין המסמן והמסומן (כאן זהו מונולוג של
רעיונות פילוסופיים ואידיאולוגיים) ובין הנחת אי-המשכיותם (קביעת
פתרון שנדמה כהיפוך וסתירה)".[17] "ההבדלים שבין היחידות",
ג'ונסון ממשיכה, "נראים כמבוססים על הדחיית (repression) הבדלים

בתוך יחידות, דרכים שבהן היחידה מובדלת מעצמה".18 זה בדיוק מה שהזז עושה פה: הוא מדחה את ההבדלים (או הסתירות) בתוך מונולוג ממושך ושופע. הקורא אינו יכול אלא לתהות על התוצאות המרומזות של ההבדלים הפועלים בתוך מה שג'ונסון קוראת "האשלייה של היפך בינארי" (ציונות/יהדות).

המונח "האשלייה של היפך בינארי" (binary opposition) קולע ביותר, מפני שאין כאן באמת "סתירה" אלא השלמה. הבעיה היא שלטקסט כבר ניתנו פירושים אין ספור ועוד יד הפרשנים נטויה. והפירוש, דומני, נמצא מחוץ לטקסט.19

ההסבר שלי הוא שהסיפור כולו מגלם את תגובתו הראשונה של הזז לשואה, את תגובתו הרגשית-והאמנותית לחדשות על השמדת יהדות אירופה שנמסרו בוודאות בסתיו, שנת 1942. התפרצותו הכאילו-פילוסופית של יודקה השתקן-המגמגם אינה אלא צעקה מרה של רגשנות, תיסכול, דחייה, שלילה, קבלת-גורל, ותקווה. כך אני מבין את ה"קרע", את הביטויים "עם אחר...ולא עם חדש ומחודש". ואת העיקר שאינו מובע כלל במסגרת הסיפור.20

ג. ע. עוז: "אהבה מאוחרת"

גם בספרו של עמוס עוז, "אהבה מאוחרת", יש היפוך גמור וסתירה יסודית לקראת הסוף, אלא שכאן ההיפוך הוא בעיקר באיפיון ובנימה, היפוך כמוס יותר במבנים הריטוריים, היפוך לא מובלט - ובזה כוחו של הסיפור.

ההיפוך נמצא במונולוג בצורת מכתב שכותב שרגא אונגר, גיבור הסיפור, להוגר, בעלה של ליובה, ידידה ושותפת ישנה של שרגא. שרגא הוא מרצה-מטיף זקן, המקשקש ללא הפוגה על האיום הנורא של הבולשביזם. הצעתו - במכתבים מדומיינים למשה דיין: לצאת במלחמת-בזק נגד האויב הסובייטי. ויש שהוא גם מדמיין אפילו את פעולת הפלישה: "...טאנקים יהודיים זוחפים...דורסים ורומסים רוצחינו (הכוונה לנאצים שעוד שולטים בוורשה")21 - ואח"כ מזרחה לרוסיה: "נופלת רוסיה כולה עיר אחרי עיר...נקמת היהודים גועשת...ומשה דיין...מקבל את כתב-הכניעה מידי הגנרל-גוברנאטור של קישינוב (דווקא!)" ולבסוף, הערתו של שרגא: "מה מופרך כל זה".22

"(ה)מכתב (ה)פרטי אל הוגו" (עמ' 76) מופיע מייד לאחר כיבוש
דמיוני זה. מבחינה ריטורית הוא שונה לחלוטין מהההתפרצות הנלהבת-
המיואשת על הכיבוש. ראשונה, יש כאן מכתב מוחש, נמסר בעל פה,
ולא רק מדומיין. שנית, הוא מדובב את הקורא הכפול (הוגו ואותנו)
לחשוב פתאום על המפעל הציוני, בעיקר על מושג *הנודמאליות*, על
אבדנה - ועל אי-קיומה - בארץ. ואשר לבולשביזם, שרגא מדבר עליו
באופן מטאפורי ופילוסופי. הטענה כנגד הבולשביזם מעוצבת מתוך
גוזמה (hyperbole); והיא משמשת סינקדוכה לשנאת היהודים בכלל.
תוך כדי כך מאופיין שרגא אונגר, בעל הטענה, כדמות שטופת
פאראנויה וטעונת בורלסקה: דמות סאטירית, קומית-פתטית ומושפלת.
אבל כאן, בסוף הסיפור, כשהופכת הסינקדוכה המוגזמת לכלל המתקבל
על הדעת (מן הבולשביזם המדומיין אל טענת האנטישמיות העולמית
והנצחית), הופכת דמותו של שרגא רציונאלית יותר, שקטה ומחושבת
יותר. שרגא משתנה והופך לדמות בעלת דעות מוכרות וסבירות.

העם היהודי, הוגו, בשום פנים איננו יכול לקום ולהסתלק לו מן
המישחק אחת ולתמיד. וכי באמת ובתמים קיווינו בלבנו להימלט
לכאן ולהקים לנו כאן ארץ חדשה ולהעמיד פתאום פני בולגאריה
או ניו-זילאנד? חשוב נא בדבר, הוגו: וכי אנחנו, כביכול, מסוגלים
לשבת כאן במנוחה אלף שנה, לחרוש אדמה כל היום ומדי ערב
לשבת ולשתות שיכר בפונדקים או לרקד עם בנות-איכרים ולקנות
ולמכור סוסים ולישון בשלום על מיטותינו כל הלילה ושוב, דרך-
שיגרה, לקום כרגיל מדי בוקר? נא. והלא שטות גדולה היא, הוגו,
לטפח בינינו מחשבות שכאלה. אני פונה אליך כאל ידיד קרוב. את
שתי עיניך אני מבקש לפקוח בחזקה. ואני אומר לך, הוגו: *כל
הזעם, וכל היאוש, כל ההתלהבות, ההיסטריקה, כל הטירוף
שבעולם*, כל המהפכות והאידיאות והקומפלקסים והייסורים
והזוועה הפנימית באשר הם, כולם מתכוונים אלינו.
כך בכל הדורות שהיו ובכל הדורות שיבואו. יש איזו תאווה איומה,
הוגו, תאווה דורסנית, משתגעת בלב כל בני העמים ובקרקעית כל
האידיאות. אני, כשלעצמי, אינני יודע לקרוא בשמה של התאווה
המאויימת הזאת. אבל אני יודע שהיא מתכוונת אלינו יומם ולילה,
מתכוונת אלינו לרעה, שוב ושוב היא נושבת על פנינו. גם כאן. גם
על המרפסת מול הים בתל אביב בלילה. 23

מבחינה ריטורית, מבעית ואיפיונית, דומה הסיום של "אהבה
מאוחרת" לסיומו של "הדרשה": היפוך פתאומי מן המוגזם אל הסביר,
מן המופרז אל המאופק, מן הצורם אל הנספג, מן השיא הדרמטי אל
האנטי-שיא. ההבדל הריטורי בולט גם בשינוי החד מדעותיו של הפרט
לרעיון   המקובל על הכלל: שהציונות היתה צריכה להוליד את
האפשרות לחיות כעם בין העמים. בדומה ליודקה, שרגא אונגר מסיים
בטיעון מושרש באידיאולוגיה של הציונות הקלאסית.

***

אפשר לומר, שבהתפרצותם והיפוכם הריטורי הבולטים,
משקפים שלושת המונולוגים האלה משברים היסטוריים, פסיכולוגיים,
ואידיאולוגיים: ירידת הגלות והקרע הפנימי של האורח אצל עגנון;
החדשות המבהילות של השואה אצל הזז; והאיום הכפול החוזר של
השואה ומצדה בימים שלפני מלחמת ששת הימים אצל עוז.

אבל מה שמאחד את המונולוגים מבחינה טקסטואלית הוא
בעיית הקריאות של הדברים, בעיית "אי-האפשרות להפריד בין הפעולה
וההערכה ובין שאלת הקריאה." 24. לפי תורת ה- Deconstruction,
"מבנה הסתירות (שראינו במונולוגים) יוצר לא התייחסות טוטאלית
ושלטת (מצד הקורא) אלא דווקא *החילוק בכל התייחסות אפשרית*."25.
זוהי הבעייה הבולטת בשלושת הטקסטים המובאים פה: הקורא נמשך
והולך וחוזר חלילה לתוך מערבולת של שיפוטים, הגדרות, היפוכים,
וערפולים. הלשון של הטקסט, לדבריו של דה מאן, "בהכרח *מטעה*
באותה מידה [שהיא] מביעה את הבטחתה על [מסירת] האמת."26.

* מאמר זה מבוסס על הרצאה שניתנה בכנס אקדמי על הספרות העברית החדשה,
  שאורגן ע"י ההסתדרות העברית באמריקה בפילדלפיה, 4-5 בינואר, 1987.

1. כך מסביר קלר את דבריו של פול דה מאן בספרו Allegories of Reading (6).
   ראה קלר (5), 257 ו-276 ואילך.

2. ברברה ג'ונסון (9), X-XI.

3. שם.

4. קלר (5), 86.

5. קלר משתמש במונח "irresolvable alternation" בהסבירו את דבריו של ג'ק
   דרידה על המושג "differance" בספרו Positions (7), 82. עיין קלר (5), 96-97.

6. 'אורח נטה ללון' (2), 427-426.
7. שם 89.
8. שם, 209. ראה גם 282.
9. שם, 100 ואילך.
10. שם, 100 ו- 128 ואילך.
11. ראה 415 ואילך.
12. ראה ברגד (4), במיוחד 65-68, ו- 82 -88.
13. ראה מ. ריפאטר (10), הטוען כנגד ט. טודורוב, ש"אי-החלטיות" היא תוצאה של "אי-דקדוקיות" (דבר מילולי שאינו מובן מתוך ההקשר), והיא משמשת דווקא ציון-דרך אל המובנות דרך האינטרפריטציה. עיין גם קלר (5), 279-276, ובמקומות אחרים. ובעניין ה-"אי-החלטיות" בשירה, ראה גם ב. הרושובסקי, (8), 18.
14. 'אבנים רותחות' (1), 230. כל הציטטות מובאות מהוצאה זו, ורובן ניתנות בגוף המאמר.
15. ראה ברגד (4), 82-84.
16. 'אבנים רותחות', 243.
17. ג'ונסון (9), 86.
18. עיין הערה 2 לעיל, וראה גם קלר (5), 242-241.
19. שם. ההדגשה שלי - ז. ב.
20. ראה ברגד (4), 86-87.
21. 'עד מוות' (3), 72. כל הציטטות מובאות מהוצאה זו.
22. שם, 73-74.
23. שם, 77-78.
24. עיין הערה 3 לעיל.
25. קלר (5), 234. ההדגשה שלי.
26. דה מאן (6), 277. ההדגשה שלי.

ביבליוגרפיה

1. חיים הזז, 'אבנים רותחות', עם עובד, 1965. (הוצאה ראשונה: 1946).
2. ש.י. עגנון, 'אורח נטה ללון', שוקן, 1960. (הוצאה ראשונה: 1939).
3. עמוס עוז, 'עד מוות', ספרית הפועלים, 1971.
4. Bargad, Warren. *Ideas in Fiction: The Works of Hayim Hazaz.* Chico: Scholars Press, 1982.
5. Culler, Jonathan. *On Deconstruction: Theory and Criticism After Structuralism.* Ithaca: Cornell University Press, 1982.
6. De Man, Paul. *Allegories of Reading: Figural Language in Rousseau, Rilke, and Proust.* New Haven: Yale University Press, 1979.
7. Derrida, Jacques. *Positions.* Chicago: University of Chicago Press, 1981.

8. Hrushovski, Benjamin, "Poetic Metaphor and Frames of Reference," *Poetics Today*, 5:1 (1984): 5-43.

9. Johnson, Barbara. *The Critical Difference: Essays in the Contemporary Rhetoric of Reading*. Baltimore: Johns Hopkins University Press, 1980.

10. Riffaterre, Michael, "Interpretation and Undecidability", *New Literary History*, 12:2 (1981): 227-242.

מתוך *'מגוון'*: מחקרים בספרות העברית ובגילוייה האמריקניים, מכון הברמן למחקרי ספרות, לוד. תשמ"ח.

'ירח בעמק אילון'
(רומן לירי לעמליה כהנה-כרמון)

"ורק העצבון, משתרג ועולה. כאדם
כמרצדה, בחשיבות חוכא." ('ירח בעמק
אילון' -עמ' 180).

הרומן הלירי הוא תופעה נדירה בספרות העברית החדשה: א.נ.
גנסין, ש. הלקין, ס. יזהר ועמליה כהנא-כרמון - זהו עיקר שלשלת-
היוחסין לז'נר מורכב זה בעברית. בדומה לקודמיו ניזון גם 'ירח בעמק
אילון' ממסורת הסיפורת הלירית האירופאית, וניכרת ביותר השפעתה
של הסופרת הבריטית, וירג'יניה וולף. מפאת שילוב מסורות זה של
ריכוז פנים-יהודי (ההוויה הישראלית) עם השימוש בקונבנציות
אמנותיות חיצוניות, חובה לראות בעיצוב יצירה זו אחת ממיטב
ההגשמות של אימרתו-הצהרתו של מ. י. ברדיצ'בסקי (ב"צורך ויכולת
בספרותנו היפה"): שעל הספרות העברית להרחיב את גבולותיה
ולהתמודד עם "שאלת הקיום, שאלת הלאום, שאלת האדם וצרכיו".

בהתאם לניסוחים האסתטיים של הרומן הלירי, מורכבת יצירה
זו משיחזור ההתרחשות החיצונית, האובייקיבית, עם ההשקפה
הסובייקטיבית, הנפשית, על אותה התרחשות. אין ל"עלילה" שום
חשיבות אלא בדרך שהיא נספגת לתוך ה"אני" ונפלטת לעיני הקורא
בתבניות מיטאפוריות. אכן יש לגשת למירקם סיפורי-לירי זה כאל
שירה לירית, בה מעוצבת משמעות הדברים בעיקר דרך קולות ה"אני"
הדרמטיים, דרך ציורים, מיבנים ריתמיים ומיטפוריים, ורציפות סמלית.
דמויות פועלות ישנן; אפיסודות דרמטיות ישנן; דיאלוגים ישנם; זרם
זמני ומשך סיפורי ישנם. אבל כל אלה באים רק כדי ליצור מסגרת
להתרחשות העיקרית, הפנים-תודעתית.

את המסגרת הסיפורית, שבתוכה טמון הדיוקן הנפשי המרכזי,
אפשר לסכם בקצרה: בנובמבר 1966 מגיע לארץ מהנדס "מומחה"
מאנגליה, מר פיליפ פורבס, שבא ליעץ ל"אשמור-תעשיות-פיתוח
בע"מ". הגברת נועה טלמור, אשתו של אשר טלמור, בעל המפעל
התעשייתי - אשה בדמי ימיה במצב של התנכרות מסויימת מבעלה -
מסיירת עם האורח בתל-אביב, באר-שבע ואילת. נוצרים ביניהם יחסי
קירבה שהולכים ומתעצמים כלשהו אך לא באים כלל לידי סיפוק.

פיליפ עוזב אחרי כחודש וחוזר לשהות קצרה בקיץ הבא, לאחר
מלחמת 1967; אך אין כל המשך לעניין, והוא הולך לדרכו.

בתוך ההתרחשות הזאת שבהווה נזכרת נועה טלמור בימים
שעברו, בהיותה סטודנטית בירושלים לפני מלחמת השחרור, עת פגשה
את אשר ונמשכה אליו לראשונה - על אף אדישותו הבולטת. על מסך
העבר מוקרנות נפשות אחדות: חברותיה של נועה בחדר, ימימה
וברוריה; ושכנן, מר רולו, גם הוא בריטי, קשיש במידת-מה מהבנות,
חוקר ארכיאולוגי, "אוסף הוכחות" לשם שיחזור תולדות תחילת
הנצרות. ועל במת ההווה עולות גם דמויות-מישנה: סוניה, מנהלת
משרדו של אשר; ומר רוטמן, העובד גם הוא במפעלו של אשר.

כל הדמויות האלה משקפות, אם במישרין ואם בעקיפין, את
הדילמה הכפולה של נועה: ההתייחסות הבעייתית בין אשה וגבר,
ותחושת הגורליות נוכח זרם החיים האדיש. סוניה מתחרה עם נועה
ביחסיה עם אשר ופיליפ; מר רוטמן מספר לנועה פרשה טראגית ארוכה
על תהילה, אשה נשואה שהתאהב בה אך היא לא השיבה לו אהבה;
ימימה, ברוריה ומר רולו חוזרים ומופיעים בהווה, במקביל להופעתו
השנייה של פיליפ; וימימה מספרת גם היא על פרשת הידרדרות יחסיה
עם בעלה ומשיכתה לרופאה, ד"ר טית, בימי ההחלמתה לאחר ניתוח
רחם. העבר וההווה, ההתייחסויות הכושלות שבין הדמויות, וסמיכות
הפרשיות הסיפוריות השונות - כל אלה משמשים בעירבוביה, כדי
להבליט את חווויית הייאוש הדומיננטית ברומן.

דרך נקודת המבט הלירית, דרך ההכרה הפנימית בהווייה,
הופכים כל האלמנטים הסיפוריים האלה לגושים סמליים בתבנית
מיטאפורית רב-גוונית אך אחידה. איחוד האובייקט והסובייקט נראה
בעיצוב דו-מסלולי אך מקביל של דמות המספר ברומן. במרכז
ההסתכלות והמסירה הסובייקטיבית עומדת נועה טלמור, לעיתים היא
עצמה משמשת דמות-מספר בלשון "אני", ולעיתים הוא מוצגת כנושא
ההתרחשות הנמסרת בפי דמות-המספר השנייה. שתיהן מכונות "אני"
(כעין זיווג של "אני" ו"אני-אחר"); ושתיהן מהוות מקורות תודעה
אחידים.

הרומן הוא רומן של התמרמרות, של טינה-ההופכת ייאוש;
ומגמתו להציג את הכרתה ההולכת ומתעצמת של הגברת טלמור
בתחושת אזלת-היד בחייה, בחוסר שליטתה על גורלה, בכשלונה
להגשים את "הרצון להיות בשיא". בחלקה הגדול נוצרת תחושת
ההתמרמרות תוך חיפושה אחר נקודת-אחיזה וטעם בחייה הסבילים,

תוך הגדרת תפקידה וצרכיה כאשה, ותוך תהליך ההבהרה בקביעת
זהותה. תהליכים נפשיים אלה מובעים ברומן דרך שלושה מוטיבים
מרכזיים חוזרים: הזיהות, העשייה, וההשתנות.

לעיתים עומדת הגדרתה העצמית של נועה טלמור איתנה: "אשה
ישראלית ממוצעת אני" (עמ' 82); או בשעת ההסתכלות בראי: "אני
אשה תל-אביבית בסביבתה הטבעית" (עמ' 119). אך תוך כדי האישור
שבהצהרות אלה ניכרים כבר מקור הטינה, הרגשת חוסר-סיפוק, הרצון
להימלט מן הנמצא ולהיות "אחרת", להחליף את צורת חייה "שאינם
יוצאי דופן". "אני אני אני" מהדהד בלבה קול תלונתו של בעלה, אשר,
כרמז למאבק שבין זיהותו השבירה וזיהותה הרופפת. שוב ושוב היא
מזדהה עם גורלן המר של נשים אחרות. למשל, היא מהרהרת על
הסבילות והשיעבוד הנראים לה בדמות אישה בדואית
פרימיטיבית,"חיה-אישה", הממתינה לבעלה מחוץ למסעדה בבאר-
שבע: "אדם לעמל יולד. ואשה כמוני לשכחה. מי ידע חייך בחושך,
באבק, אשה שחורה. הבדואים במסעדה, פני-פוקר, אין לנחש למי מהם
היא שייכת, מחכה" (עמ' 133). היא מגיבה פה לחוסר הרגישות
ולאדישות כלפי האשה בעולם, למצב האשה הנעמדת על כורחה בשולי
ההתרחשות. ניסוחים כגון "ימימה, את אני, מר חירם, אתה אני" (עמ'
177) עולים כלייט-מוטיבים חוזרים בהרהורי נועה, כדי לשקף את
זהותה המפוצלת, המורכבת מתכונות נפשיות של אחרים. ולקראת סוף
הרומן היא חושבת כך בשעה שמסתיים ה"פיקניק" עם חברותיה מכבר,
ימימה וברוריה.

> האשה נשארה, ואינה יודעת מדוע. ואינה יודעת מהו אשר עקב כך
> איבדה...ואתה, ראה מה עשית ממני. מרוצה? מאושר? או: אני
> ימימה. אשה קשה. ניצבת בפני שוקת שבורה. או: אני תהילה.
> האשה אשר יצאה מדעתה. וברוריה, אה, ברוריה, ברוריה קסומה,
> כולנו, עמך, הילדה בעיניים הסיניות אשר נדונה להבשלה איטית
> ונכונות לקראת משהו העתיד לקרות ואינו קורה לעולם (עמ' 186).

גורלה כגורלן: איבוד התמימות, חוסר התכלית בחיים. אכזבה
מרה, תחושת שגעון. וה"אתה" על פני השטח הוא אשר או פיליפ; אך
בעצם הוא כל הסדר המקובל של הדברים והיחסים בעולם של גברים.
רק מתוך הנאיביות וקוצר-ראות אפשר עוד להתקיים ולצפות להגשמה
בעתיד.

מוטיב הזהות מופיע באופן צדדי בעשרות מקומות ביצירה, והוא
מהווה איפוא דוגמה טובה של אמצעי עיצוב בתבנית המיטאפורית של
הרומן הלירי. למשל: נועה מהרהרת שבתעודת הזיהות שלה היא
"נושאת תצלום אשר שוב אינו תצלומי" (עמ' 23); פיליפ מעיר כלאחר-
יד ש'טלמור' הוא "שם ממית, שם נוטל זהות" (עמ' 34); ימימה
שואלת: "נועה, מה את" (עמ' 82); רוטמן מספר: "לא הכרתי את
עצמי" (עמ' 139); ושוב נועה, ברגע של הארה עצמית דווקא: "לרגע
אני לא אני" (עמ' 183). המוטיב משתרע גם על פני הגוף, בשינוי פני
הסביבה ובמקרים חוזרים של זיהוי מוטעה, ובהרקע מרחף לסרוגין סמל
של זיהות-לא-זיהות: "אנסטסיה לבית רומאנוב".

המוטיב העיקרי השני הוא מוטיב העשייה, היצרנות והתכלית.
עולמה של נועה, עולם הידע הנפשי והתודעה הרגישה, מתמודד ברומן
עם עולם המסחר, עולם ה"הצלחה" - עולמו של אשר. במאמר מכליל
מאשימה נועה עולם פרגמטי זה כנטול-רגש: "מגע ההצלחה, על מנת
להצליח בעסקים עליך להיות נגוע באל-אנושיות מיוחדת במינה" (עמ'
39). היא מנסה להמחיש את עצתה של ימימה: "נועה , עליך לעשות.
הכרחי לך להיות אדם עושה" (עמ' 82); אך היא נרתעת מחיי-מעש
מתוך חשש אינסטינקטיבי לאיבוד כוחות הנפש האילמים ולאיבוד
יכולת ההתבוננות הסבילה אך המעמיקה בעולם. פיליפ מעמיד
כאידיאל שלו "איש בעל כוחות היוצר". אדם שיכול "להביא לידי
פריחה את הכוחות הגלומים" (תפקיד שהוא עצמו נכשל בו ביחסיו עם
נועה). אבל נועה מהרהרת אחרת, ורואה בדבריו רק את דמותו
השלילית, המיכנית, של אשר: "סגור, מהלך. והוא ריק. צומת הכוחות
גלומים בלתי-נראים אשר עשוהו לתחנת-מעבר" (עמ' 100). אשר יש
בו, אמנם, "הכוח לחולל שינויים"; אולם, נועה מעדיפה את הספיגה
הפסיבית של עולם האשה: "אין ממחה. ומאומה אינה עושה. רק מבט
ורואה" (עמ' 40).

על אף נימת ההתמרמרות בשל הכורח לעמוד בצדדי החוויה,
משתרע אישור תפקידה הסביל של האשה על פני כל הרומן. אפילו
ימימה, הפרגמטית והאידיאליסטית, ה-"ביצועיסטית", כביכול, חוזרת
בה לאחר הניתוח. יחד עם הרגשתה שבנטילת כוח-היוצר הביולוגי
שלה כאשה ("לשם מה, איפוא, אני מוסיפה להיות קיימת") נוצרת
ההכרה בלבה שלאו דווקא בעולם הפעילות טמונים סוד ותכלית הקיום
האנושי.

כך אנו ערוכים, להיות בנמצא. נוכח מצב פחות או יותר דרמטי,
להיכנס לפעולה: המילה הנכונה, המעשה הנכון, הכלים. הלא זה
מעניין, כי המדובר באנשים אותם האנשים. במילים אחרות: אסור
לבן-אדם להתפעל, להיהפך לאופטימי, להיגרף להאמין. רק המכונה
המשוכללת בפעולה היא זו. לא התייחסות אישית (עמ' 172).

הנימה העיקרית שבמוטיב העשייה - כבמוטיב הזהות - היא
נימה אנטי-גברית, ויש ברומן הדהוד לא זעיר של רעיונות "שיחרור
האשה". אולם, מאידך ברור גם כן, שבמעמקי אותה נימה נשמעת
תלונה כוללנית יותר על אפס-כוחו של האדם בפני זרם החיים
לכשעצמם. בדומה לגברת דאלוויי של וירג'יניה וולף נדמה שמאמצה
המרכזי של נועה טלמור הוא לתבוע ולאשר את עצם ההתבוננות
בהווייה כפעולה נעלה. מתוך המושג החברתי-סטיריאוטיפי, שהאנשים
"חייבים לעשות משהו" (כדברי קלאריסה דאלווי) צצה ועולה האמונה
שהרחות הדברים תוך כדי תפיסה סבילה חובה גם ליחס לה את תוקף
הפעילות. שוב ושוב, נתקלת נועה במערבולת-עשייה (עיין, למשל,
בתיאור תל-אביב עם בעלי המלאכה המתרוצצים בה, תיאור שניתן
בלבוש ארכאי לשם הרחקה והגזמה כאחת - עמ' 146). וכל הרקע רווי
שגשוג, צמיחה, וטיפוס אל-על, לקראת שיא הפעלתנות. אולם,
בתודעתן של נועה ושל דמות-המספר אפשר להבחין בהשקפה פסימית
וסרקסטית למדי. "כל אשר למענו אמרנו לחיות, יש להתקיים בלעדיו",
מהרהרת נועה (עמ' 184). פיליפ מתפעל: "זה נפלא, איזו ארץ. אילו
אנשים. כלבבי. הכל - מאמץ משותף. איש אינו אדיש. וישר לעניין";
אבל נועה מגיבה אחרת בהרהוריה: "זה לא עוזר. לא עוזר. לא מעניין
איש. לא מסחרר" (עמ' 21). והמספר איתה: "אילת תהיה באר-שבע,
באר-שבע תהיה תל-אביב, תל-אביב תהיה לכרך" (עמ' 23). נועה אינה
משתתפת בחווית ההתקדמות. היא משקיפה מן הצד, "במלוכסן", "זרה
לסובבים", שקועה בשטף "דברים לא לי", לא מקשיבה לדוברים אליה,
מאזינה לשיחות צדדיות. היא צמאה להיות אהובה, אך נרתעת מכל
תופעה מינית גלויה וממגע חושני כלשהו. היא מנסה לשתף את עצמה
בעולם העשייה דרך מפעל משלה, יצירת מרצדות לנוי; ויום אחד היא
קמה ושוברת את תוצרת-ידה לרסיסים. היא עצמה כמרצדה: תלוייה
במצב "לימבו" בין עולם הפעלתנות ובין עמדתה הנפשית הסבילה.
בזיהותה היא מתנועעת (כשמה כן היא) בלא הפסק, אך יחד עם זאת יש

בה הרבה מן הסטאטיות והמיכניות. בעת ובעונה אחת מרגישה הגברת
טלמור שהיא גיבורה רומנטית סבילה. "כלואה במגדל", אך היא רואה
בתפקידה הפסבדואקטיבי להיות "תוף...שהמאורעות, האנשים,
המקומות מכים בו" (עמ' 59).

בעיקרו של דבר מעיד הרומן על הצורך האמביוולנטי בעולמנו
להימשך בתוך הזרם ולהפסיקו, לשם הסתכלות אל מתחת פני השטח.
אמנם, יש חליפות בחיים; אבל אין שינוי ביסודות ההוויה, שהיא בעצם
סמוייה, נפשית. וזהו המוטיב המרכזי השלישי. התבגרות והתפתחות
ישנן; חידוש, גיוון, ובנייה ישנם; תוצאות מלחמת 48' ו- 67' ישנן. אך
על הכל מתגברת הנימה האירונית והאלגית כמעט של הרגשת חוסר
ההשתנות הפנימית והאמיתית. ימימה אומרת:

"חלפו הימים. אבל לא חלפו. המדינה חידשה נעוריה. השלנו עור
ישן, אמרנו. ואף לכך מתרגלים, במהירות" (עמ' 147).

בכל הרומן חוזרות ונישנות המילים "חדש", "אחר", "שינויים",
ו-"עתיד". אך מאידך חוזרים ועולים בתבנית דמויות, שמות ותמונות
מהעולם העתיק ואף שימושי-לשון ארכאיים, כאילו להביא ראייה לכך
שהעולם הנוכחי יסודו בשכבות תת-קרקעיות בעבר ותת-מציאותיות
בהווה, וכך חוזר הגלגל חלילה.

שלושת המוטיבים הכלליים האלה מסתעפים בכל מימדי
המירקם הלירי של הרומן. הם מתעצמים בדמויות, בהתרחשויות, בטבע
וברקע, והם עומדים במרכז אותה תבנית סמלית, שהיא עיקרה של
יצירה זו. גוונים וצבעים מועדים כנגד חוסר-פיגמנטים אפרורי; צמחי-
בר לעומת פרחי-גן; חולי-רוח ושגעון מול אניני-טעם וצלילות-דעת;
לחלוחית מרעננת מול יובש מחניק; צעירים מול זקנים; פשוטי עם
במציאות מול דמויות מלכות בדמיון; מסעות-פתע לעומת טיולים
מאורגנים; מסעדות, בתי מלון ומשרדים מול הר גריזים, חקירות
ארכיאולוגיות, והכותל; סדר חיים בורגני מול פולחן עתיק-יומין; הרים
כמרחק מגרה מול הרים כממלכודת. וכך גם בלשון הדימויים ברומן:
החופש והתנועה (ברוריה היא "כציפור במעופה") כנגד הסטאטיות
והמוות (אשר הוא "ארון מומיה", ומפעלו "בית קברות"); המרוחק
והאקזוטי (הגבעות הן "עקבות מדורות-ענק", והעננים "כגמלים
הוחרדו מרבצם") כנגד הקרוב והיומיומי (הרקיע "קערה שקופה" או
"חולצה דהה", ושפת-הים "כדפנות כוס", והעננים "חלב קלוש"). אבל

בהתאם לתבנית המורכבת של הרומן הלירי אין כוונת דברים אלה חד-
צדדית. משמעויות מתנגשות מכאן ומשלימות מכאן, הכל לפי טיב
הקשרים הרב-מימדיים. אך ברור שבכל גווני רקע סמליים אלה, כולל
שימושי-הלשון, נשקף הרעיון העיקרי שברומן: אזלת-היד בפני עצם
תהליך ההתקדמות וההשתנות, על אף כושר ההסתכלות וההתבוננות
המעמיקה באותו תהליך.

> "פה פתילי-חיים יעודים אחוזים כקרנים בסבך או כבחיבוק-מוות
> לכודים. לכל עץ-אלה אבשלום תלוי. תחת הנעצוץ יעלה ברוש תחת
> הסרפד יעלה הדס. ויתן לחסיל יבולם ויגיעם לארבה. והרוח הטובה,
> באה מים, תעבור. בכנפיה תצרור את זה ואת זה ואת זה. תשאם
> באשר תשאם. תאבדם באשר תאבדם" (עמ' 160).

הרומן מסתיים בקריאת ה"גליונות" של סופר אחד, מר חירם,
(כינויו כ"בונה" אירוני ביותר) בידי הגברת נועה טלמור. בגליונות
ארבעה חלקים, כולם פיקטיביים, כביכול, חורגים בכלל ממסגרת הזמן
והמקום שביתר היצירה: תמונה של עומדים-בתור לעשיית מסיכות-
מוות; תיאור הזייתי של לונדון, עם "אני" עלום, הנואם על ערך
העבודה; הצגת סופר "הנמצא בעיקר לבדו"; וראיון עיתונאי מעושה עם
דבריו אותו סופר על דרכיו ביצירה. דברי הסופר מבהירים הן את הקשר
שבין חלקי הגליונות והן את משמעותם בהקשר הרומן כולו. דבריו על
תפקידו של הסופר, "להעמיד במלוכסן גופי דברים", מצביעים בסמוי
על תפקידו של רומן זה בפרט ועל דעתה-דרכה של הסופרת עמליה
כהנא-כרמון בכלל. מחד גיסא, "הנמצא בעיקר לבדו" לא יודע "כי
האנשים אינם אחרים מכפי שהם נראים", ואכן, באמת אין שום
אפשרות לחדור אל המציאות התת-הכרתית. אבל, מאידך, על כרחו
הסופר "שומע את הקול" הנשלח כ"טיל מבוית", והוא "אוסף עדויות"
על אף ההרגשות הסבילות, הפחד, והסבל העומדים עליו. הוא "קשוב"
ו"ער" ונאבק עם המילים כדי ליצור; אך הוא יודע "כל הזמן ידיעה
פטלית: זו שירת-הברבור שלך. שיחה אחרונה" (עמ' 201). ובמקביל
לזה ניתן להבין שהירושה הממשית היחידה שהאדם עלול להניח
בעזבונו הוא "מסיכת-מוות", כעין העתק, או תצלום, של הדמות
החיצונית בלבד.   זהו עיקר מאבקו האירוני-טראגי של הסופר. למרות
הייאוש בגלל הנראה בנולד הוא מנסה לחשוף ולהעיד; והוא מתקומם
"התקוממות אין-אונים נגד מצב זה" של קוצר-היד האנושי לתפוס

תפיסה של ממש את סיפור החיים. כך שהסופר וסיפורו - ליתר דיוק,
הסופרת ויצירתה זו המזהירה והמזעזעת - אפילו במיטב יכולתם, אין
בידם להביא מרפא לאנוש, ואין ביכולתם אלא לשחק בתפקיד החשוב
אך העצוב של המפגין הסביל, להיות אך "ציר שלוח ממחוזות נהרה"
ולשמש דוגמת-מופת, בסופו של דבר, של "תקוות-הסרק של לב יוצא".

הדואר. כ"ב באלול, תשל"ב, גליון ל"ו: 617-616.

אהרן אפלפלד: העבר האבוד דורש אזכרה

"ידעתי כיצד השתלשלו המאורעות, אך
לא ידעתי מי כיוונם" ('כפור על הארץ',
עמ' 42).

בדומה לסופר אלי ויזל מתייחס אפלפלד ברוב סיפוריו לפרשת
השואה. כמו ויזל בא אפלפלד ומבקש להאיר על פרשה שחורה זו
בכדי לגלות את יסודות הטראומה הנפשית הכבירה שבה, טראומה
עמוקה אך דמומה הזורמת תדיר בעורקי התת-הכרה של האדם. אבל
בניגוד לסיפורי ויזל אין למצוא אצל אפלפלד תיאורי זוועה ותמונות
גיהנום של השואה, ואין אצלו גם אותה נימה של תהיה פילוסופית,
חתירה לנבכי סוד הגורל ודרישת נימוקים לאור ההבנה ההיסטורית
והתיאולוגית. בסיפוריו עוסק אפלפלד יותר בימים שלאחר השואה,
בחדירה אל דרכי המחשבה וההתנהגות של היחיד הנמלט, השריד
שמנסה להקים סדר חיים חדש לאור התדהמה הפסיכולוגית.

מצב האדם בסיפורים עגומים אלה הוא ברוב המקרים מצב של
מעבר. הנפשות הפועלות רובן ככולן מוטלות בין קטבי הסכנה
והבטחון, האיום והשלווה, ההתבודדות וההשתתפות בחברה; הן
מיטלטלות, מאין ברירה, בין הקבוע והארעי, הבריאות והמחלה,
ההסתגרות והמרחב, המחבוא והחשיפה, הבריחה והשהייה; והן חיות
בעולם של תערובת הפכים נפשיים של שיכחה וזכרון, מתינות וייאוש,
הבעה ושתיקה, השתלטות והתמסרות לגורל. הדמויות נמצאות לרוב
בדרך, במסע, בין היער המסתיר והשדה החושף, בתחנות, וליד חופים
וגבולות. הן יוצאות מביתן וממקומות עבודתן - מן הקבוע והבטוח -
ומושלכות אל הרחוב, המרחק, הכפר הנידח; אל בתי מלון ואכסניות
ארעיות. האנשים בורחים מן ההרגל, מבקשים לחרוג מן המעגל הסגור,
מחפשים תקנה והצלה - ובאירוניה כבדה נגלתה להם, שהם שוב בתוך
מלכודת לא צפויה, תוך שלגים וסופות מעכבים, תוך זרם חיים חדש,
המושך לכאורה בנוחותו אך מרתיע בזרותו ובאיום המחודש שבו. מה
שנראה כפתרון הופך למצב-של-משבר, המשקף את אי-היכולת
להתגבר על אות-הקלון שבמצח הנווד הנצחי. מחד גיסא, כל תכנית
העשוייה בידי אדם רוויה היא כשלון דווקא מפאת מידת ההצלחה
שבה, מפאת כושר ההסתגלות לשיגרה החדשה. ומאידך, ההצלחה

הבלתי צפויות, העשויות בידי הגורל - גם אלה מובילות להידרדרות,
למחלה, לטירוף ולמוות.

רוב הסיפורים שבקובץ הראשון של אפלפלד ('עשן', 1962)
משקפים את המוטיבים האלה של מעבר מן הקבוע, המתוכנן והיציב
אל המדהים, המרופף והמיואש. ב"שלושה" בטוחים הנמלטים
באמונתם, ש"הכל כבר היה מאחוריהם", שבאמת הצליחו להינצל. אבל
מייד מוטלים השלושה לתוך תחושת "איזו חידה", לתוך הכרת
ההודאות של "משמעות נסתרת" הנוגסת בהם מבלי להרפות: הרי לא
עזרו לאחרים להימלט, ולעולם לא יוכלו לברוח מהרגשת אשמה זו. הם
שרויים בספק. לבסוף הם נעשים זרים לעצמם ומתרחקים זה מזה ביער.
ב"פיצויים" עוברת הגברת טראום מעולפה המסודר בארץ - לעולם של
"שיגרה עמומה", "מתינות" ו"קפדנות" - לעיר מולדתה בגרמניה,
ששם היא צריכה לקבוע במשפט את סכום פיצוייה. העברה זו מלווה
תערובת רגשית הנשקפת ברקע: הכל נראה "זר וחדש" ונשמעת, בליל-
בואה, "איזו צווחה עוקרת של קטר ועשן בהול ומאיים". לאחר ביקורי
זוועה בבית חולים הצמוד למנזר, שם היא רואה יהודים זקנים ממתינים
למוות, ובבית הקברות שם קבורים אבותיה, מתחיל מצב בריאותה
להידרדר, והיא מגיעה לסף הטירוף, כל מאמציה בחיפוש אחר צידוק
ותיקון עולים באפס וריק, בשעה שהיא נתקלת בעצם עובדות הזרות
והאבדון שבקיומה.

אירוניה טראגית פועלת גם ב"אביב קר". כשיוצאת משפחת
הפליטים מהבונקר מתחיל מעגל חייהם להתפורר. יסודות היציבות
והבטחון, שעמדו להם בבונקר, הולכים ומתרופפים בפני המציאות
החדשה, הנורמלית כביכול. כסימן מובהק לכך רואים כי צייטל, זו
הפרגמטית, שדאגה כל הזמן לשמירת הבריאות ולהמשיך קיומה של
המסגרת המשפחתית, דווקא היא מוסרת את עצמה להזיות כישוף
המגלות לה את את אבידותיה. הטראומה מכה את שורשיה לאחר האסון;
ההווה שלאחר השיחרור עומד כחוויה בלתי נסבלת לעומת ימי
הקביעות בבונקר.

בקובץ השני, ב'גיא הפורה' (1963), מתווספים למצבי המעבר,
הנדידה וחוסר השליטה המוטיבים של אי-מוצא, חוסר מטרה, חיפוש
אחר הזיהות האמיתית והיציבה, וכוח הזכרון האובד והולך. ב"קיטי"
מנסה הנזירה מריה לחנך את קיטי, הנערה היהודיה, בדרכי הקודש
והכפרה. במנזר היא מבודדת אותה יותר ויותר מהוויות העולם
ומסתירה ממנה את סוד עברה וזהותה. אבל בעת ובעונה אחת נגלות

לקיטי גם זהותה וגם רחישת התבגרותה; ובשעת גילוי כפול זה נמסרת
הבחורה להרג בידי חיילים, הדורשים קרבן לצורך פולחנם האכזרי.
ב"בגובה הקר" משתדלים הפליטים להשכיח את עברם האיום, חושבים
ליצור לעצמם זהות חדשה כליצנים בקירקס, ומשהים ככל האפשר את
הירידה מהּהר, מקום הבראתם, לעולם הממשי, לעיר, לשוק, לסדר
חיים רגיל. מאמצי השיכחה וההשהייה נכשלים בגלל תהליך ההבראה
האירוני ההולך ומתגבר על רצונם.

אילו היו יכולים להתמיד במצב מדומדם זה היו ניצלים מידי
החשבון המכרסם. אבל שמש מרפא הופיעה, החליקה על עורם,
העמידה אותם על רגליהם...השיבה להם על כורחם את המחשבה
המגששת. ('בגיא הפורה', עמ' 150).

מצב אירוני דומה נמצא ב"השיירה". עזוב לנפשו בכפר איטלקי
לאחר הפלגת אוניית-הפליטים, מבקש הגיבור, שטולצמן, להשתרש
בחברה החדשה. הוא מצליח במסחרו השחור, מתידד עם הכומר,
השוטרים וילדי המקום, ולרגע נוצרת לו דמות אחרת, דמות של אדם
חסון ואיתן ובטוח בעצמו. אך ברוב הטובה דווקא - כולל השיחרור
מזכרונותיו, מזהותו הקודמת, מ"עצמו, כביכול" - טמון גם כשלונו.
גופו מסתרבל, והוא נעשה "נטול גמישות" ומאבד את כושר
"הדריכות". לבסוף הוא חוזר לחוף וממתין לשיירה שתבוא לאסוף
אליה.

דמות המספר בסיפורים אלה משקפת את המתיחות האירונית בין
כוח השיתוף ובין אונס ההרחקה במצב הדמויות. תפקידו העיקרי של
המספר הוא בעיצוב אווירה רווייית מתח פסיכולוגי, ודרכו בכך כפולה
היא: לעיתים עומד המספר מחוץ להתרחשות ומתאר את הדמויות
כלכודות בידי חידה גורלית, ואין אף ביכולתו הוא למצוא להן פתרון.
ולעיתים עומד המספר תוך קירבה יתירה; הוא נכנס כאילו לתוך מוחן
של הנפשות ומוסר את רחשן-לחשן מבפנים. הסימנים הבולטים
לתערובת זו שבהשקפה הם השימוש הגובר והולך בדיבור סמוי
(כשמסוננים דברי הדמות דרך תודעתו של המספר) ובמסירת התגובות
האמוטיביות דרך לשון של נוכחות ("עד כי יכולת לחוש", "עד שכמעט
חשת"). בדרכים אלה נעשה המספר המדווח - ואף הקורא - שותף
להרגשות המתבטאות במסופר ובו בזמן גם מעין עד-ראייה לתמורות
הנפשיות שבו.

באותה קירבה רגישה מבחינים היטב בקובץ השלישי, 'כפור על
הארץ' (1965). ה"אתה" מקבל כאן הבלטה יתירה; הדמויות פונות אף
לעצמן בכעין עימות; והמספר והקורא הופכים לאחיהן בצרה. הצרה
היא לרוב צרת היחיד הנתקל הנתקל בשיגרה ובציפייה שאבד עליהן הכלח;
באמצעי שליטה והצלה שהתהרופף כוחם; בחזרה אל המוכר, שהפך
בינתיים לזר לחלוטין. ומעל לכול חופפת דממה עצומה. נותק כמעט
כליל כושרו של דו-שיח חי. בשל אזלת-היד לעומת עוצמת הזמן
וההשתנות נמנעת כל אפשרות של פעולה חיובית, של התקרבות אל
מחוז החפץ, של הימלטות מאימת הקפאון. האשלייה בלב הפליטים -
"לרגע נדמה כי מעולם לא היתה מלחמה" - הופכת לוודאות ההכרה
בחוסר היכולת להחזיר את האבוד, את ה"משהו שנשתייר מימים
אחרים, משהו שאדם יודע שהיה בו". כאן ובקובץ הרביעי, 'בקומת
קרקע' (1967), מתאבקים לשוב, להמשיך, להיזכר; אבל מוצאים
ש"נשתנו העיתים", שהם אחוזים בעולם הזרות ועומדים חשופים בפני
איתני "התנאים החדשים" ו"קסומים במעגל ההשתנות". מאידך, מהווה
הזכרון הכוסס גם טראומה נפשית הדורשת שיכחה והסתגלות לקראת
הבאות. מתח זה שבהתערובת העבר והעתיד, הידוע והסמוי, מביא את
הנפשות בסיפורים אלה לידי אילמות, חוסר שליטה בקיומן, וכניעה
לגורל האומר "משא עגמומי שאין לו פשר".

בסגנונו מושפע אהרן אפלפלד מנימת הפרדוכסליות וההחדירה
הפסיכולוגית של ג. שופמן, מהטון הלירי-האלגי המביע עגמימות
וגורליות פאתטית בסיפורי מ. י. ברדיצ'בסקי, ומהמבע המאופק-אירוני
של ש. י. עגנון. לשונו של אפלפלד מקורית מאוד ומצטיינת ביכולתן
להמחיש מימדים נפשיים ע"י צירופי שמות עצם של מצב ואופי
סטטיים עם פעלים סבילים המדגישים חוסר תנועה וכניעה. הוא מרבה
בצורות כגון "גמישות", "צניעות", "איטיות", "קלילות" ו"השתנות"
כדי להטעים שנפשותיו תמיד תפוסות הן בידי המצב, בתוך סיטואציה
הדורשת פתרון שבפעולה - ונמצא שאך לאלוהים פתרונים והפעלה.
אפקט זה של אזלת-יד מובלט גם ע"י פעלים בצורת בינוני הפעול -
"חבוקים", "עמוסים", "חשופים", "דחוקים" - וצורות סביל אחרות.
הסטטיות והסבילות מתגברות גם דרך הסתמיות והעירפול המכוונים
בסגנון. המילה "משהו" וצירופים כגון "איזו וודאות", "איזו עגמה"
ו"איזו ערטילאות" באים להדגיש שוב את הרגשות אי-המוצא וחוסר
נקודת האחיזה, ואת טילטולי הנפש וסבכי התעתועים של הדמויות.

בבואו לתאר את מצב נפשו של האדם מישראל לאחר הטראומה

של השואה, נדמה שגם אפלפלד עצמו חש את המתח הכביר בין יצר
השתיקה והאילמות ובין רגש הייעוד למסור, להביע ולהעיד. דילמה זו
מתבטאת במקומות אחדים בסיפוריו: הילד-המספר ב"אביב קר"
נתאלם בשעת היציאה מהמחבוא. כשנחטף אחיו בידי גויה הוא אומר
בצער שבריפיון נפשי:

אלי לא חזר הדיבור. רציתי לומר משהו ולא יכולתי. נדמה היה לי,
שאילו היה חוזר אלי הדיבור הייתי יודע לייעץ. בדידות גדולה ירדה
עלי... ("עשן", עמ' 55).

הארכיאולוג-המספר ב"מקום אחר" ('כפור על הארץ', עמ' 138-
149) ניטלטל בין עבודת החשיפה ובין הרצון להשאיר את עברו
במכוסה, בין הזהות המציאותית ובין המשיכה אל המיתוס הרחוק.
והמרצה הנודד-המספר ב"הבשורה" מלא ספיקות הוא על תפקידו. אבל
הוא מודה, "שחייבים להביא את הבשורה, לעשות הכול כדי להפיצה"
(שם, עמ' 99). אך הדוגמה המרכזית של מתח זה נראית ב"בגובה הקר"
('בגיא הפורה', עמ' 135-153), שם מובעות במישרין השקפות על
הצורך במישהו, בסופר, שיבוא ויספר את הדברים כהווייתם. ובדברים
אלה מסוכם תפקידו המוסרי של אהרן אפלפלד, תפקיד נורא ואיום
המוטל על האמן העומד כשליח-ציבור, נרעש ונפחד בין האזכרה
וההשכחה, בין ההסתגרות וההתקשרות, בין המלה הגואלת ועדות
מדהימה ומרתיעה.

היה צורך באיש אחר, במספר, שיבוא לכאן, ילקט את סיפוריהם של
האנשים ויצרף אף סיפורו הוא, שהרי הוא ניחן בסגולות קור
מסויימות, המאפשרות לו ראייה כלשהי. הלוואי שלא ייפגע...סיפורו
הוא חבוי עמו, סיפוריה של עדת חבריו יחיו בו כזיקוקי אור
המתערבלים במעלות שמים. והבשורה? שהרי לכך, ואולי רק לכך
התכוון ביושבו לבד על הדפים המצהיבים...ואולי מן הדין שיישכח.
מה זכות לו לספר סיפורה של העדה הזאת...